UNDERSTANDING
Yacht Racing Rules
THROUGH 1992

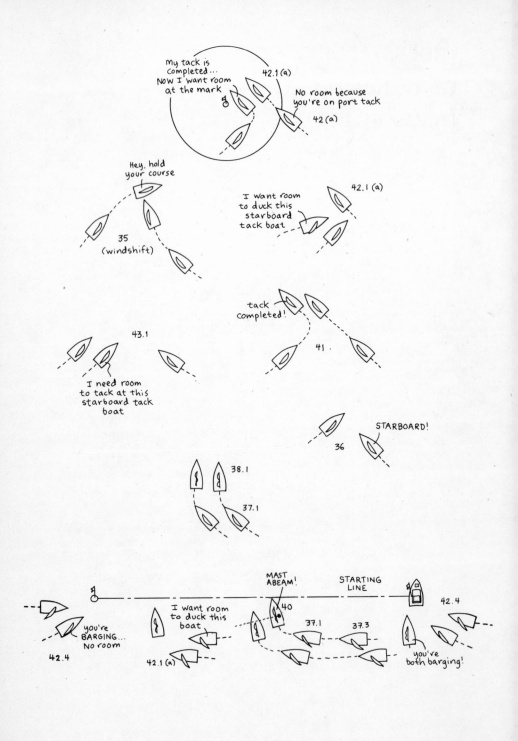

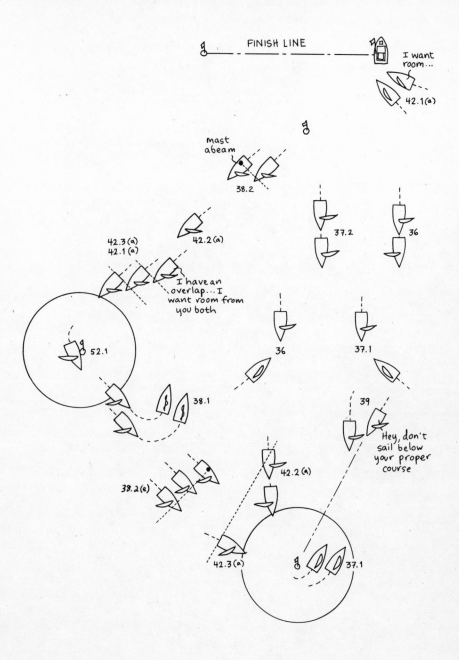

OTHER BOOKS BY DAVE PERRY

Winning in One-Designs

UNDERSTANDING THE

Yacht Racing Rules

THROUGH 1992

Dave Perry

Illustrations by Brad Dellenbaugh

A Perigee Book

Perigee Books are published by
The Putnam Publishing Group
200 Madison Avenue
New York, NY 10016

Library of Congress Cataloging-in-Publication Data

Perry, Dave.
    Understanding the yacht racing rules through 1992 / Dave Perry;
illustrations by Brad Dellenbaugh.

        p.   cm.
    "A Perigee book."
    Includes index.
    ISBN 0-399-55002-X   ISBN 0-399-55004-6 (pbk.)
    1. Yacht racing—Rules.   I. Title.
GV826.7.P48   1989   88-35949 CIP
797.1′4—dc19

Printed in the United States of America
1 2   3   4   5   6   7   8   9   10

Contents

Preface   11

Acknowledgments   13

Introduction—How to Learn the Most from
    This Book   15

Code   19

1   An Overview of the Rules System   23

    How the rules got to where they are today; and
    where all the rules are located.

2   A Simplified Version of the Yacht Racing
    Rules   30

    An explanation of the basic terms used in the rules;
    and a list of the basic rules useful to know when new
    to sailboat racing.

3   Principles Underlying the Yacht Racing
    Rules   35

    A useful discussion of the major principles underly-
    ing the actual rules themselves.

4   The Fundamental Rules (Part I)   51

    A complete discussion of the four Fundamental
    Rules: (A) Rendering Assistance, (B) Responsibility
    of a Yacht, (C) Fair Sailing, and (D) Accepting Penal-
    ties.

5   The Definitions (Part I and Part VI)   62

    An explanation of the definitions of terms used
    throughout the rules, including those found in Part
    I, Part VI, and elsewhere in the rule book.

6   Rights and Obligations When Yachts Meet
    (Part IV–Section A)   91
    A complete discussion of the preamble to Section A,
    and Rules 31–34.

7   Principal Right-of-Way Rules and Their
    Limitations (Part IV–Section B)   110
    A complete discussion of Rules 35–41.

8   Rules That Apply at Marks and Obstructions and
    Other Exceptions to the Rules of Section B
    (Part IV–Section C)   150
    A complete discussion of Rules 42–46.

9   Other Sailing Rules (Part V)   205
    A complete discussion of Rules 52, Touching a
    mark, and 54, Propulsion.

10 Protests, Penalties and Appeals (Part VI)   220
    A complete discussion of Rules 68.1–68.4, Protests
    by Yachts, and 75, Gross Infringement of Rules or
    Misconduct.

11 The Sailboard Racing Rules and
    Their Enforcement   232
    A discussion of Appendix 2, Sailboard Racing
    Rules, and rules enforcement in boardsailing.

12 How to Prepare a Protest and a Defense,
    by Bill Ficker   237
    A comprehensive discussion on how to best prepare
    for a protest hearing, how to properly present a
    protest or defense, and how a protest hearing should
    be run.

    Advanced Rules Quiz   252

Appendix A: Significant Changes in the
1989–1992 International Yacht Racing Rules   257

Appendix B: Tables   263
 1. Distance, Speed, and Time Relationships
 (D=R×T)
 2. Alteration (in feet) per Change in Course (in
 degrees)

Appendix C: General Information on the
Rule Books and Judging   267
 USYRU, CYA, and IYRU addresses; how to pur-
 chase the IYRU rule book and the updated USYRU
 Book of Appeals and IYRU Cases; how to become a
 USYRU Certified Judge.

Appendix D: The 1989–1992 International
Yacht Racing Rules, Including Appendices
1, 2, 3, 5, 6, and 14   269

Appendix E: Answers to the Advanced Rules
Quiz   339

Appendix F: Index of Rule Numbers and
Titles, with Cross-Reference Chart for New Rule
Numbers   343

Preface

Each sailor who reads this book will be able to say honestly that they do finally know and understand the rules completely. I realize that a rules book doesn't often make for the best bedtime reading; but I've made a conscious effort to write in an easy to follow, conversational style. In addition, I've taken the time to go into each rule in enough depth so that you can feel confident that you actually do understand what the rule means and how it applies to your racing; and Brad has provided his usual clear and humorous diagrams that make understanding the rules even easier.

If you're new to sailboat racing, Chapter 2 covers the basic terms you'll hear throughout the book and around the race course; and it lists the basic rules which you will need so you can get out there and start having fun without feeling that you're lost and in everyone's way. But, after reading Chapter 2, you should really take the extra time to read through the rest of the book. Obviously you won't be able to visualize all the situations discussed, but at least you will have been exposed to the big picture right off the bat; and I can promise that your understanding of the rules will happen much faster because you will know how to answer most of your own rule questions as they arise—which they will!

If you are already an experienced racer, I'm confident that you will find this book an interesting and useful reference, as well as a good opportunity to "bone up" on the latest rule changes and interpretations. Wherever possible, I have quoted from the United States Yacht Racing Union (USYRU) Appeals and International Yacht Racing Union (IYRU) Cases so that you will know **their** authoritative interpretation and explanation of the rules. I have also gone into depth in areas which commonly cause the most problems or raise the most questions. As a result, this reference will also be extremely useful to sailors serving as judges on a protest committee. The most useful appeals are quoted or referenced with the discussion of each rule; and each discussion goes into sufficient depth to provide the answers or at least the guidelines to resolve most protests or questions which come up. Both competitors and judges will find the extensive use and reference to the appeals very useful and time-saving when they are either lodging a protest or trying to resolve one in the hearing.

On the subject of the protest hearing, Bill Ficker, in Chapter 12, provides the most comprehensive and useful advice I have seen in writing on the subject. The protest hearing is the sailor's court where rules conflicts and questions are initially heard, debated, and resolved. Bill goes into depth on how sailors can best prepare for the hearing and then present their case. Through his explanations he also provides excellent advice to members of protest committees on how to conduct the hearing.

It is nearly impossible to race sailboats without getting involved in some rules-related situations, whether it's in a crowded mark rounding, a protest hearing, a measurement problem, or an appeal. I'm also firmly convinced that the Finn sailor who was disqualified, based in part on the precedent set in IYRU Case 78, from the 1984 Finn Olympic Trials which he had otherwise won, would not have even attempted what he did had he simply read or known about IYRU Case 78. So it is my hope that this book, which blends the rules and the appeals together, will answer most of your rules questions and expand your knowledge and awareness of what is in the USYRU and IYRU appeals so that you can continue to satisfy your own rules curiosity into the future, and feel confident that you in fact do understand the rules yourself.

Good Sailing,
Dave Perry

Acknowledgments

I'd like to thank the following people, and for the reasons given:

My father, Hop Perry, who began my rules interest and taught me the first rules I knew; Harry Anderson, who patiently tolerated my endless rule questions during his every visit to Yale from '73 to '77, and who answered each with the same high care and interest to explain exactly why he gave the answer he did; Gregg Bemis, whose countless hours of conversation on the rules I've cherished; Bill Bentsen, who by his example has shown and inspired me to be a strict analyst of the exact word in each rule so as only to learn and interpret what the rule writers wrote, and who was a tremendous help in getting preliminary drafts of the new rules; Tom Ehman, who shares my insatiable curiosity to understand the rules and with whom I have no inhibition in discussing even the most unlikely possible contortions which boats might get themselves into: Andy Kostanecki and Dick Rose, with whom I shared my first experience at writing a rule and who were wonderful to work with; Lynn Watters, who helped me understand some of the new rule changes; and the USYRU office, which was a great help in getting the final draft of the new rules.

I would also like to thank the many friends with whom I've enjoyed much open-minded and friendly, thoughtful debate on the rules, completely devoid of any self-righteousness or the ill effects of taking debate personally; and all the sailors I've met while sitting on protest committees, who have given clear and honest testimonies so that the facts of what happened were clear, enabling everyone involved to learn from and enjoy the more intellectual challenge of applying the rules to the seemingly endless variety of situations we find ourselves in while racing.

Also, this book has been greatly enhanced by the contributions from my wife, Betsy, Bill Ficker, and the tireless support and assistance of Doug Logan and the late Allen Klots. I can't say enough about the talent and energy of my friend Brad Dellenbaugh, whose illustrations are an equal half of making this book fun and effective. Finally, I want to acknowledge all those sailors who took the time to write to me with their critical comments and suggestions for the improvement of this book.

As individual words form together to create a rule, so have all these people formed together to become my teacher in a subject that never ceases to give me pleasure each time I feel I know and understand a rule a little more clearly. To all of you, I dedicate this book.

Introduction: How to Learn the Most from This Book

Give me a fish and I'll eat for a day; teach me to fish and I'll eat for the rest of my life.

It is one goal of this book to help you learn and understand the rules and the appeals better. It is an equal goal to help you see how you can continue to answer your own rules questions as they arise, whether in the position of a competitor, a race committee member, or a judge. Here are some suggestions that will make it much easier for you to accomplish both.

DON'T TRY TO MEMORIZE THE RULES

It is the wrong approach to try to memorize the eight situations where *port-tack* has right of way over *starboard-tack*, just as it's confusing to try to simply memorize the entire text of Rule 42. Each rule has a clear purpose, which I have tried to explain thoroughly. You'll learn and remember the rules faster and more clearly if you take a step back and try to see exactly what actions each rule is trying to produce or eliminate. For example, when you are over the starting line at the gun you have taken an unfair head start on your competitors. You can remedy your mistake simply by returning behind the line and starting properly; and it makes complete sense that while you are returning you have no rights over boats that have started correctly. This is the **purpose** of Rules 51 and 44, which you can easily understand and apply in your racing without knowing the exact wording of each rule.

LET GO OF PREVIOUS MISCONCEPTIONS OF THE RULES

Most sailors have lives filled with more on their minds than just sailboat racing. As a result, it is understandable that their rules knowledge may be a tad out of date or that they possibly learned a rule incorrectly from another sailor whose rule knowledge wasn't accurate. My advice is: Read this book with an open mind. Be careful not to hurry through sections that you feel you already know. Read each word and discussion carefully. It's too common and easy to superimpose what you "think" a rule says, and in many cases this causes you to miss a subtle difference in what the rule is actually saying. I've also found that people are often reluctant to admit, even to themselves, that something they've believed for years may actually be wrong. However, the rules are accurately constructed and well interpreted in the appeals, leaving very little room for other interpretations; and sailors seriously interested in understanding the rules will find pleasure in relearning a rule correctly, when necessary.

WHEN ALL ELSE FAILS, READ THE DIRECTIONS

It is usually not difficult to answer your own rules questions if you follow this route. When you have a question, first look in the contents of the IYRU rule book at the titles of the Parts, then the Sections, and finally the rules themselves to find the one(s) that might pertain to your situation. (See Appendix F.) For example, if it involves two or more boats, the appropriate rule(s) are probably in Part IV. To find the rule(s), first determine what the relationships of the boats were just before, during, and just after the incident. For instance, were they converging for some time or did one of the boats suddenly alter course and cause the convergence; were they on the same or opposite *tacks;* were they *overlapped* or not, and so forth. Also determine where they were on the course—i.e., were they behind the starting line, near a *mark,* or halfway down a reaching leg? Then look through the titles of the rules in Part IV for the description most similar to the situation.

When you have found the rule you feel applies, read it out loud. As Bill Bentsen, Chairman of the USYRU Racing Rules Committee for many years, says, "Before answering a rules question I always re-read the rule first." Then read the discussion of the rule in this book, along with each appeal referenced in the discussion.

It is also good advice to re-read the definition, found in Part I, of each italicized word in the rule. If you are still not confident in the answer, write down your question in the back of your rule book and discuss it with the local rules expert or one of the USYRU Certified Judges in your area.

NOTE: Wherever possible, I have quoted from or referenced a USYRU Appeal or IYRU Case in my explanation and discussion of the rules. When no published appeal exists, I have offered my own personal opinion on the rule. These personal opinions reflect my best, studied judgment at this time, and do not constitute the official opinions of USYRU or any other body.

USEFUL FEATURES OF THIS BOOK

Appendix F will help you find the discussions of the rules you're interested in. Also, the tables in Appendix B will prove very useful when either preparing for a protest or hearing one. The "blimp's eye" chart in the front of the book should be very useful when you're involved in a protest but you're not sure what rule number applies. The chart shows an entire race course with the rule numbers for the common situations in each location.

Throughout the discussions of the rules, I have quoted extensively from the USYRU *Decisions of the Appeals Committee* and the IYRU *Interpretations of the Yacht Racing Rules*. These quotations are set in Helvetica typeface to immediately distinguish them from the text. When used, the official wording of an IYRU racing rule is set in Helvetica typeface. When a term defined in Definitions, Part I, is used in its defined sense, it is printed in *italic type*. When a term defined in Part VI is used in its defined sense, it is printed in **bold type.** In addition, I have used **bold type** to emphasize words or phrases throughout my explanations and discussions of the rules.

Having raced, taught the rules, and judged extensively at all levels of our sport, I have seen and heard where the common rules problems and questions occur. As a result, I have located throughout the text the most commonly asked rules questions, indicated by the sailor's head in the margin. Undoubtedly you'll recognize many of the questions as ones you might still have. Also located throughout the text are discussions relating to specific rules for boardsailors. These are highlighted by the boardsailor in the margin. Whenever a discussion of a significant rule change occurs, a "NEW" starburst appears in the margin.

I have also included a new Advanced Rules Quiz. The idea of the quiz is for you to check the progress of your own rules understanding. Work through each question as if you were a judge on the Olympic Jury. Then check your "decision" with the answers in Appendix E. When you can accurately answer all 10 questions with confidence, you have reached an advanced level of rules understanding.

Sailing is one of the few sports where men and women can compete either with or against one another at all levels; and though the sport is completely integrated, the omnipresent singular male pronoun "he" does much to belie that fact. Not being a fan of "he or she" or some of the other awkward pronoun conventions, I have found good counsel from Casey Miller and Kate Swift, authors of the *Handbook of Non-Sexist Writing*. They argue—from history—that even as the solely plural "you" became in time a pronoun that could be both plural and singular, so the normally plural "they" must begin to be used with singular antecedents, as well as plural. They further point out that this has already begun to become rather common. ("Anyone using this beach after 5 P.M. does so at their own risk."—rather than "at his or her own risk.") So, following their advice, I have in this book consistently used "they" and "their" with singular antecedents.

Finally, this book will be published each four years with the revisions of the IYRU Yacht Racing Rules. As it is my goal to provide a useful and accurate reference for all sailors, I welcome your comments and suggestions concerning improvements and inaccuracies. Please send them to my attention by May 1, 1992, or sooner at: 1100 Pequot Avenue, Southport, CT 06490.

And now, enjoy your understanding of the rules!

Code

Throughout this book, in order to consolidate space and to conform to the appeals, I have used the following code:

S—*starboard-tack* yacht
P—*port-tack* yacht
L—*leeward* yacht
W—*windward* yacht
A—yacht *clear ahead*
B—yacht *clear astern* (behind)
M—middle or intervening yacht
I—inside yacht (at a *mark* or *obstruction*)
O—outside yacht (at a *mark* or *obstruction*)

When combined, the codes work like this:

SL—the yacht is on *starboard-tack* and *overlapped* to *leeward* of the other yacht.
PI—the yacht is on *port-tack* and *overlapped* on the inside of the other yacht.

UNDERSTANDING THE

Yacht Racing Rules

THROUGH 1992

1

An Overview of the Rules System

Here is an overview of the system developing the rules and their interpretations and where the rules are located.

BRIEF HISTORY

Up through the early 1920s different parts of the world had their own versions of racing rules. Then, as more sailors started traveling to other countries for international regattas, the European and United States yacht racing associations agreed on a common set of right-of-way rules in 1929. However, as racing grew in popularity and the boats were getting smaller, the existing rules were not clear and precise enough to make them easily enforceable.

In the mid-1930s Mike Vanderbilt, defender of the America's Cup in the J-boats *Enterprise* (1930), *Rainbow* (1934), and *Ranger* (1937), began work on a new draft of the rules, based on the three basic relationships: boats on the same tack, boats on different tacks, and boats in the act of changing tacks. In 1948 the North American Yacht Racing Union (NAYRU), predecessor to the United States Yacht Racing Union (USYRU) and the Canadian Yachting Association (CYA), adopted Vanderbilt's draft as their official rules.

In 1949 the International Yacht Racing Union (IYRU) created a Racing Rules Committee to study the various racing rules that were being used throughout the world. From 1950 to 1959, Mike

Vanderbilt and Gregg Bemis of the United States worked hard with others, including Gerald Sambrooke-Sturgess of Great Britain, to draft one set of rules under which the entire world would race. In 1960 the IYRU adopted a draft, largely based on the "Vanderbilt draft," and these rules came into effect in 1961. Since then, racing throughout the world has been done under the same rules.

THE RULES AND HOW THEY ARE UPDATED

These are the International Yacht Racing Rules. Each national authority (the USYRU in the United States) adopts these rules for racing in its own country. Some rules permit each national authority to make some additions or modifications, called "prescriptions." So when racing in a different country, a sailor need only learn what prescriptions, if any, that national authority has made. But notice that there are no modifications permitted to the Definitions and Right-of-Way rules, thus ensuring that these remain identical throughout the world.

Beginning in 1961 the IYRU's policy has been that it contemplates no changes in the rules for a four-year period. These periods are timed so that a set of rules will be in effect through the Olympic Games. After each Olympics the IYRU, at their annual meeting in November, adopts a draft of the rules for the next four years. This draft represents the hard work and scrutiny of the rules given by sailors around the world during each four-year period. Sailors communicate their ideas to the Racing Rules Committee in their country, which also studies the rules for areas of improvement. These suggestions are passed along to the IYRU Racing Rules Committee, which meets every year and publishes the new draft every fourth year.

Notice that the IYRU is very interested in having sailors study the rules for improvements. Rule 3.1 restricts which rules the sailing instructions can alter, but continues, "when so prescribed by the national authority, this restriction shall not preclude the right of developing and testing proposed rule changes in local races." The USYRU so prescribes.

USYRU APPEALS AND IYRU CASES

What is an "appeal"?

If you are penalized in a protest hearing and you feel that the **protest committee** applied the rules incorrectly to the facts they found, you can "appeal" their decision to a "higher court." In the United States the "highest court" is the USYRU Appeals Committee. Their decisions are published regularly. When they decide an incident that to them sets a precedent, is a clear interpretation of a rule, or the like, they can submit the appeal, along with their decision, to the IYRU Racing Rules Committee, which in turn can publish this appeal in their book. Notice that the IYRU does **not,** in most cases, decide appeals; they simply publish ones submitted by national authorities that they feel are important interpretations.

The USYRU's *Decisions of the Appeals Committee* and the IYRU's *Interpretations of the Yacht Racing Rules* are available from the USYRU office. USYRU members receive new decisions of the USYRU Appeals Committee free of charge when they are published. (See Index C.)

What is the status of the USYRU's *Decisions of the Appeals Committee* and the IYRU's *Interpretations of the Yacht Racing Rules?*

The appeals of the national authorities (the USYRU in the United States) and the IYRU cases are not rules. They are "authoritative interpretations and explanations of the rules." (See IYRU regulation 6.3.3.) Sailors and **protest committees** can and should refer to the appeals for guidance.

The IYRU's interpretations, called cases, carry supreme weight worldwide. In referring to the appropriateness of citing IYRU Case 78 as a precedent in the 1984 Finn Olympic Trial disqualification of the sailor who otherwise had won, the USYRU Executive Committee said, "IYRU Case 78 is an official interpretation of the rules for the sport of yacht racing adopted by the international federation and is therefore the standard for the sport." Clearly, when a situation is identical to a published IYRU interpretation, the IYRU case serves as a precedent.

Similarly, the USYRU Appeals Committee's decisions carry supreme weight within the United States; and in fact their appeals are highly regarded throughout the world. They do not, however, have the same weight as the IYRU cases outside the United States, and they may sometimes be disregarded in favor of the host country's national Appeals Committee's decisions.

In IYRU Case 131/USYRU Appeal 252 it was asked, "May a USYRU member yacht club . . . state . . . that, while appeal is not denied, end-of-regatta standings and awards will not be affected by any appeals decisions? Answer: No. An appeal involves not only the adjudication of a dispute on the meaning of a rule but also, in the event of a reversal of the decision of the protest committee or district appeals committee, an adjustment of the results of the race and of the final standings of the regatta on which the awards are based."

How does the appeals process work?

The appeals process is clearly described by Rules 77 and 78. Notice that the procedures for filing an appeal have been changed significantly.

Notice that only someone **directly involved in a protest** can appeal (Rule 77.1).

Also notice that the **facts,** as found by the original protest committee, **cannot** be appealed (Rules 74.1 and 77.4). If after a hearing you, as a **party to the protest,** feel the **protest committee** found the wrong facts, you can ask them to **re-open** the hearing under Rule 73.6.

In short, if you want to appeal in the United States, you must **request** a written copy of the decision and diagram, if relevant, from the **protest committee** (74.6[b]). You must now file your appeal with the appropriate "intermediate level" appeals committee within **fifteen days** after receiving the written decision, along with any appropriate fee. Your appeal must contain the

grounds for the appeal—i.e., why you believe the decision or action was incorrect (78.1[a]). Furthermore, your appeal must contain any of the documents listed in Rule 78.1(b) that are in your possession. From then on you simply wait. The appeals committee meanwhile must send your appeals package to the **protest committee,** which in turn must send back to the appeals committee any missing documents plus any comments on the appeal it wishes to make. The appeals committee will then send your complete appeals package to all other **parties to the protest,** who are welcomed to submit comments of their own. (See Rule 78.) When you are not satisfied with the decision of the "intermediate level" appeals committee or when there is no such committee, you may have your appeal sent to the USYRU Appeals Committee.

Finally, Rule 77.3 permits a yacht club or association that is a member of USYRU to send directly to the USYRU Appeals Committee a **question** involving **solely the interpretation** of the racing rules. And in fact many of the present appeals are answers to these questions, which may or may not be based on actual facts.

When can a sailor not appeal?
Rule 1.5 is very clear on this. The right of appeal may be denied only:

(a) When there is a properly constituted international jury in accordance with Rule 1.4 and Appendix 8, International Juries.

(b) When it is a "ladder event" such that the results of the race or series will determine who qualifies for the next stage of the event. An example is a district class championship that qualifies sailors for the national class championship.

(c) When a national authority so prescribes for a particular event open only to entries under its own jurisdiction.

Notice that when the right of appeal is to be denied the organizing authority **shall announce** its intention in the **notice of race** or regatta and in the **sailing instructions** (Rule 2[m] and 3.2[b][xxx]).

What's the best way to use the appeals books?
Both the USYRU Appeals Committee's *Decisions* and the IYRU's *Interpretations* are easily designed for quick reference. One index lists each appeal referring to a particular rule, and another gives a short description of each appeal. Instead of

reading the appeals book from front to back, you should read each appeal pertaining to a particular rule. The appeals themselves are each very short. You are given the facts, a diagram when relevant, and then the decision. What I like to do is read the facts, close the book, think out what my decision would be, then compare it with the actual decision.

WHERE THE RULES ARE LOCATED

The rules are located in the following places. (See Part VI, Definitions—Rules.)

1. The IYRU rule book and the prescriptions of the national authority. The USYRU sells one "rule book" that includes the IYRU rules, appendices, and USYRU prescriptions. Parts or the whole of an Appendix rank as a rule when so prescribed in the sailing instructions. See its Table of Contents for an overview of where each IYRU rule is located and what each Appendix covers.

2. Class rules. Each class publishes rules specific for that class, which are available from the class secretary. (Contact the USYRU for class office addresses.) For instance, in 1974 the Iceboat Racing Rules specified, "When two yachts sailing *off-the-wind* are on the same *tack,* the *leeward yacht* shall keep clear."

3. Club or "local" rules. On the narrow Mill River in front of the Pequot Yacht Club in Southport, Connecticut, the frostbiting starting line runs from shore to shore. In order that leeward end of the line starters can't call for "room to *tack*" moments after the start, the local rule states that Rule 43 ("sea-room") cannot be called until twenty seconds after the starting signal. And the Inland Lake Yachting Association, recognizing that the large scow spinnakers result in poor visibility, creating a possibly dangerous situation, used to have a special rule saying, in part, that a yacht in the act of setting, carrying, or lowering a spinnaker shall have the right-of-way over all other yachts not sailing on the same leg of the course as she. That has now been deleted.

4. Notice of the race or regatta. Rule 2 lists the information contained in the Notice.

5. The Sailing Instructions. Rule 3.1 reads, "These rules shall be supplemented by **written** sailing instructions that shall rank as rules." The sailing instructions are required to tell you when class and "local" rules apply, as well as when parts or the whole of an Appendix shall apply. They may even alter certain IYRU rules. (See Rule 3.1.) Rule 3.2 lists all the information the sailing instructions must contain. Notice that Rule 3.4(b) prohibits any oral instructions unless there is a procedure specifically set out in the sailing instructions. This is obviously to avoid confusion and potential prejudice to sailors not hearing about a change. (See also USYRU Appeal 97.)

Every sailor should take a few minutes to read the sailing instructions for a race or event.

A good race committee will not answer oral questions concerning any rule or sailing instruction, for the above-stated reason. You should give them your question(s) in writing in ample time for them to consider their answer, seek the judges' opinions (when necessary), and post each question with its answer in writing on the official notice board.

2

A Simplified Version of the Yacht Racing Rules

If you are just getting into sailing and racing, you've probably noticed that there are a few different words and phrases used around the track. Clearly, we wouldn't be using them if they didn't make things easier; so here are some illustrations to help you understand what some of these terms mean.

SIMPLIFIED RULES

There's no disagreeing that there are a lot of rules to know in racing sailboats. But just as in every other sport, you don't need to know and completely understand them all before you go racing. I love to play soccer, and I've got the basic rules down: Keep my hands off the ball, try to kick the ball into the goal to score, try not to kick the other guys in the shins, and stop when the ref blows the whistle. I'm still a bit hazy on what "off-sides" means, what the difference between an "indirect" and a "direct" kick is, and just how many elbows in the ribs I'm supposed to peacefully accept as part of the game. But I still have a great time playing, and I learn a bit more about the rules each time I go out.

Here then are a few basic rules you should know so that you can get into racing without feeling like you're just in everyone's way. At first, take the racing easy just to get the feel of how it works; and never be worried about asking too many questions—that's exactly how we all learned what was up. Of course, the one danger in learning just the basic rules is that there will be places on the course where there are exceptions or where the actual rule has more detail. So you should really take the time to read through this book. It's written in language that is easy to understand. The more you race, the more situations you'll run into that are exactly as covered and described here, and the sooner you'll be comfortable enough to get in there and mix it up out on the course.

These are the basic rules that apply when you and another boat are about to hit. (When one boat has the "right-of-way," that means that the other boat is required to keep clear—i.e., not to interfere with the right-of-way boat.)

1. If you are on **opposite** *tacks* (booms on different sides), the boat on *starboard-tack* has the right-of-way over the boat on *port-tack* (just as at a four-way stop, the car on the right gets to go first). (Rule 36.)

2. If you are on the **same** *tack* (booms on the same sides), the *leeward* boat has the right-of-way over the *windward* boat; and a boat coming up from behind can't hit the boat ahead (just as on the road). (Rule 37.)

3. If you are changing *tacks*—i.e., *tacking* or *gybing,* you have **no** right-of-way over a boat sailing in a straight line (just as you

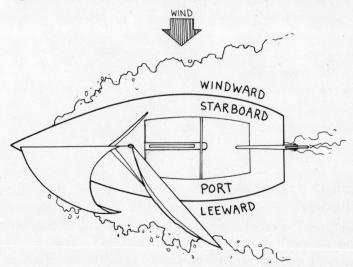

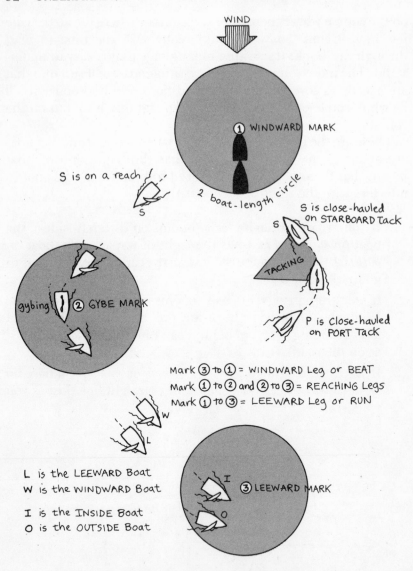

WIND

① WINDWARD MARK

S is on a reach

2 boat-length circle

S is close-hauled on STARBOARD Tack

TACKING

P is close-hauled on PORT Tack

gybing ② GYBE MARK

Mark ③ to ① = WINDWARD Leg or BEAT
Mark ① to ② and ② to ③ = REACHING Legs
Mark ① to ③ = LEEWARD Leg or RUN

L is the LEEWARD Boat
W is the WINDWARD Boat

I is the INSIDE Boat
O is the OUTSIDE Boat

③ LEEWARD MARK

cannot pull out onto a road immediately in front of a car driving down the road). (Rule 41.)

4. Before most races, the race committee will give each competitor a copy of the sailing instructions (SI's), which contain the specific information on how the races will be run. Included in

the SI's will be the timing system for the starts. If not, ask someone on the race committee to explain their system. There will be an imaginary line between two *marks* called the "starting line." You must be completely behind this line at your start. If you are not, simply turn back and get behind the line. However, while you are returning, you must stay clear of all boats that *started* correctly. (Rule 44.)

5. Before the race starts, the *leeward* boat can turn toward the wind (*luff*) to keep a nearby *windward* boat from passing, but they must turn slowly and smoothly. However, after the *leeward* boat has crossed and cleared the starting line, it can *luff* suddenly and as sharply as it wants. For this reason, it is risky to sail near the *windward* side of another boat. (Rules 38 and 40.)

6. When you are two boat-lengths from a *mark* or *obstruction,* any boat between you and the *mark* or *obstruction* has the right-of-way while you are passing or rounding it. (Rule 42.)

7. One large exception to basic rule 6 (above) is at the **starting** *marks,* where *windward*/inside boats do **not** have the right-of-way. If the *windward*/inside boat tries to squeeze in between a starting *mark* (like a race committee boat) and the *leeward* boat, they are "barging," which is definitely illegal but unfortunately very common. (Rule 42.4.)

8. If you touch any *mark,* you can simply do two full circles as a penalty. Nevertheless, while you are doing your penalty circle, you must keep clear of the boats rounding the *mark* correctly. (Rules 45 and 52.)

9. When you have the right-of-way and are near a boat that is trying to keep clear, you must **hold your straight-line course** until the other boat has gone by. You also have the responsibility to try to avoid all collisions if possible. (Rules 32 and 35.)

10. When you know that you have interfered with a right-of-way boat, you must drop out of the race immediately. (Fundamental Rule D.) Because this is such a strong penalty, **be extra careful when you are near other boats.** Sometimes the sailing instructions permit an alternative penalty that is less

severe, such as doing two complete penalty circles (a "720") or taking a percentage penalty. (Appendix 3.)

If you have the right-of-way and another boat interferes with you, you can "protest" them by putting up a flag immediately. Then at the *finish* you tell the race committee which boat you are protesting, and onshore you fill out the protest form the race committee will give you. Soon afterward, the race committee will hold a hearing at which both sides have the opportunity to tell their story, and then the committee will make its decision. (Rules 68 to 74.)

3

Principles Underlying the Yacht Racing Rules

The rules contain many principles that, when thoroughly understood, make the rules themselves much easier to learn and apply. Studying these carefully will not only help you to see how the rules all interact, but will also help you immensely when you have to make quick decisions out on the race course around other boats. All these principles are expanded upon in the USYRU Appeals and IYRU Cases.

WHEN THE RIGHT-OF-WAY SHIFTS FROM ONE BOAT TO ANOTHER

You're sailing on a run on *port-tack* with another *port-tack* boat just to *windward*. As the *leeward* boat, you have the right-of-way (Rule 37.1) and everything is under control. You have the "sword," so to speak, and they must stay out of "its" way. Suddenly, the *windward* boat throws its boom over to the other side. Now they're on *starboard-tack*, and you're on *port*. As right-of-way boat, **they** now have the "sword" (Rule 36), but they can't just turn and hit you. It's a long- and well-established principle that when the right-of-way shifts between boats, the new non–right-of-way boat, called the "give-way boat," is entitled to "room and opportunity" to get clear of the right-of-way boat. This same principle applies to a right-of-way boat that acquires a **temporary obligation** to give way.

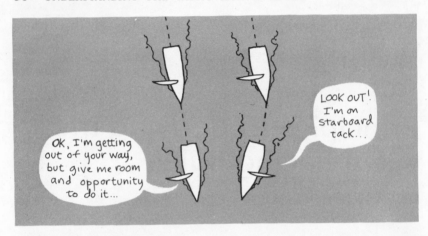

IYRU Case 46 says, "It is a general principle in the rules that when the right-of-way suddenly shifts from one yacht to another, the yacht with the newly-acquired right-of-way must give the other yacht time for response and a fair opportunity to keep clear."

This principle is loudly echoed in many appeals, including USYRU Appeals 139 and 221 and IYRU Case 53. And, in fact, it is written right into several of the rules. For instance:

- Rule 37.3 says, "TRANSITIONAL: A yacht that establishes an *overlap* to *leeward* from *clear astern* shall initially allow the *windward* yacht ample room and opportunity to keep clear."

- Rule 41.2 says, "TRANSITIONAL: A yacht shall neither *tack* nor *gybe* into a position that will give her right-of-way unless she does so far enough from a yacht on a *tack* to enable this yacht to keep clear without having to begin to alter her course until after the *tack* or *gybe* has been completed."

- Rule 42 begins to apply "when yachts are about to round or pass a mark . . . or an obstruction." Often a right-of-way boat coming into a *mark* will be the outside or give-way boat during the actual rounding. Recognizing this potential shift in right-of-way, the phrase "about to round or pass" builds in a transitional period to let the outside boat begin to keep clear before getting to the *mark* or *obstruction*.

- See also Rules 42.3(a), 42.4, 44.1(b), and 46.2.

Protection is not continuing.

However, the protection of "room and opportunity" is not continuing. In the video game *Deluxe Asteroids* a tiny rocket ship tries to blast apart large rocks that will blow up the ship if they hit her. When there are just too many rocks about to hit, the player can press a button, putting a protective force shield around the ship. At first, the rocks bounce off the shield, but after a few seconds the shield begins to fade and disappear.

The "room and opportunity" to respond to a newly acquired obligation to keep clear is a "shield" for the new give-way boat. It is very strong initially, but fades in strength as the seconds go by. Also, for you to be entitled to the protection of the "shield," you must, at the moment you become the give-way boat, make an immediate and careful attempt to begin to get clear of the right-of-way boat. If you delay even for a few seconds or choose an unsuccessful means of keeping clear, you lose the protection of "room and opportunity," and you run the risk of fouling the right-of-way boat.

USYRU Appeal 233 says, "It is to be kept in mind that a windward yacht's right to 'room and opportunity to keep clear' under both Rule 37.3 and Rule 40 is a shield and not a sword for W." IYRU Case 11 states, "L was bound by Rule 37.3 to allow W ample room and opportunity to keep clear, but this obligation was not a continuing one and in this case the overlap had been in existence for a considerable period during which nothing had obstructed W's room."

IYRU Case 116/USYRU Appeal 126 makes the point that the give-way boat must respond immediately: "When W lost right-of-way as a yacht clear ahead, she was entitled by Rule 37.3 to 'ample room and opportunity' to fulfill her newly acquired obligation under Rule 37.1 to keep clear of the leeward yacht, and since she at once trimmed sails and headed up and kept clear thereafter, her appeal is sustained." In USYRU Appeal 150, "P had ample time to avoid her (S), yet made little effort to do so. Thus disqualification of P . . . is upheld." And in USYRU Appeal 233, L established an *overlap* to *leeward* from *clear astern* before the start. W, in trying to keep clear, *luffed* sharply, the corner of her port transom hitting L amidships. The Appeals Committee reasoned that because L could only *luff* slowly before the start (Rule 40), "W made an unnecessarily extreme luff, hitting L, thereby infringing Rule 37.1."

A right-of-way boat does not have to anticipate losing right-of-way.

A right-of-way boat does not have to anticipate that it will lose its right-of-way. IYRU Case 116/USYRU Appeal 126 is clear on this point: "A yacht clear ahead need not anticipate her requirement to keep clear as a windward yacht under Rule 37.1 before the yacht clear astern establishes an overlap to leeward."

RIGHT-OF-WAY BOATS HAVE OBLIGATIONS ALSO

The rules clearly tell us that whenever boats come together, some of the boats have the right-of-way and some must give way. The rules then go on to put specific obligations on **each** boat. The give-way boats must keep clear of the right-of-way boats; and the right-of-way boats must not alter their course so as to interfere while the give-way boats are trying to keep clear. It's just like driving. If you see a car coming at you in your lane, the first thing you'd do besides slow down would be to stay in your lane (hold your course). Of course, as soon as you decided that the other car might hit you, you'd do whatever was necessary to avoid or mini-mize the collision.

Rule 35 reads, "When one yacht is required to keep clear of another, the right-of-way yacht shall not so alter course as to prevent the other yacht from keeping clear; or so as to obstruct her while she is keeping clear." Rule 32.1 reads, "When a collision has resulted in serious dam-

age, the right-of-way yacht shall be penalised as well as the other yacht when she had the opportunity but failed to make a reasonable attempt to avoid the collision." IYRU Case 51 reads, "The rules of Part IV are specifically framed to avoid collisions. All yachts, whether or not holding right-of-way, are at all times bound to keep a good lookout." (See the discussion of Rules 32 and 35.)

"SHALL" VS. "CAN" AND "MAY"

Understanding the rules requires that we take each word literally. **The Introduction to the rule book reads, "In translating and interpreting these rules, it shall be understood that the word 'shall' is mandatory, and the words 'can' and 'may' are permissive." Thus, Rule 31.2 tells us, "A yacht may be penalised, before or after she is *racing*, for seriously hindering a yacht that is *racing*. . . ."** In other words, she doesn't have to be, but the **protest committee** may disqualify her if they feel it is appropriate. **However, Rule 36 reads, "A *port-tack* yacht shall keep clear of a *starboard-tack* yacht."** Here the **protest committee** has no choice. If they decide that the *port-tack* yacht did not keep clear, they must penalize her.

"ONUS OF PROOF" (SOMETIMES CALLED "BURDEN OF PROOF")

The introduction to Appendix 6, Recommended Protest Committee Procedure, states:

In a protest hearing, the protest committee should give equal weight to the testimony of all principals; should recognize that honest testimony can vary and even be in conflict as a result of different observations or recollections; should resolve such differences as best it can; should recognize that no yacht is guilty until her infringement has been established to the satisfaction of the protest committee; should keep an open mind until all the evidence has been submitted as to whether the protestor or the protestee or a third yacht, when one is involved in the incident, has infringed a rule.

However, to help the **protest committee** make a decision in situations that can often boil down to one person's word against another's, some rules build in a specific "onus" on one of the boats. It is then up to the boat with the "onus" to satisfy the **protest committee,** when there is a dispute, that they fulfilled their obligations under the **rules.** If not satisfied by the burdened boat's testimony and evidence, the **protest committee** will usually rule against them. A built-in "onus" appears in Rules 41.3, 42.1(c), 42.1(d), and 43.2(b)(iii).

Other rules, by the use of adjectives and other words, tilt the rule toward one boat, giving her the *benefit of any doubt.* Examples are the words "clearly" in Rule 39, "obvious" in Rule 44.2, "ample" in Rules 37.3 and 44.1(b), "presumably" in the definition of *proper course,* and "seriously" in Rule 31.2.

Finally, USYRU Appeals 32 and 137 and IYRU Case 113 discuss an "onus" on a *port-tack* boat under Rule 36. (See the discussion of Rule 36.) So when maneuvering near other boats, it's important to try hard to stay away from conflicts where you will have the "onus."

A BOAT THAT MAY HAVE FOULED CONTINUES TO HAVE RIGHTS WHILE STILL RACING

One noticeable phenomenon in racing is that if a lot of boats can gather in one location on the course, they will. Peter Isler calls it the "magnetic boat" syndrome. He theorizes that when boats get near each other, a force is generated that sucks the boats together with no mercy on the sailors. The more boats in an area, the greater the suction. Though not that appealing to most sailors, these multiple boat incidents are enjoyed by boat builders and by **protest committees,** who get the "fun" of sorting them out.

In attempting to untangle a multiple foul incident, an important decision is whether all these fouls are one related incident or several separate incidents that happened one after the other. IYRU Case 108 reads, "It is well established that the rules governing the manoeuvering of yachts in any given situation apply only as long as the relationship between the yachts remains unchanged." USYRU Appeal 185 concerns a boat that while "barging," hit the *leeward* boat and immediately thereafter hit the race committee boat. The Appeals Committee said, "The dual violations committed by W in colliding with L, and immediately thereafter with the committee boat, occurred in such close proximity as to constitute a single foul, not two. A yacht need be penalized only once for a single foul, even though more than one rule has been infringed, as occasionally occurs."

In IYRU Case 108, yacht A, a *windward* boat, *bore off* below her *proper course* while another boat, yacht B, was trying to pass to *leeward*. Then yacht B *luffed* up across yacht A's transom and yacht A *luffed* also, hitting B. The decision read, "While A was a yacht clear ahead and to windward, she was subject to Rule 39; when, however, B, having been clear astern, established an overlap to windward on A, a new situation existed in which A had luffing rights under Rule 38.1. . . . The protest committee found as fact that A was well within three of her own boat lengths of B whilst still bearing away, and on that ground correctly decided that A had infringed Rule 39 and penalised her. . . . When A luffed and B failed to keep clear, B infringed Rule 37.1 and is to be penalised. . . ." USYRU Appeals 31 and 51 concur with this principle.

At the root of this principle is Fundamental Rule D, Accepting Penalties: "A yacht that realises she has infringed a rule shall either retire promptly or accept an alternative penalty when so prescribed in the sailing instructions. However, Rule 34 states, "When a yacht that may have infringed a rule does not retire or exonerate herself, other yachts shall continue to accord her such rights as she has under the rules of Part IV." In other words, just because a boat may have been wrong in a previous situation, she is still governed by all the right-of-way rules if she keeps **racing.** (See discussion of Fundamental Rule D and Rule 34.)

INNOCENT VICTIM

In multiple-boat fouls, often one boat is forced to foul another boat by a third boat. When the **protest committee** decides that this was the case, the boat that was forced to foul another is considered an "innocent victim" and is not penalized. When this happens to you, be sure to protest the boat that forced you to foul, and then ask to be held blameless under 74.4(b), which reads, "When the protest committee . . . decides that: in consequence of her neglect of any of the rules a yacht has compelled other yachts to infringe any of the rules, she shall be disqualified ... and ... the other yachts shall be exonerated." Remember, "shall" is mandatory. (See USYRU Appeal 242.)

However, USYRU Appeal 11 warns, "It is reasonable to assume that all yachts in a race know and will obey the rules but discreet to anticipate that in some circumstances they may not." If you are a give-way boat, you must try your hardest to keep clear of the right-of-way boat. If you will need to hail another give-way boat for room to keep clear, do it soon enough so that if they don't respond, you still leave time and space to keep clear of the right-of-way boat yourself. Claiming "innocent victim" is only a strong defense when you are **forced** to foul **despite your best efforts** to keep clear. (See also USYRU Appeal 71 and IYRU Case 114/USYRU Appeal 37.)

DO THE RULES TAKE INTO CONSIDERATION THE ABILITY OF THE SAILORS?

The rules are very unforgiving to faulty boat-handling. Actually, it would put **protest committees** in a very touchy position if they could excuse a *port-tack* boat who rammed a *starboard-tack* boat because "it was only the skipper's fourth day out in a sailboat" or because the skipper had "quite a good time at the party last night" or because a sailor "just lost control of the boat." A **protest committee** can be sensitive and understanding to a sailor in the way they handle the hearing and explain the decision, but they must be firm in their application of the rules to the situation.

The rules do, however, factor in other considerations such as the speed and sailing characteristics of the boats (IYRU Case 14/USYRU Appeal 91 and IYRU Case 55/USYRU Appeal 145), the wind and sea conditions (Rule 54 and USYRU Appeals 119 and 153), the length of the boats (Rules 39 and 42.3[a][ii]), the amount and difficulty of handling required for maneuvers (IYRU Case 55/USYRU Appeal 145), and the maneuverability of the boats (clearly a sailboard in light air will usually require more room to *gybe* than in heavy air, due to its having no rudder).

HAILS

How much hailing or talking to the other boats do the rules require? The rules themselves are very careful not to require very many hails. The reasons are: (1) these are international rules governing people who speak many different languages; (2) it's often hard to hear, as in heavy air or on large noisy boats; and (3) some people's voices are just louder than others.

In fact, there are only five **mandatory** hails in the entire rule book. (A hail by a right-of-way boat when her alteration of course may not be foreseen and that results in serious damage is not mandatory because of the words "**may** be disqualified," but in principle it is expected [Rule 32.2, Hailing].)

The mandatory hails are:

1. Hailing "Mast Abeam" or "Obstruction" or words to that effect, under Rule 38.2(c).
2. Hailing for "room" to *tack* at *obstructions* and responding under Rule 43.
3. Hailing when anchored or aground and in danger of being fouled by another yacht, under Rule 46.4.
4. Hailing (the word "protest" always suffices) when the "720" rule is in effect under Appendix 3,1.3, or when racing a sailboard under Appendix 2,5, or whenever else the sailing instructions may require a hail to signify an intent to protest. (See also Rule 68.2.)

5. Hailing when acknowledging an infringement (instead of flying code flag "I") when racing sailboards and when the percentage penalty is in effect under Appendix 3,2. (See Appendix 2,6.)

When a hail is required, it must be loud and clear so that the other boats affected can easily hear and understand the hail. When a *leeward* boat wants to hail for "room to *tack*" under Rule 43.1, IYRU Case 117/USYRU Appeal 147 states, "Failure of a windward yacht to hear a properly executed hail would not necessarily relieve her of her obligations to a leeward yacht under Rule 43. Where, however, the leeward yacht, as in the case with L, observed no response after her hail, a second more vigorous hail would be required to constitute adequate notice of her intention to tack. Since the protest committee found that W did not hear the hail even though the two yachts were approximately two boat-lengths apart, and since L made no attempt to hail further, it is held that the hail was inadequate."

And in IYRU Case 101 a *leeward* boat that was entitled to *luff* did so suddenly. The *windward* boat hailed "Mast Abeam," but L did not hear the hail and continued to *luff* until there was a collision. The decision reads, "Rule 38.2(c) is not satisfied by a hail that is not loud enough to be heard. In this case, while L is still in doubt, she has a right to luff until W succeeds in informing her that she has attained 'mast abeam.' If W's first hail was inadequate, a second louder hail was required."

Also, when a hail concerning the rules is made, it is to be taken seriously. IYRU Case 107 says, "A yacht that deliberately hails 'Starboard' when she is on port-tack has not acted correctly and is liable to disqualification under Fundamental Rule C—Fair Sailing." (See the discussion of Fundamental Rule C, Fair Sailing.)

In IYRU Case 130/USYRU Appeal 191 two boats were fast approaching the "two boat-length circle" at the leeward *mark.* While more than two boat-lengths from the *mark,* the boat that was *clear ahead* (O) hailed "no overlap." The boat that was establishing the inside *overlap* from *clear astern* (I) immediately *bore off* and hit the rudder of O. The decision reads, "The facts show that when I bore off and hit the windward side of O's rudder she thereby established that at that time she overlapped O. In as much as O was then very close to, but more than, two lengths from the mark and I was overtaking O, it is inescapable that not only was the inside overlap established at a distance meeting the requirement of Rule 42.3(a)(ii) but also that it would have still existed when O came within two lengths of the mark.

"O's hail 'no overlap' is not to be assumed to be a bluff or inappropriately timed but simply a mistake in judgment, and its clear implication is that in O's opinion I had no right to room and was expected to round astern or outside. I, if she acted immediately, as she did, was entitled to rely on such a hail and if it was incorrect O must accept the responsibility for the resulting contact."

However, the rules **strongly encourage** hailing in two situations. Anytime you have the right-of-way and you make an alteration of course that might not be foreseen by boats around you, and a collision resulting in serious damage occurs, you can be disqualified if you did not hail the other boats first, except if you are *luffing* after you have *started* and cleared the starting line. Second, when rounding or passing *marks* or *obstructions*, the rules encourage you to talk to the other boats about *overlaps,* no *overlaps,* how much room you need, and the like. (See Rules 32.2 and 42.1[f].)

Clearly, the racing is a better sport when people talk with one another. Even in international competition, most of the sailors know the basic English words "starboard," "room" or "water" at the *mark,* and "no" (useful in many situations). When in doubt, you can further communicate by waving your arm (when you want someone to cross you, for instance) or banging on your deck (when you want to get someone's attention). As Bill Bentsen has said, you can rarely get into trouble because you hailed, but you can often get into trouble for not hailing.

THE SHARP LUFF

You're sailing down the reach going nice and fast, and passing just to *windward* of another boat. Everything's going well. Suddenly, wham, the *leeward* boat jams it up hard with no warning at all. Your spinnaker drapes all over their shrouds and the two hulls crash together. Upset, you let the other guy know you're not happy, or words to that effect, and protest.

The rules are quite verbal on this maneuver and very sympathetic to the *leeward* boat's tactic. The reason is that when a boat is passing to *windward* of another, the *windward* boat has a tremendous advantage in that they can cut off the wind getting to the *leeward* boat and easily pass them. If the *leeward* boat was unable to protect herself, the game would not be as challenging.

The rules governing a *luff* read, "Before a [right-of-way yacht] has *started* and cleared the starting line, any *luff* on her part that causes another yacht to have to alter course to avoid a collision shall be carried out slowly and initially in such a way as to give a *windward* yacht room and opportunity to keep clear." (See Rule 40.) But "After she has *started* and cleared the starting line, a yacht *clear ahead* or a *leeward* yacht may *luff* as she pleases, subject to the *proper course* limitations of this rule." (See Rule 38.1 and USYRU Appeal 42.)

"If after starting and clearing the starting line, a leeward boat can luff as fast and as suddenly as she wants, provided the windward boat has not reached the 'mast abeam' position during their overlap [Rule 38.2, Proper Course Limitations], what about Rule 35 saying that a right-of-way boat can't interfere while I'm keeping clear?"

Rule 35(a) reads, "The right-of-way yacht shall not so alter course . . . except to the extent permitted by Rule 38.1, Luffing Rights." Also, Rule 32.2 explicitly says that even if the *luff* causes a collision resulting in serious damage, no hail is necessary. However, **Rule 32.1 always applies,** putting an obligation on **all** right-of-way boats to avoid collisions that might result in serious damage.

My opinion is that the rule writers are sending a clear message: When a *windward* boat is passing close to *windward* of a *leeward* boat, the *leeward* boat's major defense is a sharp *luff,* and the *windward* boat must anticipate this. I have heard it voiced that this is a "dirty tactic" to use. My feeling is that under some circumstances it is an inappropriate tactic, whereas in others it is the best and only tactic. The factors to consider are: 1) who the sailors in the *windward* boat are, i.e., do they know the rules, are they experienced sailors, do you know them personally; 2) what kind of boats are involved; 3) what the wind and wave conditions are; 4) what caliber of regatta it is; and 5) if it is the best tactic in that situation. Also, by hailing a warning first, you greatly minimize the chance that a boat will try to pass to *windward,* or if they do, that a *luff* will result in a collision.

TEMPORARY OBLIGATIONS

It's a common complaint that the rules are difficult to learn because they have too many exceptions in them. If someone tries to simply memorize them, this may be true. But when you take a step back and look at the race course, the reasons for the exceptions become clear and easily understandable.

Section C of Part IV contains all the rules that govern when boats are rounding or passing *marks* or *obstructions.* It also contains the rules that apply to boats that have *started* prematurely, hit a *mark,* or run into some kind of trouble like running aground or capsizing. In these situations, boats that may have previously held the right-of-way are handed **temporary obligations.** For example, you *start* on *starboard-tack* but are over the line early. You *bear off* to go back behind the line and find yourself on a collision course with a *port-tacker* who has *started* correctly. **You** still are the *starboard-tack* boat (Rule 36), but because you *started* prematurely and are in the act of returning, you have a **temporary obligation** to keep clear of all other boats that have *started* correctly (Rule 44.1[a]). As soon as you get back behind the starting line you can assert your *starboard-tack* rights again (Rule 44.1[b]). The same is true when you hit a *mark.* While you are doing your "720," you have a **temporary obligation** to keep clear of all other boats. However, as soon as you complete the "720" and are on a *proper course* to the next *mark,* you get all your rights back (Rule 45.1).

It's no secret that most collisions and fouls in racing occur at the *marks.* Obviously, when you have every boat headed for one fixed point, there's going to be a jam-up. Rule 42 provides the rules governing boats as they are rounding or passing *marks* and *obstructions.* Simply put, when *overlapped* boats are rounding or passing a *mark* or *obstruction* on the same side, boats on the outside have to give boats on the inside "room" to round or pass. So if you are the *leeward* boat and there's a boat to *windward* that will be on the inside track around the *mark,* you have a **temporary obligation** to provide enough "room" so that the inside boat can round the *mark.* (See the discussion of Rule 42.)

FAIR SAILING AND SPORTSMANSHIP

Our sport is unique compared with a lot of other sports. I was watching a pro tennis singles match (two players) and became amused as I counted at least ten referees: one calling each of the four lines on each side, one calling the net, and an umpire to settle disputes. Even at the highest levels of racing we "call our own lines," and the sport is much the better for it.

The rules are written so as to make competitor enforcement easy and so as to provide for fairness, equity, and conformity among all the players. Fundamental Rule C, Fair Sailing, reads, "A yacht, her owner and crew shall compete only by *sailing,* using their speed and skill, and, except in team racing, by individual effort, in compliance with the rules and in accordance with recognised principles of fair play and sportsmanship." When one boat is forced to foul another boat through no fault of her own, Rule 74.4(b) allows that boat to be excused from blame. If one boat feels they have been materially prejudiced by the race committee or another competitor, they can ask for redress under Rule 69, but Rule 74.2(c) reminds the **protest committee** to make as equitable an arrangement as possible for **all** yachts concerned.

Concern has been expressed at times that a yacht will exploit the rules and then seek redress, for instance by letting herself be intentionally hit and damaged by a give-way yacht when she was doing poorly in a race. USYRU Appeal 159 reiterates IYRU Case 38 by saying, "So far as the fears expressed by the race committee are concerned regarding the possible exploitation of such a situation by an unscrupulous helmsman, the rules are framed to ensure that, as far as possible, yachts compete against one another safely and equitably. The rules are not based upon contemplation of misuse. Should isolated cases of misuse occur, Rule 1.6 and Fundamental Rule C suffice. Each case should be dealt with on its own merits. A race committee should not let the possibility of misuse of Rule 69 in some other case affect its decisions in a case before it regarding the applicability of Rule 69 and the nature of the relief to be granted." (Rule 75 also suffices in a situation of intentional misuse.) USYRU Appeal 182 reads, "The important point for a race committee to keep in mind is equity—the equal treatment of all competitors." (See also the preamble to Appendix 6, Recommended Protest Committee Procedure.)

It's very clear that the rule writers want sailing to remain competitor-enforced as opposed to positioning referees all over the race course. They have done a very good job at assigning specific and clear rights and obligations to boats in any situation that might arise on the race course so that collisions are minimized and tactical opportunities are made more challenging and fun.

In turn, it is up to us, the sailors, to use the rules as they are written and intended.

It was very upsetting to even hear the accusations that some of the very top boats in the 1981 Southern Ocean Racing Circuit had filled their water tanks, rolled extra sails inside other sails, and otherwise connived to receive lower ratings than they actually deserved, just as it is upsetting to hear someone obviously lie in a protest hearing as to what happened on the course or why they did something. At the 1984 U.S. Olympic Trials for Finns, a sailor who otherwise had sailed a great series *started* prematurely (the jury found as fact that he had done so intentionally) in the last race so as to try to prevent the one sailor who could beat him (and to do so he had to win the last race) from winning the last race. Prior to the race some other excellent sailors were of the opinion that by sailing so well in the first nine races, he had earned the privilege of *starting* prematurely to ensure his win.

You don't earn the privilege of infringing a rule. The nature of the sport is such that without rules the game would be useless to play; yet with the competitors on their own to sail by and enforce the rules themselves, the enforcement system is very fragile. It is too easy to lie in a protest hearing or subtly rock a boat upwind and down, just as it would be too easy to win if you could start halfway up the beat with the others behind the starting line.

In this edition of the yacht racing rules, the rule writers have taken some strong measures to amplify the message that sailboat racing should be synonymous with good sportsmanship and integrity with regard to fair play.

1. They have incorporated the terms "fair play" and "sportsmanship" into Fundamental Rule C.

2. They have underscored the principle of self-penalty, which is the foundation of our competitor-enforced rules system, by bringing it forward as Fundamental Rule D, and by incorporating the word "shall," thereby making it mandatory to comply with the rule.

3. They have addressed the continued abuse of Rule 54, Propulsion, by defining the term "sailing" and placing it in Fundamental Rule C, Fair Sailing; by providing a more "black and white" Rule 54; by permitting **protest committees** to disqualify yachts under Rules 54.2 and 54.3 without a hearing (though a competitor is guaranteed a hearing upon request); and by denying competitors disqualified under Rule 54 from

dropping that score in series permitting "throw-out races." [Note that by prescriptions the USYRU modifies the **rules** such that, in the United States, a Rule 54 DSQ **can** be dropped, and a **protest committee** can only act under Rule 54 without a hearing if the sailing instructions permit them to do so.]

4. They have further denied competitors from dropping disqualifications under Fundamental Rule C, Fair Sailing, or Fundamental Rule D, Accepting Penalties.

One problem is that some feel that the rewards from winning justify cheating, such as the "good feeling" of winning, the attention and hype, the benefit to business and sponsors, and so on. Obviously, this is a personal decision that all sailors must make for themselves. The hope is that the temptations to cheat can't possibly overpower the realization that once people start bending or ignoring the rules, or develop their own "common law," the whole exercise of playing the game becomes useless for everyone involved.

Rule 75, Gross Infringement of Rules or Misconduct—see the discussion of Rule 75 provides the external "weight" to encourage strict and voluntary rule observance. However, people who race should **want** to know that **everyone** whom they've spent the time, money, and energy to race against is sailing within the rules; and when they know or suspect that someone isn't, rather than joining in, they should take action under the rules to encourage the others to stop.

As four-time Olympic Gold Medalist Paul Elvstrom, generally accepted as the world's most successful sailboat racer, has said, "You haven't won the race if in winning the race you have lost the respect of your competitors."

4

The Fundamental Rules (Part I)

The first rules in the rule book are unnumbered. They are entitled "Fundamental Rules" and address four very important issues: helping others when in a position to do so, responsibility for one's own safety, fairness while **racing,** and responsibility for accepting a penalty when in the wrong.

RENDERING ASSISTANCE, FUNDAMENTAL RULE A

Every yacht shall render all possible assistance to any vessel or person in peril, when in a position to do so.

This rule is the first fundamental rule, reaffirming that this principle must be the one to which all sailors hold above all others. The rule book is very supportive of this principle. Remember that the word "shall" is mandatory. If it were proved that a sailor was in a position to render assistance but did not do so, they would be liable for disqualification or further penalty under Rule 75.

• Rule 46.2 reads in part, "A yacht shall not be penalised for fouling a yacht in distress that she is attempting to assist."
• Rule 54.1 reads, "Unless permitted by rule 54.3, a yacht shall race only by *sailing.* Fundamental Rule A, Rendering Assistance, . . . over-ride(s) rule 54."
• Rule 58 reads in part, "No person shall board a yacht except for the purposes of Fundamental Rule A, Rendering Assistance."

- Rule 59 reads in part, "No person . . . shall leave, unless . . . for the purposes of Fundamental Rule A, Rendering Assistance."
- Rule 60 reads in part, "Except as permitted by . . . Fundamental Rule A, Rendering Assistance . . . a yacht shall (not) receive outside assistance."

In addition, if you have lost time and/or places as a result of a rescue, you are permitted to ask for redress under Rule 69(b) and to have the race committee consider giving you compensation for the time and/or places lost. In the event you go to a rescue, try, if possible, to accurately note the time and your position when you began sailing to the rescue and the time when you got back in the race. On boats in offshore races it is common to keep a log of times and positions to help the race committee provide the fairest compensation.

A now famous instance of these rules at work is the rescue made by Canadian Finn sailor Larry Lemieux in the 1988 Summer Olympic Games held in the rough seas off Pusan, South Korea. While in second place midway through a race, Larry noticed a fellow racer in the water separated from his boat and having great difficulty. Larry went to the sailor's rescue, succeeded in getting him safely back to his boat, and after the race requested redress under Rule 69(b). The Olympic Jury awarded Larry points equal to finishing second in that race.

Several appeals speak clearly on the subject. IYRU Case 66/USYRU Appeal 161 reads:

"FACTS AND CONCLUSIONS: The circumstances involved only one yacht. Shortly after jibing around a reach mark, the crew of Polecat fell overboard. It took her helmsman several minutes to take down the spinnaker and get the yacht in condition to be able to get back to the crewman in the water, during which time the yacht made little or no forward progress. While this was going on a spectator boat picked up the crewman and offered to take him ashore. Instead he was put back on board and Polecat resumed the race. After finishing and returning to the club, Polecat elected to retire in view of Rule 60, Outside Assistance. Subsequently she requested reinstatement on the grounds that, in the interests of safety, the penalty of retirement points was too severe.

"DECISION: While Rule 60 generally precludes a yacht from receiving

outside assistance, it also contains a specific exception in the circumstances of Fundamental Rule A where the assistance is rendered to a
vessel or person in peril. In the best interests of safety a man overboard
normally should be considered to involve some degree of peril; no
countervailing circumstances appear here. Further, Polecat met the
requirements of Rule 59, namely the man overboard was back on board
before she continued in the race for the protest committee found that
Polecat made 'little or no forward progress' during the recovery opera-
tion. Accordingly Polecat's appeal is sustained and she is reinstated in
her finishing position."

USYRU Appeal 75 reads:

"FACTS: The race committee reported that Catamaran #15 capsized
at the windward mark and received assistance in righting from a spectator who dove from the committee boat, swam to the Catamaran and
assisted in righting it, and then swam back to the committee boat. The
race committee proceeding in accordance with Rule 70.2 disqualified
Catamaran #15 for having received outside assistance, and she
appealed the decision.

"DECISION: Rule 60 asserts that a yacht shall not receive outside
assistance while racing with three exceptions: (1) a person may come
aboard to attend to an injured or ill member of the crew as provided in
Rule 58; (2) she may receive assistance when a person is in peril as
provided in Fundamental Rule A; and (3) she may receive assistance
from the crew of a vessel fouled as provided in Rule 55. The facts
submitted by the race committee do not indicate that any of the exceptions was applicable in the situation. Therefore the decision of the race
committee is affirmed, and the disqualification of Catamaran #15 for
infringement of Rule 60 is sustained."

IYRU Case 38 reads:

"SUMMARY OF THE CASE: One of the dinghies capsized during the
race. Upon reaching her, a second yacht asked if she needed assistance. Told that she did, the second yacht came alongside and took the
two crew members aboard. Then all hands worked to right the first yacht,
which took several minutes, owing to the fact that her masthead was
stuck in soft mud. During the interval, a third yacht came by and the
helmsman of the assisting yacht hailed her that there was no point in
continuing to race for he intended to claim that the race should be

abandoned. Upon reaching shore the assisting yacht requested redress, inasmuch as her action in rendering assistance had prejudiced any chance of her winning or placing in the race. The request cited Rule 69, and the redress sought was abandonment.

"The race committee considered several factors in its decision. First, the helmsman of the capsized yacht was a highly-experienced sailor. Secondly the wind was light, and the tide was rising and would shortly have lifted the mast free. Thirdly, she did not ask for assistance; it was offered. Therefore, neither yacht nor her crew was in peril. Accordingly, the request for redress was refused. Nonetheless, since the second yacht's hail to the third yacht had prejudiced the latter's finishing position, the race committee decided to abandon the race under Rule 5.4 ('Reasons directly affecting . . . the fairness of the competition') and ordered it to be resailed.

"While the result was the same as the assisting yacht had sought, she appealed on principle. Her reasoning was that, while Fundamental Rule A requires that 'every yacht shall render all possible assistance to any vessel or person in peril when in a position to do so,' it does not place any onus on a yacht rendering assistance to decide, or to defend, a decision that peril was involved. As to the comment given to the third yacht, she was free to make whatever use of that information she saw fit—i.e., to continue racing or not.

"In commenting on the appeal, the protest committee argued that it must have some discretion in the application of Fundamental Rule A in order to be able to guard against unscrupulous competitors who might, for example, demand to be given assistance when not actually in peril, or cause abandonment of a race in which they would otherwise finish last or not at all. Also, it offered further reasons for considering the capsized yacht not to have been in peril:

1. both crew members were wearing personal buoyancy;
2. the yacht had built-in flotation; and
3. a rescue launch, while not in the immediate vicinity at the time, was in attendance on the race course.

"DECISION: Appeal upheld, to the extent that the protest committee should reconsider its decision with respect to Rule 69. A yacht in a position to assist another that may be in peril is bound to do so. That she offers assistance not requested is irrelevant. That a race committee, later assessing the many factors that may cause a vessel or person to be in peril, concludes that no peril existed is likewise irrelevant.

"A yacht that, in rendering assistance, prejudices her finishing position, may seek redress, even when subsequent examination shows that no peril has arisen. From the evidence in this case, there seems little doubt that the appellant prejudiced her finishing position. While a decision to take action under Rule 69 lies within the discretion of the protest committee it ought to have agreed that Rule 69 applied and have decided what action was to be taken.

"In regard to the committee's expressed fear of possible exploitation by an unscrupulous helmsman of such a situation, the rules are not based upon contemplation of misuse. Should instances of misuse occur, Fundamental Rule C—Fair Sailing, and Rule 1.6 suffice.

"A protest committee's options are not confined to abandoning or cancelling a race. Rule 74.2 states that a protest committee, after satisfying itself that redress is warranted, 'shall make as equitable an arrangement as possible for all yachts concerned.' To abandon or cancel a race merely because one yacht at the rear justifiably seeks redress might be more inequitable to all the other yachts.

"Depending upon circumstances, such an arrangement could include one of the following options:

1. to arrange a sail-off between the prejudiced yacht and those ahead of or close by her at the time, if they could be identified;
2. to award the prejudiced yacht breakdown points;
3. if the incident occurred close enough to the finishing line for her probable finishing position to be determined with some certainty, to consider her as having finished in that position;
4. to award the average points scored in the other races of a series, less the score of her worst race, when a discard is allowed."

RESPONSIBILITY OF A YACHT, FUNDAMENTAL RULE B

It shall be the sole responsibility of each yacht to decide whether or not to *start* or to continue to *race*.

There have been attempted lawsuits brought unsuccessfully against race committees by sailors who have had accidents during races in strong winds. Their contentions have been, in part, that the race committee has jeopardized their safety by holding races in severe conditions. USYRU Appeal 209 is crystal clear: "The decision whether to start, postpone, or abandon a race is a matter solely within the jurisdiction of the race committee. Under Fundamental Rule B—Responsibility of a Yacht, each yacht has the sole responsibility to decide whether or not to race. If a yacht decides not to race, she cannot claim her finishing position was prejudiced. If she disagrees with the race committee's judgement, her recourse is to the Commodore of the host club." Notice that it is the **yacht's** responsibility to decide. Every sailor on a yacht has the responsibility to voice their opinion as to whether or not to *start* or to continue to race. Nothing in this rule protects an owner, skipper, or helmsman from a liability suit by their crew.

One related topic is the Life Jacket Signal (Code Flag "Y"). Many race committees utilize this provision of Rule 4.1, which reads, "Code Flag 'Y'—Life Jacket Signal, means: Life jackets or other adequate personal buoyancy shall be worn while *racing* by all helmsmen and crew, unless specifically excepted in the sailing instructions." However, the rule continues, "Notwithstanding anything in the rule, it **shall** be the individual responsibility of each competitor to wear a life jacket or other personal buoyancy when conditions warrant. A wet suit is not adequate personal buoyancy." The message is clear: Whether or not the race committee flies International Code Flag "Y," it is **your** responsibility to decide when to wear your life jacket, and whether to stay out on the water or return to shore when conditions become worse.

FAIR SAILING, FUNDAMENTAL RULE C

A yacht, her owner, and crew shall compete only by *sailing*, using their speed and skill, and, except in team racing, by individual effort, in compliance with the rules and in accordance with recognised principles of fair play and sportsmanship. A yacht may be penalised under this rule only in the case of a clear-cut violation of the above principles and only when no other rule applies, except rule 75, Gross Infringement of Rules or Misconduct.

As was discussed in Chapter 3 under "Fair Sailing and Sportsmanship," the rule sets down the principle of fairness and sportsmanship under which we all should agree to race. We agree to be fair, to be good sports, to attempt to win using superior boat speed and racing skills as opposed to other means, and to not receive any help from other boats or people on the race course, though in team racing we can obviously get help from our teammates (Appendix 4).

Notice also the first line requiring us to compete only by *sailing*. The inclusion of this new definition is a clear message that the abuse of Rule 54, Propulsion, must stop; and that the intentional use of kinetics is not fair sailing.

Notice that a yacht cannot be penalized under Fundamental Rule C unless no other rule applies to the particular situation. In addition, there must be a "clear-cut" violation of the Fair Sailing principles. In IYRU Case 107, "a more experienced helmsman of a port-tack boat hailed 'Starboard' to a beginner who, although on starboard-tack, not being sure of himself and probably being scared of having his boat holed, tacked to port to avoid a collision. No protest was lodged. One school of thought argued that it is fair game, because if a helmsman did not know the rules, that was his own hard luck. The other school rejected this argument, on the grounds that it was quite contrary to the spirit of the rules to deceive a competitor that way. It is known that such a trick is often played, particularly where novices were involved, and therefore guidance was sought on whether a protest committee should or should not take action under Fundamental Rule C—Fair Sailing.

"ANSWER: A yacht that deliberately hails 'Starboard' when she is on port-tack has not acted correctly and is liable to disqualification under Fundamental Rule C—Fair Sailing."

In deciding whether to apply the Fair Sailing rule, I feel it is important to consider the **motive** for the action—i.e., was it an intentional violation of one of the Fair Sailing principles? Here are some examples:

• A *port-tack* boat is reaching by to *leeward* of a *starboard-tack* boat before the start. Suddenly, the *starboard-tacker bears away* and hits the *port-tacker*. Clearly, this isn't fair. However, Rule 35 requires that a right-of-way boat not alter her course in such a way as to prevent another boat from keeping clear. As the *starboard-tacker* did alter her course and the *port-tacker* had no chance to keep clear, the *starboard-tack* boat is disqualified under Rule 35 and the Fair Sailing rule cannot be used.

Now, the same two boats are passing. This time the *starboard-tack* boat does not alter her course but just as the boats are passing, her boom suddenly flies out and hits the *port-tacker's* shroud. If it was determined that S's skipper let the boom out **intentionally** to hit the boat on *port,* I would disqualify S under the Fair Sailing rule.

• Two boats come off the starting line side by side in very light air. Suddenly, the *leeward* boat rocks hard to *windward,* the tip of her mast hitting the tip of the *windward* boat's mast. The *leeward* boat did not alter course and held the right-of-way. If it was determined that the action was done solely to try to touch the *windward* boat, I would again disqualify her under the Fair Sailing rule. I would apply the same reasoning to a *leeward* boat whose crew goes out on the trapeze in light air or otherwise reaches out and touches the *windward* boat for the sole purpose of "fouling the other boat out."

Notice that now the penalty for infringing the Fair Sailing Rule is more severe. Rule 74.5(c) reads, "When a scoring system provides that one or more scores are to be excluded in calculating a yacht's total score, a disqualification under Fundamental Rule C, Fair Sailing . . . shall not be excluded."

If a **protest committee** wants to give a penalty more strict than disqualification in a race for a situation where they feel a principle of the Fair Sailing rule has been intentionally violated but where another rule also applies, they can use Rule 75.1. (See discussion of Rule 75.)

One common practice that I feel strongly is **not** a violation of Fair Sailing or a gross breach of sportsmanship is the tactic whereby one competitor tries to put boats between themselves and another competitor at the finish. The likely scenario is: On the last beat of the last race, Boat A is winning the race and Boat B is in second. If Boat B finishes second, they win the series; but if

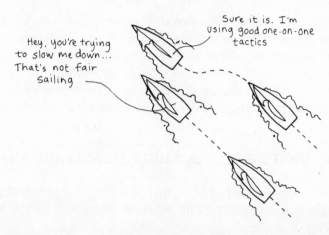

Boat B finishes worse than fifth, then Boat A will win. Beginning the final beat, Boat A turns around and sails back toward Boat B. Because she is not on a "free leg," Rule 39 does not apply and Boat A may sail where she pleases provided she keeps clear when required. Boat A positions herself on Boat B's wind and proceeds to slow Boat B for the entire leg. At times, Boat A is sailing only "half speed" in order to further slow Boat B. Finally, at the finish, Boat B crosses in eighth place.

As long as Boat A has violated none of the rules (in which case Boat B would simply protest), nor acted in collusion with any other boat, she has not violated the Fair Sailing rule. She has raced by individual effort and fair sailing.

The use of the word "speed" does not imply that it is a violation of the Fair Sailing rule to sail slowly, either intentionally or unintentionally. There are many circumstances during a race in which it is a good tactic to slow down, such as when early before a start, on the outside of a group of boats at a *mark,* or pinned to *windward* of a *leeward* boat that is *luffing* you. Besides, many races and series are won by boats that were not the fastest but were the smartest, the most skillful and consistent, or even the luckiest.

Though some may shiver at the notion that it is okay for one boat to actively try to hinder another boat's race, the racing rules themselves are in no way constructed to discourage, inhibit, or prevent this. In fact, it is quite common for one boat to try to *start* close to *leeward* of another for the purpose of hindering the other's *start,* to intentionally *tack* on someone's wind on a beat, or to *luff* a boat downwind. In addition, it is quite common for sailors to be aware of "who their competition is" from the outset of a race or series and to actively seek opportunities to hinder them early on. As long as it's done on a one-to-one basis and within the yacht racing rules, there is no problem.

ACCEPTING PENALTIES, FUNDAMENTAL RULE D

A yacht that realises she has infringed a rule shall either retire promptly or accept an alternative penalty when so prescribed in the sailing instructions.

The principle in Fundamental Rule D, that you penalize yourself when you know you are in the wrong, is the foundation for our competitor-enforced, "no-referee" rules system. The rule writers have made a significant change by giving it prominence as a Fundamental Rule and by using the phrase "shall either retire or accept an alternative penalty." Now, when you know you are in the wrong, you are **required** to drop out or accept the alternative penalty if it applies (e.g., a "720," 20 percent, or the like). If you do not immediately penalize yourself, you are deliberately infringing a **rule**—i.e., cheating. If the fact becomes later known to the **protest committee,** you will be disqualified under Fundamental Rule D. The significance of that is that a disqualification under Fundamental Rule D cannot be "dropped" in series which permit you to "throw out" your worst score (see new Rule 74.5[c])!

A common scenario is the sailor who is in an incident, completes the race, and then comes ashore and tells the race committee he is withdrawing. If during the race he wasn't sure if he was wrong, he is certainly entitled to keep racing. And if upon further reflection and/or discussion ashore he realizes he was wrong, he can (and is required to) drop out immediately. However, if ashore he admits he knew he was wrong and now wants to retire, the race or **protest committee** can call a hearing under Rule 70.2(b) alleging infringement of Fundamental Rule D.

A **protest** should arise only when both boats **honestly** feel they are in the right. People who "never drop out," even when they know they are in the wrong, because they think they have a chance to "win" the **protest** in the hearing just waste the time of all the people involved in the **protest** and diminish the quality of the racing.

5

The Definitions (Part I and Part VI)

DEFINITIONS. ALL PREAMBLES AND DEFINITIONS RANK AS RULES

The Definitions are the "dictionary" of the rule book. Words and terms like "finishing," "tacking," and "proper course" are specifically defined so that there is no question or debate as to their meaning. When a word or term defined in Part I of the rule book is used in a rule, it is printed in *italic* type. Many people have their own perceptions as to the definitions of these terms, based on either a knowledge of previous years' definitions or a quick read-through recently. Before studying the rules, be sure to study the Definitions, and then actively check back to them as you go through each rule, and you'll find that in a short time you will be confident of each rule's full meaning.

SAILING

A yacht is *sailing* when using only the wind and water to increase, maintain, or decrease her speed, with her crew adjusting the trim of sails and hull and performing other acts of seamanship.

The insertion of the term "sailing" as a definition, and the very first definition, represents the clear message that the intentional use of kinetics by racing sailors is not part of the sport and must stop. The term "sailing" has been incorporated into many rules, significantly:

Fundamental Rule C, Fair Sailing

"A yacht, her owner, and crew shall compete only by *sailing*."

Rule 54, Propulsion

"Except when permitted by rule 54.3, a yacht shall compete only by *sailing,* and her crew shall not otherwise move their bodies to propel the yacht."

The definition is clear and represents no change in fundamental philosophy as to how boats are to be propelled. The definition recognizes that the people on board (the crew, which includes the helmsman) must move on board the boat making adjustments, etc. in order to maximize the use of the power of the wind and water. It is Rule 54 that provides the explicit restrictions on crew activities that in and of themselves propel the boat.

RACING

A yacht is *racing* from her preparatory signal until she has either *finished* and cleared the finishing line and finishing *marks* or retired, or until the race has been *postponed, abandoned, cancelled,* or a general recall has been signalled.

You actually begin *racing* at the preparatory signal. In a 10–5–GO sequence, the five-minute signal is usually the preparatory (Rule 4.4[a]). In a 3–2–1–GO sequence, it's usually the two-minute signal. Check the sailing instructions for the race to find out when the actual preparatory signal is. Also, Rule 53.1 reads, "A yacht shall be afloat and off moorings at her preparatory signal, but may be anchored." (See Rules 53.2 and 53.3.)

You are no longer *racing* when you have *finished* **and** cleared the finishing line. USYRU Appeal 99 reads, "It is held that when no part of a yacht's hull, equipment or crew is still on the finishing line, she has cleared it."

STARTING

A yacht *starts* when, after fulfilling her penalty obligations, if any, under Rule 51.1(c), Sailing the Course, and after her starting signal, any part of her hull, crew or equipment first crosses the starting line in the direction of the course to the first *mark*.

You cannot *start* until **after** the starting signal for your class. If you are not completely behind the starting line at the starting signal, you are considered a "premature starter" (PMS), and you must return behind the line to *start* correctly (Rule 51.1[b]).

Notice that you *start* when, **after** the gun goes off, **any** part of your hull, crew, or equipment first crosses the starting line. There is no mention of **normal position** here. If your bow person is calling the line from the pulpit and inadvertently sticks their hand over the line just before the gun, or if your crew, by going out on the trapeze, mistakenly puts their head over the line one second before the gun, you are a "premature starter." The same is true if anchored and your anchor and anchor line are over the starting line.

Notice that the phrase "fulfilling her penalty obligations" refers only to Rule 51.1(c). Rule 51.1(c) is the "Round-the-Ends rule." Rule 51.1(c) is in effect whenever International code flag "I" has been displayed.

(See Rule 4.1 ["I"-Round the Ends Starting Rule].) Notice that the race committee can signal the Round-the-Ends rule on **any start** it wants, by raising International Code Flag "I" (a yellow flag with a black dot in the center) **before or with** the preparatory signal. When it is lowered, accompanied by one long sound signal, one minute before the starting signal, it means that the one-minute period of Rule 51.1(c) has begun.

The purpose of the rule is to keep people from charging over the line early and making it difficult for the race committee to have a fair start. The way it works is, if you are on the course side of the starting line or its extensions during the minute before your starting signal, you must return behind the line by going

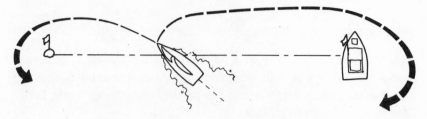

Forty seconds before the starting signal, A goes over the line. Before starting, she must go around one of the ends, which she can do immediately if she chooses—that is, she does not have to wait for the starting signal before going around the end.

around one end or the other at some point before *starting* correctly. Notice you can get back around an end immediately. You don't have to wait for the gun to go off.

USYRU Appeal 182 suggests to race committees, "Notification of yachts over the line in the minute before the start when the Round-the-Ends rule is in effect is entirely permissible under the rules provided the procedure is covered in a sailing instruction. The sailing instruction should state the nature of the notification—a hail of the yacht's number, ... a sound signal for each yacht, or whatever."

Notice the significant change in how to exonerate yourself if you hit one of the starting *marks* after the preparatory signal (i.e., while you are *racing*). Now all you have to do is get clear of other boats as soon as possible and do a "720" (two complete 360-degree turns in the same direction, including two *tacks* and two *gybes*). (See Rules 52.2[a] and 45.1.) That means that if you hit a starting *mark* by accident with the end of your boom at four minutes to go, you can immediately exonerate yourself!

The reasoning behind the "softening" of the penalty (prior to this you had to wait until the starting signal before re-rounding) was to bring the "punishment" more in line with the "crime." Generally, no real advantage is gained by cutting starting *marks* close enough to hit them well before the *start;* and the less time there is before the *start,* the more "severe" the penalty becomes.

FINISHING

A yacht finishes when any part of her hull, or of her crew or equipment in normal position, crosses the finishing line in the direction of the course from the last *mark*, after fulfilling her penalty obligations, if any, under Rule 52.2(b), Touching a Mark.

You *finish* when any part of your hull, or of your crew or equipment in **normal position,** crosses the finish line—i.e., when it first crosses. Again, in a strong adverse current, for example, all you need to do is get your bow across to get your finishing position or time. Rule 51.5 makes it clear that "it is not necessary for a yacht to cross the finishing line completely; after *finishing,* she may clear it in either direction."

Notice that the crew or equipment must be in **normal position.** "Normal position" is generally defined as the position where your crew or equipment is normally located in the existing wind and sea conditions (IYRU Case 101), so you can't come into a close downwind finish and suddenly let your spinnaker halyard and sheets out two feet, or come into a close upwind finish in light air and suddenly have your crew jump out on the trapeze to put their head across the line.

If you touch a finishing *mark* before you have cleared the line and *marks,* Rule 52.2(b) reads, "When a yacht touches a finishing *mark,* she shall not rank as having *finished* until she first completes her turns and thereafter *finishes.*" This is a much more severe penalty than before. After touching the *mark* you must get clear and do a "720"

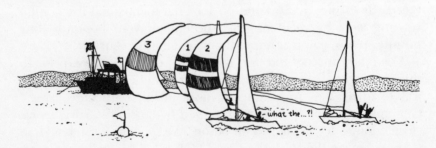

Boat 3's spinnaker is not in normal position.

(two **complete** 360-degree turns in the same direction, including two *tacks* and two *gybes*). Once you have completed your turns you may *finish.*

It is not uncommon to see a capsized boat drifting across the finishing line. It's perfectly normal for a boat to capsize, and a capsized boat that has not received outside assistance (Rule 60) is still *racing* (Rule 46.1). Of course, a boat that intentionally capsizes because they think they can *finish* more quickly may have to satisfy the **protest committee** that that particular capsize was **normal.**

Sometimes, when coming up to a finishing line, it is not always clear which way to go across it. USYRU Appeal 84 says, "A yacht *finishes* when any part of her hull, or of her crew or equipment in normal position, crosses the finishing line in the direction of the course from the last *mark*. It is ruled that 'the last *mark*' means the last turning mark prior to the finishing line." It is clear that the finishing line will usually be between two *marks* (one or both of which may be race committee boats) and that you simply cross the line in the natural direction from the last *mark* you rounded.

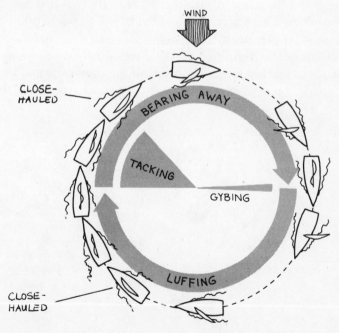

LUFFING

Altering course towards the wind.

What is confusing is that we use the word "luffing" to describe many things in the sport. When our sails are flapping we say they are "luffing" or that our boat is "luffing"; and when we turn up sharply toward the wind to cut off a *windward* boat, we say we are "luffing" the *windward* boat.

But, in the rules, the word "luff" means only **one** thing: the **alteration** of a boat's course toward the wind. Notice that the boat must be **turning.** Anytime you are turning your boat toward the wind, you are *luffing*.

TACKING

A yacht is *tacking* from the moment she is beyond head to wind until she has *borne away* to a *close-hauled* course.

This definition has been greatly simplified by removing all references to "beating to windward." Now there is just one definition for when a *tack* is complete, regardless of what point of sail the boat is on just prior to *tacking*.

Here's how the definition works, assuming you're *tacking* from **port-tack** to **starboard-tack.** You push the tiller over and the boat heads up. Though you are intending to *tack,* your *tack* doesn't

HEY... you haven't completed your tack

YES, he has ... they've changed the rule. Even when not beating to windward a tack is complete when the boat has borne away to a close-hauled course

begin until your bow **crosses** head to wind. Prior to that moment, you are *luffing* on *port-tack*. Your *tack* begins when the bow crosses head to wind, and it ends when you are **aiming** on a *close-hauled* course. Whether your sails are full or your boat has full speed **does not matter** to the definition.

There are still a lot of people using the phrase "full and by" to describe the completion of a *tack*. This was the wording in the 1949 NAYRU rules, but it has never appeared since! Do not use the phrase "full and by," as it is a clear signal that your rules knowledge may be well out of date.

IYRU Case 58 says, "L was wrongly disqualified, because her intention to tack was of no relevance. It was established as fact that, during her preliminary luff, she did not go beyond head to wind. Therefore, while she intended to tack, she in fact had exercised only her right to luff as permitted by Rule 38.1." IYRU Case 77 continues, "The race committee found as fact that, in attempting to round the mark, P luffed and passed beyond head to wind. She was thereafter, by definition, in the act of tacking and, having collided with S while so doing, was properly disqualified under Rule 41.1." IYRU Case 32 concludes, "A yacht has completed her tack when she is heading on a close-hauled course, regardless of her movement through the water or the sheeting of her sails." USYRU Appeal 135 summarizes, "In other words, when a yacht which tacks in 90 degrees has turned through an arc of 90 degrees she is on her new close-hauled course, whether or not her sails are full, and has completed her tack."

BEARING AWAY

Altering course away from the wind until a yacht begins to gybe.

This is the opposite of *luffing*. The definition of when a boat is beginning to *gybe* is covered in the definition of *gybing*.

GYBING

A yacht begins to *gybe* at the moment when, with the wind aft, the foot of her mainsail crosses her centre line, and completes the *gybe* when the mainsail has filled on the other *tack*.

Whereas the definition of *tacking* is based on the boat's actual position relative to the wind, the definition of *gybing* is based on the foot of the mainsail. On a conventional mast-and-boom rig, the foot of the main is usually attached to or very close to the boom. In this case, the *gybe* begins when the boom **crosses** the centerline of the boat, and the *gybe* is complete when the sail fills with wind on the other side. This will happen almost immediately and definitely well before the boom goes all the way out. Therefore, a boat is *gybing* only for a brief second or two. On a sailboard it's common to *gybe* by swinging the sail forward over the bow. Again, the *gybe* begins when the foot of the sail crosses the board's centerline and is completed when the sailor begins to trim the sail so that it fills with wind.

ON A TACK

A yacht is *on a tack* except when she is *tacking* or *gybing*. A yacht is on the *tack* (*starboard* or *port*) corresponding to her *windward* side.

If you are not in the act of *tacking* or *gybing,* you are *on a tack.* Notice there is no such beast as "on a gybe"—i.e., you are never on starboard *gybe.* Your *tack (port* or *starboard)* is determined by your *windward* side—i.e., if your port side is your *windward* side, you are on *port-tack.* To determine your *windward* side, see the definitions of *leeward* and *windward.*

CLOSE-HAULED

A yacht is *close-hauled* when *sailing* by the wind as close as she can lie with advantage in working to windward.

Because of the variety of boats and of people sailing them, this is one of the trickiest points of sail to define, though the definition has remained unchanged and very workable since 1930. Basically put, your *close-hauled* course is the course you sail in trying to get to the windward *mark* as fast as possible. In light and lumpy seas your *close-hauled* course will probably be a slightly lower course than in medium winds and smooth seas. In handicap racing, two boats of different sizes and designs will undoubtedly have slightly different *close-hauled* courses as well.

CLEAR ASTERN AND CLEAR AHEAD; OVERLAP

A yacht is *clear astern* of another when her hull and equipment in normal position are abaft an imaginary line projected abeam from the aftermost point of the other's hull and equipment in normal position. The other yacht is *clear ahead.* The yachts *overlap* when neither is *clear astern;* or when, although one is *clear astern,* an intervening yacht *overlaps* both of them. The terms *clear astern, clear ahead,* and *overlap* apply to yachts on opposite *tacks* only when they are subject to Rule 42, Rounding or Passing Marks and Obstructions.

Forgetting for a moment what *tack* the boats are on, let's look at two boats sailing near each other. To figure out if they are *overlapped,* take one of the boats and draw a line down its centerline. Then find the aftermost point of its hull or equipment **in normal position.** Draw another line perpendicular to the centerline and through the aftermost point. If the other boat's hull and equipment **in normal position** are completely behind that line, they are *clear astern* and you are *clear ahead.* If they are across that line at all, then neither of you is *clear astern* of the other; therefore you two are *overlapped.*

Now let's say you were *clear ahead* of the other boat by five feet. Put a third boat **in between** you two. If the first boat, who was *clear astern,* now *overlaps* this middle boat and the middle boat *overlaps* you, the definition says that now the first boat is *overlapped* with you.

One point worth discussing is determining the aftermost point of the hull and equipment in normal position. It literally means the point on the boat that is the farthest aft—i.e., the point that would hit a wall first if the boat were backed into one. This raises the point that the definition doesn't specify "above" or "below" the surface of the water, nor do any of the appeals. Because the intent of the rules is to provide practical and enforceable rules under which to sail, common sense suggests that the *overlap* is based on the aftermost point **above** the surface of the water. But

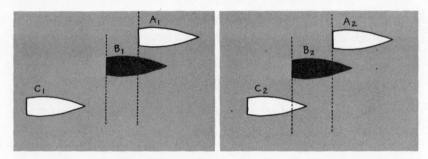

In position 1, A and B are overlapped, and C is clear astern of both A and B. In position 2, C is overlapped with B, and because B is overlapped with A, C is now technically overlapped with A.

this would certainly include the trailing edge of a rudder or aft tip of a rudderhead. Notice also the term "normal position" again. (See the definition of *finishing*.) If your auxiliary engine is tilted up, then in all likelihood the propeller is the aftermost point; and if you've been sailing the race with it up, you can't come into a *mark* and quickly swing the engine down just to break an *overlap* by making your boat shorter.

Notice that the terms "clear astern," "clear ahead," and "overlap" do not apply to boats on opposite *tacks*, **unless** they are about to round or pass a *mark* or *obstruction*. So two boats side by side on opposite *tacks* halfway down the run are **not** *overlapped*, but when they get down near the "two boat-length circle" at the *mark*, they are considered to be *overlapped*. (See Rule 42.)

Also, Rule 38.2(b) puts a **special limitation** on the term "overlap" that **only applies** to boats wanting to *luff* sharply near each other. (See the discussion of Rule 38.2[b].)

LEEWARD AND WINDWARD

The *leeward* side of a yacht is that on which she is, or when head to wind, was, carrying her mainsail. The opposite side is the *windward* side. When neither of two yachts on the same *tack* is *clear astern*, the one on the *leeward* side of the other is the *leeward yacht*. The other is the *windward yacht*.

SPECIAL SAILBOARD DEFINITION
(APPENDIX 2,1.1)

The *windward* side of a sailboard is the side that is, or, when head to wind or with the wind astern, was, toward the wind, regardless of the direction in which the sailboard is *sailing.* However, when *sailing* by the lee (i.e., with the wind coming over her stern from the same side her boom is on), the *windward* side is the other side. The opposite side is the *leeward* side. When neither of two sailboards on the same *tack* is *clear astern,* the one on the *windward* side of the other is the *windward* sailboard. The other is the *leeward* sailboard.

Remember that in the definition for *on a tack* we are told that whether you are on *port-* or *starboard-tack* is determined by your *windward* side—i.e., if your *windward* side is your starboard side, you are on *starboard-tack.*

For all boats **except sailboards,** the *windward* and *leeward* sides are determined by where the **mainsail** is. If your mainsail (think of your boom) is on the port side, then the port side is your *leeward* side and the starboard side is *windward.* This makes sense because the wind is blowing **over** the starboard side **pushing** the mainsail to *leeward.*

If the boat is head to wind, your boom will be in the middle of the boat. You have not **crossed** head to wind, so you are not *tacking,* therefore you are still *on a tack.* If the main **had previously** been on the port side, then the port side is still your *leeward* side and you are still on *starboard-tack.*

Picture yourself sailing *close-hauled* on *port-tack* (boom on the starboard side) in light air. Now heel the boat sharply to *windward.* The boom falls to the port side of the boat. Are you now on *starboard-tack?* Though the definition merely states, "The *leeward* side . . . is that on which she is . . . carrying her mainsail," it is my opinion in applying the **rules** and definitions that they refer to where the **wind** would **naturally** push the sail, not to where some force other than the wind, such as your arm or gravity, would force it to go. So if you are sailing along on *starboard-tack,* go head to wind, and push the boom out on the starboard side to back down, you are still on *starboard-tack* as long as your bow doesn't

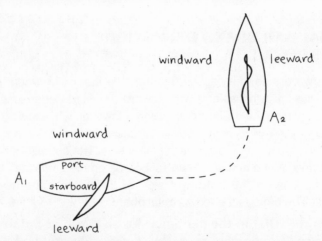

In position 1, A's mainsail is on the starboard side. Therefore A's starboard side is the leeward side, her port side is the windward side, and she is on port-tack. In position 2, A is head-to-wind. Her windward side is still her port side, so she is still on port-tack.

cross head to wind. The moment it crosses head to wind, you are *tacking* until you fall off to a *close-hauled* course.

The other issue is sailing "by the lee." You're sailing on a run on *starboard-tack* in a Laser (no side shrouds) with a superlong mainsheet. You turn past dead downwind and let out your mainsail. Now the wind is hitting your *leeward* (port) side first **but** your mainsail is still being carried on the *leeward* (port) side. You continue to turn, letting your main out farther and farther until the wind is hitting your port side at a 45-degree angle. If your boom was not capable of being let out more than 90 degrees to the centerline, as is the case in most boats with side shrouds, the wind would have **pushed** the boom over to the starboard side, *gybing* the boat. Because the Laser has no side shrouds, an unnatural situation develops. Though there's no appeal to provide a guideline, it is my opinion that at some point a boat sailing "by the lee" should be considered on the other *tack,* even though her boom has not actually crossed the centerline. My opinion is that anytime a boat is sailing much past 15 degrees beyond dead downwind, it should be considered to be on the other *tack.* Notice that the sailboard definition clarifies this for sailboards.

Finally, there is the definition of *windward* and *leeward* boat. If the boats are **on the same tack** and they are **overlapped,** the one on the *leeward* side of the other is the *leeward* boat. The other is the *windward* boat. Notice that if they are **not** *overlapped,* they are not *windward* and *leeward* boats, they are *clear ahead* and *clear astern.*

PROPER COURSE

A *proper course* is any course that a yacht might *sail* after the starting signal, in the absence of the other yacht or yachts affected, to *finish* as quickly as possible. The course *sailed* before *luffing* or *bearing away* is presumably, but not necessarily, that yacht's *proper course.* There is no *proper course* before the starting signal.

This is probably the most difficult and misunderstood definition in the book, though it is very important, particularly in applying Rule 38. A good analogy is that of a Time Trial. You and nine other sailors show up to race around a fixed-length triangle course, one at a time; the one with the fastest time wins. Around the windward-reach-reach course there are windshifts, grandstands, and a small manmade island on the second reach for the press and photographers.

You *start.* You've already calculated the fastest path up the first beat, accounting for windshifts, waves, current, time lost while *tacking,* and so on. Down the first reach as you approach the grandstand area, you notice it's creating a huge wind shadow, so you *bear away* to avoid the light air and break through to leeward as quickly as possible. On the second reach you've calculated that passing to leeward of the press island is the shortest, fastest route to the leeward *mark.* You *finish.*

The next boat *starts.* But this boat goes a different way up the beat. And it doesn't think the grandstand's wind shadow is that bad, so it doesn't *bear off* as much. And finally it passes the press island to windward and *finishes.* Both boats were trying to race and *finish* as quickly as possible, and so they were both sailing *proper courses.* In fact, all the boats may have had different opinions as to the fastest course that day. The course each boat sailed was a *proper course.*

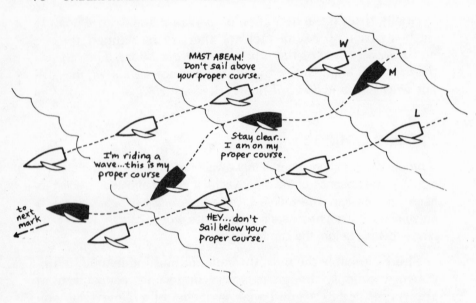

M is surfing waves in order to increase her speed in an attempt to arrive at the next mark as quickly as possible. Therefore, her luffing and bearing away are justifiable changes in her proper course; M has not infringed any rules.

USYRU Appeal 127 substantiates that there may be more than one *proper course* based on people's different viewpoints on what will get them to the next *mark* more quickly. "It is possible therefore that there may be several proper courses at any given moment depending upon the particular circumstances involved." However, because it is often difficult to prove when someone is actually on a *proper course* as opposed to sailing extra high or low for tactical purposes, IYRU Case 25 suggests, "Which of two different courses is the faster one to the next mark cannot be determined in advance and is not necessarily proven by one yacht or the other reaching the next mark ahead. Two of the criteria for a proper course are whether the yacht sailing it has a logical reason for its being a proper course and whether she applies it with some consistency."

For some, the phrase "in the absence of the other yacht or yachts affected" in the definition is confusing. This doesn't mean "in the absence of all the boats in the race." The key word is

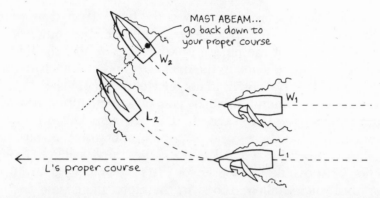

L has luffed above her proper course solely to try to prevent W from passing her. In W's absence, L would not have luffed at all. Therefore, when W reaches the "mast abeam" position, L must immediately return to her proper course.

"affected." Let's say you and another boat are sailing down a reach. The other boat is to windward and has "mast abeam"; therefore, you are not permitted to sail *above* your *proper course* (Rule 38.2[a]). You're sailing on a *proper course* to the gybe *mark* and catching up to a group of boats (*obstructions*) in front of you going slowly. Now you have to decide whether to *luff* up and try to pass the group to windward, or *bear away* and try to pass to leeward. You decide that you will arrive at the gybe *mark* faster by *luffing* and passing the group to windward, but by *luffing* you will

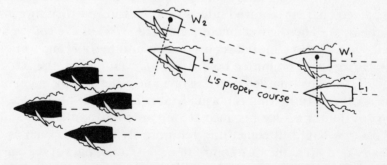

In position 1, L decides that she will arrive at the gybe mark faster by luffing and sailing to windward of the pack in front of her. Because she would do this even in the absence of W, it is a legitimate new proper course for L, and W, as windward boat, must keep clear.

collide with the *windward* boat. W is the boat **affected** by your course and even in **her absence** you would change your *proper course.* The point of the phrase is: your *proper course* should be based on what will get you to the next *mark* and ultimately to the *finish* as quickly as possible, and not on a temporary change based on a tactical consideration such as a *luff* to cut off a nearby *windward* boat. (See IYRU Case 97/USYRU Appeal 215.)

Notice also that there is no *proper course* **before** the starting signal. That's because a *proper course* is the course sailed to *finish* as quickly as possible. Obviously, you can't start racing toward the *finish* until you are allowed to *start;* therefore, there is no *proper course* until after the starting signal is made. (See USYRU Appeal 227.)

MARK

A *mark* is any object specified in the sailing instructions that a yacht must round or pass on a required side. Every ordinary part of a *mark* ranks as part of it, including a flag, flagpole, boom or hoisted boat, but excluding ground tackle and any object either accidentally or temporarily attached to the *mark*.

A *mark* can be an inflatable ball, a bell buoy, a large power boat, an island, or any object the sailing instructions so indicate. Notice that often the sailing instructions require that government *marks* be passed on their required side as you sail from one turning *mark* to the next. These government *marks* are *marks* of the course as well. On a starting line between a race committee boat and a buoy, the **entire** race committee boat is a *mark* even though the actual end of the line is marked by a flag or some other specific point on the boat. Anything that is normally attached to the object is also part of the *mark*—for instance, a long antenna, a mizzen boom, or a large flag; but something temporarily attached, such as a whaler tied up to the race committee boat, is not part of the *mark* **unless** the sailing instructions indicate otherwise.

Notice that the ground tackle—i.e., the anchor line and chain—is **not** part of the *mark*. So on a race committee boat with a high bow, where fifteen feet of anchor line may be above the water, the anchor line is simply ground tackle, ranking as an *obstruction* to any boat in danger of running into it, and the *mark* begins at the bow of the boat. USYRU Appeal 59 reads, "The existence of the ground tackle of marks, wholly or partially submerged and only partly or not at all visible, is a common hazard to racing yachts and observation and discretion is required in allowing for its presence. Ground tackle, as stated in the Definition of Mark, is not a part of a mark and therefore no penalty attaches to touching it. If, however, fouling its ground tackle causes the mark to be drawn against the yacht, the mark has been touched and the yacht involved must act in accordance with Rule 52."

Also note that the entire object is the *mark,* not just the above-water part. The 1949 NAYRU rules read, "Every ordinary above-water part of such object . . . is part of the Mark, but no part below water." This was changed in the 1961 IYRU rules. One exception to this is when the *mark* is an island. IYRU Case 94 explains:

"When the sailing instructions prescribe that an island is to be rounded or passed on a required side, it ranks by definition as both a mark and an obstruction. In its condition as a mark, only its above-water parts must be considered; as with the ground tackle of an ordinary mark, its below-water parts, the submerged portion below the water's edge, need not. Therefore, a yacht that goes aground in shoal water near that island is not touching a mark within the meaning of Rule 52. She merely fouls an obstruction.

"On the other hand, a yacht that touches any above-water part, including a projecting rock or jetty, of an island that ranks as a mark infringes Rule 52 and is subject to the exoneration provision of that rule. There is an exception, however, when it is necessary for her to be hauled out on that island for the purpose of Rule 55 or to effect repairs, reef sails, or bail out as permitted by Rule 53.2. Rules 53 and 55 then over-ride Rule 52, because they serve a practical purpose and those permissible actions of the yacht in no way interfere with the proper sailing of the course."

OBSTRUCTION

An *obstruction* is any object, including a vessel under way, large enough to require a yacht, when more than one overall length away from it, to make a substantial alteration of course to pass on one side or the other, or any object that can be passed on one side only, including a buoy when the yacht in question cannot safely pass between it and the shoal or object that it marks. The sailing instructions may prescribe that certain defined areas shall rank as *obstructions*.

This is another commonly misunderstood definition. An *obstruction* is **anything** on the race course large enough to require you to make a substantial alteration of course to avoid it if you are about to hit it. In determining how large the object must be to be considered an *obstruction,* the definition offers three criteria.

One, the amount of course change required is based on the length of your boat and is measured from a point one of your boat's overall lengths away from the object. This strongly suggests that you keep a lookout for anything ahead of you, as opposed to suddenly finding yourself about to hit something right in front of you and needing to slam your tiller over to miss it.

Two, the definition says, "to pass on one side **or** the other." Therefore the size of the alteration is **not** based on what is necessary to pass the object in the shortest route possible, but on what is necessary to pass on the near side of the other—i.e., the largest possible alteration necessary.

Three, the size of the course change must be "substantial"— i.e., a large course change. In a twenty-foot boat, a course change of 10 degrees moves the bow three and a half feet. Done when one boat-length away, a 10-degree alteration will clear a seven-foot object on either side. (See Index B, Table 2.) **As my general rule** I would say that a course change less than 10 degrees is not "substantial"—i.e., a stationary object clearly less than one-third your boat's length would not be an *obstruction,* though a moving object will require a larger alteration to get around it. Obviously, a lobster pot or an average-size channel marker is not going to require you to alter your course substantially, but a race commit-tee boat, a breakwater, a large clump of seaweed, or another sailboat in a race will.

A powerboat can be an *obstruction* if it's large enough. When a race committee decides to use a powerboat as one end of the starting line, the powerboat becomes a *mark* also. Notice that it doesn't cease to be an *obstruction*. It is always an *obstruction*, but now it also happens to be a *mark*.

Notice also that another boat in a race is an *obstruction* when you are required to not hit it. Therefore, a right-of-way boat is always an *obstruction* to a give-way boat. IYRU Case 91 reads, "With respect to 'A' [which is *clear ahead*], both yachts [clear] astern are subject to Rule 37.2. [A yacht *clear astern* shall keep clear of a yacht *clear ahead*.] 'A' thus ranks as an obstruction to both." (See also USYRU Appeal 192.)

However, a give-way boat can be an *obstruction* when the right-of-way boat is **required** not to hit her. Rule 32 **requires** the right-of-way boat to try to avoid collisions resulting in serious damage or else risk disqualification. Therefore, when confronted with the need to alter course to avoid a serious collision with the give-way boat, the right-of-way boat can rely on the rules concerning the passing of *obstructions*—i.e., Rules 42 and 43 (IYRU Case 19). Similarly, when L and M are sailing above their *proper courses* and W suddenly gets "mast abeam," L and M are **required** by Rule

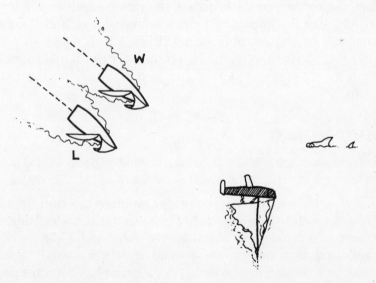

Rule 46.1 (b) requires L and W to keep clear of the capsized yacht. Therefore, the capsized yacht ranks as an obstruction to L and W.

38.2(a) to return back down to their *proper courses*. While still above her *proper course*, M is **required** not to hit W and can ask L for room to keep clear of the *obstruction* (W). (See IYRU Case 4.)

Otherwise, give-way boats are **not** *obstructions* to right-of-way boats. IYRU Case 45 reads, "Under Rule 36 [a *port-tack* yacht shall keep clear of a *starboard-tack* yacht], S held right-of-way over both port-tack yachts, PL and PW. Consequently, PW did not rank as an obstruction to S."

POSTPONEMENT

A *postponed* race is one that is not started at its scheduled time and that can be sailed at any time the race committee may decide.

A race can be *postponed* only if it has not been started. Once a race has been started it can only be stopped before the first boat *finishes* by *abandonment* or *cancellation*. A *postponement* is signaled, under Rule 4.1, by raising International Code Flag "AP," Answering Pendant (red and white vertical stripes), and is usually accompanied by two sound signals. (Check your sailing instructions.) When the *postponement* has ended, the race committee will lower the "AP" flag accompanied by one sound signal, and the next signal will be the warning signal (Rule 4.1[a]). Note also that under Rule 4.1(b) and (c) the race committee can signal a specific length for a *postponement*, or it can *postpone* to a later day (Rule 4.1[d]).

ABANDONMENT

An *abandoned* race is one that the race committee declares void at any time after the starting signal, and that can be re-sailed at its discretion.

Once a race has started, the race committee can stop the race by *abandonment* under Rule 5.4. This is signaled under Rule 4.1 by raising International Code Flag "N" (blue and white checkerboard) and is usually accompanied by three sound signals. (Check your sailing instructions.) A race that has been properly *abandoned* may be resailed. If the race committee plans to resail the race shortly, they can raise "N" over "X" (blue cross on white background). After an *abandonment* the next signal will be the warning signal.

Notice that the race committee is governed by Rule 5.4 when deciding whether to *abandon* or *cancel* a race. Rule 5.4 (iv) reads, "After the starting signal, the race committee may . . . *abandon* or *cancel* the race: . . . for any other reasons directly affecting the safety or fairness of the competition."

"Does this mean the race committee can abandon a race in progress when a large windshift occurs?"

Yes, when in its Judgment the windshift has made the race an unsatisfactory test of skill and therefore "unfair." The parenthetical phrase "(other than changes in the weather conditions)" that followed "reasons" in the 1985–88 rules has been deleted. In essence, this returns the rule to the same wording it had in the 1977 and 1981 edition of the IYRR. A 1979 Norwegian Yachting Association appeal, published by the IYRU as their Case 110, gave the interpretation that windshifts were a common occurrence in yacht racing and that, though unpredictable windshifts sometimes introduced a "lottery" element into a race, they did not affect the "fairness" of the competition.

According to the Chairman of the IYRU and the USYRU Racing Rules Committees, the opinion of the IYRU RRC has changed. The deletion of the parenthetical phrase is intended to permit race committees to exercise their good judgment and blow a race off if a major windshift ruins the contest. This "intent" is amplified in the USYRU prescribed optional instruction in Appendix 12,12.3, the reason for the prescription being to encourage race committees to alert sailors of their rightful prerogative by printing the same in the sailing instructions. IYRU Case 110 is now deleted.

Clearly it is desirable to reduce the number of subjective decisions a race committee can make once the race has started and they can see who is or isn't doing well. Therefore, it is my opinion that once a race has been started, race committees should make every attempt to anticipate and react to windshifts and to reposition *marks* in order to keep the race "fair" before deciding to *abandon*.

A race can be *abandoned* under Rule 5.5 after it is *completed* subject to Rule 74.2(b), Consideration of Redress. This means that before a race committee decides to *abandon* or *cancel* a race that has been completed, it must "satisfy itself by taking appropriate evidence that it is aware of the relevant facts and of the probable consequences of any arrangement, to all yachts concerned for that particular race and for the series, if any, as a whole."

CANCELLATION

A *cancelled* race is one that the race committee decides will not be sailed thereafter.

A *cancelled* race is signaled under Rule 4.1 by raising International Code Flag "N" over the First Substitute (a yellow triangle inside a blue triangle), and the race committee is governed by Rules 5.3 and 5.4. When a race is *cancelled* it cannot be resailed. A race can be *cancelled* under Rule 5.5 after it is completed, subject to Rule 74.2(b), Consideration of Redress. See related discussion under "Abandonment."

OTHER DEFINITIONS THAT APPEAR IN THE RULE BOOK

Room (found in Rule 42.1[a])

Room is the space needed by an inside *overlapping* yacht that is handled in a seamanlike manner in the prevailing conditions, to pass in safety between an outside yacht and a *mark* or *obstruction,* and includes space to *tack* or *gybe* when either is an integral part of the rounding or passing manouevre. (See the discussion of Rule 42.)

DEFINITIONS (FOUND AT THE BEGINNING OF PART VI IN THE RULE BOOK)

When a term defined below is used in its defined sense in Part VI (Rules 68–78) and associated appendices it is printed in **bold type.** The definitions rank as rules.

Rules—

(a) These racing rules, and

(b) the prescriptions of the national authority concerned, when they apply, and

(c) the sailing instructions, and

(d) the appropriate class rules, and

(e) any other conditions governing the event.

Protest—

An allegation by a yacht under Rule 68, Protests by Yachts, that another yacht has infringed a **rule** or **rules.**
The term **protest** includes when appropriate:

(a) a request for redress under Rule 69, Requests for Redress; or

(b) a request for a hearing under 70.1, Action by Race or Protest Committee, or Appendix 3, Rule 2.6, Alternative Penalties; or

(c) a notification of a hearing under Rule 70.2, Action by Race or Protest Committee; or

(d) an investigation of redress under Rule 70.3, Yacht Materially Prejudiced; or

(e) a report by a measurer under Rule 70.4, Measurer's Responsibility.

Notice that for one yacht to **protest** another, they must comply with all the requirements of Rule 68.

Party to a Protest—

The protesting yacht, the protested yacht, and any other yacht involved in the incident that might be penalised as a result of the **protest;** and the race committee when it is involved in a protest pertaining to rule 69(a), Requests for Redress, or Rule 70, Action by Race or Protest Committee.

It is important to understand exactly who is, and is not, a **party to a protest.** The **rules** in Part VI, Section B, provide many specific rights for **parties to a protest** and many requirements of the **protest committee** regarding **parties to a protest.** Furthermore, only a **party to a protest** may appeal a decision of a **protest committee** under Rule 77.1.

When a yacht lodges a **protest** they automatically become a **party to the protest,** as does the yacht they are protesting. When their **protest** is a request for redress under Rule 69(a), the race or **protest committee** whom they are alleging materially prejudiced their finishing position becomes a **party to the protest.** Often, in the course of a hearing, a third yacht will become implicated and brought into the hearing. If they become a "suspect" capable of being penalised for infringing a **rule,** they too become a **party to the protest.**

"If after acting on a request for redress the protest committee abandons the race in which I was first, can I consider myself a 'party to the protest' because I was 'penalised' and as such appeal the decision?"

Absolutely not. Rule 74.4 discusses "penalties," using disqualification as the usual penalty. You were not given a specific penalty when the race was *abandoned.* Obviously *abandonment* changes series results, moving some competitors up and some down. You may have been disappointed by the *abandonment,* but you were not "penalised" by it. A "penalty" results from a rule infringement either accepted voluntarily by the infringer or imposed by a **protest committee** decision. Because you were not at risk of penalty in the incident you are not a **"party to the protest"** and are not entitled to appeal.

On the other hand, you certainly can request redress under Rule 69(a) claiming that the action of the race or **protest committee** in *abandoning* the race materially prejudiced your finishing position. Then, once the **protest committee** has made a decision, you may appeal that decision. Notice, however, the decision in USYRU Appeal 230, "A yacht is not entitled to redress for proper action by the race (or protest) committee simply because alternative action also available to the committee would give her a better standing in the series." If you choose to request redress, you must be prepared to demonstrate why the committee's decision was improper.

(See USYRU Appeals 208 and 276, and IYRU Case 119.)

Protest Committee—

The body appointed to hear and decide **protests** in accordance with Rule 1.4, Protest Committee or Jury, namely:

(a) the race committee or a sub-committee thereof; or

(b) a separate and independent protest committee or jury; or

(c) an international jury.

The race committee can be the **protest committee** under Rules 1.3 and 1.4. Therefore, when it is written that the "race committee shall decide," the term "race committee" encompasses **protest committee.** Often the race committee will initiate a protest under Rule 70.2 and then be the **protest committee** for the hearing; or the race committee will hear a **protest** against itself. This is certainly permissible, though Appendix 6,2.1(d) reads, "When a hearing concerns a request for redress under Rule 69 or Rule 70.3 involving a member of the race committee, it is desirable that he is not a member of the **protest committee** and would therefore appear only as a witness."

USYRU Appeal 111 reads, "The race committee in initiating action under Rule 70.2 is not in a position of a prosecutor, but of an umpire, with one rather significant difference. An umpire who sees what he believes to be an infringement, rules forthwith, and his decision is usually final. A race committee or a member thereof in a similar situation, however, calls a hearing to give the 'apparent infringer' an opportunity to provide evidence as to the facts or support his action by a rule in his favor. The race committee at such a hearing is still in the position of an umpire. It should be noted that 'race committee' as used here includes protest committee, as provided by Rules 1.3 and 1.4." (See also USYRU Appeal 209.) (The **protest committee's** procedures are outlined in Appendix 6.)

Interested Party—

Anyone who stands to gain or lose as a result of a decision of a **protest committee** or who has a close personal interest in the result.

Rule 71.2(a) reads, "No member of a **protest committee** shall take part in the discussion or decision upon any disputed question in which he is an **interested party,** but this does not preclude him from giving evidence in such a case." (See also Appendix 6,2.1[b].)

The appeals give some guidelines to the interpretation of "interested party." USYRU Appeal 124 claims that "a contestant is an interested party." USYRU Appeal 175 qualifies that statement by explaining that a contestant who retires from a single race that is not a part of any series of races, and who is asked to hear a **protest** that does not affect the overall winners, is not considered an "interested party" on these grounds alone because they do not "stand to gain or lose as a result of their decision." (See also USYRU Appeal 176.)

Often race committee members will initiate a **protest** against a boat—for example, under the Propulsion rule (Rule 54). They are allowed to be both a member of the **protest committee** as well as the protestor. (See USYRU Appeal 209 and the discussion of Part VI, Definitions—**protest committee.**) However, they must disclose all their evidence and testimony as a witness in front of the **parties to the protest** (Rule 73.4 and Appendix 6,2.1[c]).

Other persons not specifically addressed in the appeals are parents (or offspring), instructors or coaches, employers or employees, sponsors or financial contributors, and members of the same yacht club, association, or even a fellow sailor with the same nationality. In the right set of circumstances any of these persons could be judged to be an **interested party.** If you feel any members of a **protest committee** are **interested parties,** you may object. Rule 71.2(b) reads, "A **party to the protest** who wishes to object to a member of the **protest committee** on the grounds that he is an **interested party** shall do so before evidence is taken at the hearing or as soon thereafter as he becomes aware of the conflict of interest." Appendix 6,2.1(b) continues, "The **protest committee** shall . . . ask the **parties to the protest** whether they object to any member on the grounds of 'interest.' Such an objection shall be made before the **protest** is heard." (See USYRU Appeal 175.)

In evaluating a member of a **protest committee** as a potentially **interested party,** the important criterion is: Will their hearing of the facts, their finding of the facts, and their application and interpretation of the rules be hindered by any prejudice or favoritism toward or against any of the **parties to the protest?** If a member of the **protest committee** honestly feels that any predisposition on their part will affect their decision in the hearing, they should respectfully decline to serve; and when you honestly feel or suspect that a **protest committee** member's decision-making ability might be affected for some reason, you have a right to say so, and to state your reasons.

CAPSIZED AND RECOVERING (RULE 46.3 AND APPENDIX 2—SAILBOARD RACING RULES)

Rule 46.3—

A yacht is capsized from the time her masthead is in the water until her masthead is clear of the water and she has steerageway.

Appendix 2,1.2—

(a) *Capsized*—A sailboard is *capsized* when she is not under way due to her sail being in the water or when the competitor is waterstarting.

(b) *Recovering*—A sailboard is *recovering* from a *capsize* from the time her sail or, when waterstarting, the competitor's body is raised out of the water until she has steerageway.

Note the changes in the sailboard definition of "capsized" and "recovering," and the inclusion of a definition of "capsized" for sailboats. The primary difference for sailboards is that the new definition addresses the "way" of the sailboard rather than the location of the masthead. For sailboats, it is the location of the masthead that determines when the yacht is capsized. Given that it is possible to "capsize" a boat without the very top of the mast touching the water, I interpret "masthead" to include the top few feet of the mast.

Note also that a sailboat is considered "capsized" while recovering from her capsize (i.e., other boats must continue to stay clear of her), whereas a sailboard is considered "recovering" once her sail or the competitor's body is lifted from the water (i.e., she cannot obstruct a sailboard or boat under way). (See Appendix 2, 3.3, "Recovering from a Capsize," and the discussion of Rule 46.)

6

Rights and Obligations When Yachts Meet (Part IV—Section A)

The rules that govern when racing boats meet are in Part IV of the rule book. Though Part IV is entitled "Right of Way Rules," the rules are actually written to say which boat must **keep clear** of the other; for example, Rule 36 says, "A *port-tack* yacht shall keep clear of a *starboard-tack* yacht." This means that not only must the *port-tack* yacht **not hit** the *starboard-tack* yacht, she must also not get so close that the *starboard-tack* yacht has to **alter course** to avoid hitting the *port-tack* yacht. Therefore, in learning the rules, it is more helpful to learn which boats do **not** have the right-of-way in meeting situations, as these are the boats with the requirement to keep clear.

In addition to the right-of-way rules, Part IV also contains rules that put restrictions on the right-of-way boats. In other words, a right-of-way boat cannot just go anywhere she wants. So it is equally important to see what restrictions the rules place on right-of-way boats in various situations.

Finally, there are times on the race course when a boat that holds the basic right-of-way, such as a *leeward* boat, may find herself on the outside of another boat while rounding a *mark*. While rounding the *mark*, the outside/*leeward* boat might have a **temporary obligation** to give an inside/*windward* boat "room" to round the *mark*. Part IV is clearly constructed so that when one rule conflicts with another it is easy to know which one overrides the other. The basic right-of-way rules are found in Section B, while the **temporary obligation** rules (which apply at *marks, obstructions,* when returning to correct a premature *start,* when re-rounding after hitting a *mark,* and when anchored, aground, capsized, or rescuing a person overboard) are found in Section C. As the preamble to Section C instructs, "When a rule of this section applies, to the extent to which it explicitly provides rights and obligations, it over-rides any conflicting rule of Section B . . . except Rule 35."

RIGHTS AND OBLIGATIONS WHEN YACHTS MEET

Preamble to Part IV

The preamble to Part I, Definitions, reads, "All preambles . . . rank as rules." The preamble to Part IV reads in part, "The rules of Part IV apply only between yachts that either are intending to *race* or are *racing* in the same or different races . . . from the time a yacht intending to *race* begins to sail about in the vicinity of the starting line until she has either *finished* or retired and has left the vicinity of the course."

The rules of Part IV do not apply in any way to a vessel which is neither intending to *race* nor *racing;* such vessel shall be treated in accordance with the International Regulations for Preventing Collisions at Sea or Government Right-of-Way Rules applicable to the area concerned.

The rules of Part IV also do not apply to yachts intending to *race* or *racing* in the same or different races when Rule 3.2(b)(xxviii), Race Continues After Sunset, applies. (See Appendix 9.)

First, notice that the rules apply to boats *racing* in different races. Rule 71.3 reads, "A **protest** occurring between yachts competing in separate races organised by different clubs shall be heard by a combined committee of the clubs concerned."

Second, notice that when you intend to *race,* the IYRU racing rules apply from when you begin to sail about in the vicinity of the starting line until you have left the vicinity of the course after *finishing* or retiring, and they only apply between yachts intending to *race.* This distinction may be important in resolving a financial claim after a serious collision when the boats were not actually *racing.*

SECTION A—OBLIGATIONS AND PENALTIES

Rule 31   Rule Infringement

Rule 31.1

A yacht may be penalised for infringing a rule of Part IV only when the infringement occurs while she is racing.

The preamble to Part IV is useful in establishing who held right-of-way in the event of a **protest** for an incident while not *racing*. But you can only be disqualified or otherwise penalized under the racing rules (Rule 74.4) in a race if the rule infringement occurs while you are *racing*. Remember, under the definition, you are *racing* from your preparatory signal until you have cleared the finishing line and finishing *marks* or retired. (See Definition of *Racing*.) So if your preparatory signal is five minutes before your starting signal and you foul someone with four and a half minutes to go, you can be disqualified. Remember also that you are no longer *racing* the moment your transom clears the finishing line and *marks* (USYRU Appeals 99 and 136 and Rule 51.5).

Rule 31.2

A yacht may be penalised, before or after she is *racing,* for seriously hindering a yacht that is *racing* or for infringing the sailing instructions.

This makes it clear that once you are no longer *racing,* you have an **obligation** to stay clear of boats that are still *racing*. "Seriously hinder" implies that you have interfered with another boat's forward progress or maneuverability in a "significant" way. How significant is "significant" will be up to the **protest committee,** but some guidelines might include: Was the hindrance intentional; did the hindrance cause a collision or an alteration of course to avoid a collision; in one-design racing, did the hindrance cause a loss of place; in handicap racing, did the hindrance cause a loss of time? The principle of the rule is that once a boat *finishes* it should not be able to interfere with a boat still *racing;* but the use of the words "may" (permissive, not mandatory) and "serious" (implying more than a minor hindrance) makes it clear that the infraction must be serious.

Remember that a yacht can also be disqualified before or after she is *racing* for: 1) "a gross infringement of the rules or ... a gross breach of good manners or sportsmanship" under Rule 75 (see the discussion of Rule 75); 2) infringing the sailing instructions; or 3) not complying with the rules of Part III, which includes Rule 26 concerning sponsorship and advertising. (See Index D.)

Rule 32.1   Avoiding Collisions

When a collision has resulted in serious damage, the right-of-way yacht shall be penalised as well as the other yacht when she had the opportunity but failed to make a reasonable attempt to avoid the collision.

This is a significant change in the rules. Under the previous Rule 32, even when the right-of-way boat was found to have failed to make a reasonable attempt to avoid a collision resulting in serious damage, it was not mandatory to penalize her. By using the word "shall," now her penalty is required!

The intent of Rule 32.1 is crystal clear. Every boat, including a right-of-way boat, **must** make an attempt to avoid collisions, and particularly collisions that risk injury to people or damage to boats; and by making the application of a penalty mandatory, the rule writers are strengthening this very important principle.

The difficulty in applying Rule 32 is that it requires our judgment as to what is "opportunity," a "reasonable attempt," and "serious damage." Here is my opinion based on the rule, the appeals, the dictionary, and my interpretation.

1. The rule is addressing only an action or inaction of the right-of-way boat.

2. The **protest committee** penalizes the boat per Rule 74.4, which requires disqualification unless the sailing instructions for that race provide for some other penalty.

3. The word "shall" makes the penalty mandatory.

For Rule 32 to be involved, the **protest committee** must be satisfied from the weight of the evidence (i.e., there is no "onus" on the right-of-way boat) that:

1. the right-of-way boat had the **opportunity** to make a reasonable attempt to avoid the collision,
2. the right-of-way boat did not make a **reasonable attempt** to avoid the collision, and
3. the collision directly resulted in **serious damage**.

"Opportunity"

The dictionary offers the following definitions:

opportunity: a suitable occasion or time; the right moment to take action toward a definite goal.

In deciding whether the boat had the "opportunity" to have made a reasonable attempt, the circumstances and the time frame of the incident must be reviewed carefully. However, I would think that the cases will be rare where the right-of-way boat simply had no opportunity to even attempt to avoid the collision. Furthermore, I would argue that a right-of-way boat that intentionally alters course onto a collision course with another boat (e.g., a sharp *luff*) loses the protection of the consideration of "opportunity" because she clearly had the opportunity to avoid the collision altogether had she not altered course. I would also say that "opportunity" is a moment in time. Therefore a yacht that can't take avoiding action due to some boat-handling difficulty had the "opportunity" but was unable to take advantage of it.

An appeal illustrating an example of when the right-of-way boat might not have had the opportunity to respond is IYRU Case 53/USYRU Appeal 140, in which two *port-tack* yachts "were approaching the windward *mark*. The yacht to *leeward* and *clear ahead* [LS] *tacked* to *starboard* and was immediately holed on her *leeward* (port) side by the *windward* yacht. The new *starboard-tack* yacht was disqualified under Rule 41.2. At the time of contact the new *starboard-*

tack yacht had completed her *tack,* therefore she held the right-of-way and Rule 32 did not apply to the *port-tack* yacht. If however the collision had occurred while the new *starboard-tack* yacht was *tacking,* the *port-tack* yacht would not have been in violation of Rule 32 because 'the fact is that she had practically no time to do anything after she had discovered that LS had tacked. . . . She was entitled to time for response under Rule 32, as under many other rules, but did not have it.' "

"Reasonable Attempt"

The dictionary offers the following definitions:

reason: a sufficient ground of explanation or a logical defense.
reasonable: agreeable to reason; possessing sound judgement; not extreme or excessive.

attempt: to make an effort towards; to try.

In judging "reasonable attempt" it is implicit that when two boats near each other, the right-of-way boat is first bound by Rule 35, Limitations on Altering Course, to hold her course—i.e., her straight-line or compass course. However, she may alter her course when, **in her judgment,** a collision is probable if she continues to hold her course (USYRU Appeal 157). Rule 32 serves to strengthen this latter responsibility of the right-of-way boat by saying that she **must** make a "reasonable attempt" to avoid the collision altogether **if** the resulting collision might result in "serious damage." So as she approaches the other boat, the right-of-way boat must continually assess the situation in terms of, "What are the probable chances that I may hit this other boat or vice versa?" This judgment should factor in what the response(s) have been from the other boat, whether the other boat is keeping a good lookout, what the sailing conditions are like and how well a boat of the class involved maneuvers in such conditions, who the sailors in the other boat are, and if there is anything at all peculiar about the way their boat is being handled.

My opinion is that a "reasonable attempt" would be the sailor's best attempt at avoiding or minimizing the impact of the collision, factoring in the amount of **warning** they had that a give-way boat might not keep clear, the **time** they had to consider what their best attempt might be, and the **amount** and **difficulty** of the boat and sail handling involved. Also factored in to a **much lesser degree** would be the competency of the sailors and the condition of their equipment and boat—i.e., their steering gear, cleats, and so on. However, the rules do not make allowances for poor seamanship, and I would be hesitant to excuse a right-of-way boat who failed to make a "reasonable attempt" due to poor sailing skills. In other words, "reasonable," to me, would be defined in terms of what an average sailor possessing average sailing skills could be expected to do in a similar situation.

In USYRU Appeal 159, P began to bear off to pass astern of S when a strong puff hit both yachts, forcing P into the wind with the result she was unable to keep clear and the yachts collided stem to stem. S, who was disabled by the loss of her headstay, powered into port and promptly requested redress. P promptly retired. The district appeals committee denied the request for redress and suggested that S came close to infringing Rule 32.

The USYRU Appeals Committee replied, "To hold that [S] should have anticipated the developments that occurred and, accordingly, should have borne off (a highly dangerous maneuver under the circumstances) or tacked is not supported by the rights given her by Rule 36 nor is it consistent with the obligation imposed upon her by Rule 32, Avoiding Collisions, since up to the last few seconds before the collision she had good reason to believe that [P] was in fact keeping clear."

IYRU Case 51 concerns a collision where P, a 5–0–5, and S, a Soling, were rounding the same leeward mark in opposite directions. Needless to say, the 5–0–5 received most of the damage as the Soling's bow "sliced through P's hull and side buoyancy-tank abaft the mast, the force of the impact knocking P's crew overboard . . . unhurt." The decision reads, "The rules of Part IV are specifically framed to avoid collisions. All yachts, whether or not holding right-of-way, are at all times bound to keep a good lookout. As S hailed 'Starboard' and saw that P was not responding to her hail and appeared to be out of control, it is evident that S could and should have taken avoiding action earlier. As she made no attempt to avoid a collision in time for such action to be effective and serious damage resulted, she is disqualified under Rule 32."

Finally, in USYRU Appeal 80 the Appeals Committee judged that a hail was a part of making a "reasonable attempt" to avoid a collision.

See also USYRU Appeal 266.

"Serious Damage"

The dictionary offers the following definitions:

serious: having significant or dangerous possible consequences, not trifling or inconsequential.

damage: loss or harm resulting from injury to person, property, or reputation.

injury: to harm, impair, or tarnish the standing of; to inflict material damage or loss on.

USYRU Appeal 12 concerns a *windward* boat and a *leeward* boat that had light beam-to-beam contact with slight damage. W was originally disqualified as *windward* boat, and L was disqualified for failing to avoid a collision. The Appeals Committee said, "The disqualification of L for infringement of Rule 32, Avoiding Collisions, is not justified by the facts. It is permissive, not mandatory, and designed so as not to penalize a right-of-way yacht merely for touching another yacht which should have kept clear." Clearly, Rule 32 is not a good defense for the boat on *port-tack* that gets "nicked" by a *starboard-tacker* ducking its transom.

IYRU Case 36 is the definitive answer to the question, What constitutes "serious damage"? "It is impossible generally to define the term 'serious damage' as used in Rule 32. In determining whether or not the damage resulting from a collision is serious, consideration must be given to: its extent and cost of repair relative to the size and value of the yacht concerned; whether or not it was feasible or prudent for her to continue to race; and whether the damage markedly affected her disablement and materially prejudiced her finishing position."

Their first consideration is the "extent and cost of repair relative to the size and value of the yacht concerned." To me, the "cost of repair relative to the size and value of the yacht" is a faulty barometer at best for judging "serious damage." My personal opinion is that the "cost" of something in terms of dollars is not made more or less significant in the light of the value of the boat.

For instance, I think it is unrealistic to say something like, "If the cost of repair is 10 percent of the boat's value, the damage is 'serious.' " Using this guideline, a $500 repair on a Soling (less than 5 percent of the value of a new Soling without sails, trailer, and the like) would not be considered serious, whereas in fact $500 is quite a large outlay of cash for most people. Another problem becomes assessing the "value" of the boat—i.e., the "new" value, "present market" value, "all-up" value including sails, racing gear, etc., or just "hull" value. Also, the **protest committee** will have to decide if the repair was reasonably priced.

Therefore, to me, a twelve-inch surface scratch in the gel-coat of a Lightning, which does not affect the overall speed, performance, or maneuverability of the boat but which might cost upward of $300 to make it look like new again (especially if the scratch cuts across several colors), would not be considered "serious damage" within the context of Rule 32.

Nevertheless, a similar scratch that penetrated the fiberglass, thereby requiring immediate repair after the race so that further damage didn't result or so that the future speed, performance, or maneuverability of the boat wasn't affected, would begin to fall into the "serious" category. If the extent of the repair were such that it could be handled that evening by the sailors involved with a minimum of hassle and expense, I would be inclined not to rule it "serious." But if the repair required more professional work **and** if the sailor indicated that they felt the nature and expense of the repair made the damage "serious," I would be more inclined to agree after judging the facts.

To me, the overriding consideration is the amount and extent of the damage itself. "Extent" includes the extent to which the speed, performance, or maneuverability of the boat was affected by the damage, and whether the damage required immediate repair to prevent further damage or subsequent loss of speed, performance, or maneuverability. Certainly, if the damage was such that as a direct result the boat was forced to discontinue the race, the damage was "serious" (USYRU Appeal 140).

IYRU Case 36 offers two further considerations: "whether or not it was feasible or prudent for her to continue to race; and whether the damage markedly affected her speed **and** [emphasis added] materially prejudiced her finishing position." (See also USYRU Appeals 223 and 253.)

Here are some examples of possible "serious damage":

- If the give-way boat **can** safely continue in the race and loses no finishing places **as a direct result of the collision in question,** the damage was **not** "serious."

- If the give-way boat attempts to continue in the race but does lose finishing places, and it is later determined by the **protest committee** that her attempt to repair the damage, "jury-rig" the problem, or to sail the boat up to its potential was unreasonable or unseamanlike, then it cannot be ruled that her loss was "clearly and demonstrably" proved. In this case, however, the **protest committee** might find that it had not been "prudent" for her to have **attempted** to continue, but again it should consider what was "prudent" for an average sailor in the same situation possessing average sailing skills and experience.

- If the collision involves Star boats, Snipes, or the like, and the whisker pole (which was being properly carried in a seamanlike manner) of the give-way boat was lost overboard, and the recovery or unsuccessful but reasonable attempt thereof resulted in a loss of finishing position, then there **was** "serious damage."

- If the collision results in a broken boom near the finish and the give-way boat loses no places but cannot repair or replace the boom before the second race of that day, the damage is "serious"; but if the damage was to something that could normally be repaired or replaced on the water, such as a bent guy-hook, the damage would not be "serious."

I would also be inclined to apply the same logic to a personal injury caused by the collision. Neither Rule 32 nor the definition of damage limits the injury or disablement to just property or the boat. Furthermore, two boats are considered to have collided even if the crew of one pushes off on the crew of the other. (See Rule 33 and USYRU Appeal 232.) If the injury is such that the boat cannot continue in the race because, in the judgment of the sailors involved, the injured sailor needs immediate medical attention, and it was found that the sailors involved showed sound judgment under the circumstances, I would judge the injury "serious" whether or not it was later determined that the injury required the immediate medical attention or not. And again I would judge the injury "serious" in terms of the nature and extent of the injury and of the attention needed, rather than the cost of the attention.

CONCLUSION

To make Rule 32 operative, three things must be decided. One, was a right-of-way boat involved in a collision that resulted in "serious damage"; two, did the right-of-way boat have the "opportunity" to make an attempt to avoid the collision; and three, did the right-of-way boat make a "reasonable attempt" to avoid or minimize the collision? If **either** the damage is decided to have been not serious, **or** if it is decided that the right-of-way boat did not have the opportunity or did make a reasonable attempt to avoid or minimize it, then the rule cannot be applied. As a juror I would focus on the **opportunity** and the **attempt** to avoid the collision before I considered the damage; and to penalize the right-of-way boat, I would have to be satisfied from the **weight of the evidence submitted** that the right-of-way boat was negligent or had shown very poor judgment or seamanship. Notice that the **judgment** of "reasonable attempt" and "serious damage" are not Facts Found and therefore are subject to appeal.

Rule 32.2   Hailing

(See Chapter 3, Principles—Hails)

Except when *luffing* under rule 38.1, Luffing after Clearing the Starting Line, a right-of-way yacht that does not hail before or when making an alteration of course that may not be foreseen by the other yacht may be penalised as well as the yacht required to keep clear when a collision resulting in serious damage occurs.

There are two clear principles here. One: If you have the right-of-way and you plan to alter your course or are altering your course in such a way that a collision resulting in serious damage is likely to occur, you should hail the other boat. This principle goes hand in hand with Rule 32.1, which says that the right-of-way boat should attempt to avoid collisions, and included in the attempt is hailing (USYRU Appeal 80).

Two: If you plan to *luff* sharply **after** *starting* **and** clearing the starting line, and there is a boat just to *windward*, you do **not** need to hail before or while you are *luffing*. This is a clear message to *windward* boats to look out at all times! But if the sudden intentional alteration of course by the *leeward* boat causes a collision that results in serious damage to either boat, I would argue that she failed to make a reasonable attempt to **avoid** the collision and therefore was in violation of Rule 32.1. (See Chapter 3, Principles—The Sharp Luff.)

In principle it is a good sailing practice always to tell the boats nearby when you plan to change your course.

RULE 33 CONTACT BETWEEN YACHTS RACING (RULE 33 DOES NOT APPLY TO TWO SAILBOARDS THAT HAVE TOUCHED EACH OTHER, APPENDIX 2,3.1.)

When there is contact that is not both minor and unavoidable between the hulls, equipment or crew of two yachts, both shall be penalised unless either:

(a) one of the yachts retires in acknowledgement of the infringement, or exonerates herself by accepting an alternative penalty when so prescribed in the sailing instructions, or

(b) one or both of these yachts lodges a valid **protest.**

One by-product of the rapid growth of inexpensive single-handed racing boats in the 1970s and 1980s is a considerable rise in the number of unprotested and unacknowledged collisions on the race course. Unfortunately, this trend has caused many veterans and newcomers to the sport to become discouraged and leave the sport. Rule 33 was designed to address this problem. Its principle is clear: If you and another boat touch, one of you must acknowledge that you are wrong by accepting your penalty, or one or both of you must protest.

Let's look at some situations. If you hit another boat and feel you are in the right, you should protest them. (See the discussion of Rule 68.) If you decide not to protest them because you see that they are protesting you, you are taking a big chance. If for any reason **their protest** is later found invalid (i.e., they didn't fly their flag at the first reasonable opportunity, they didn't notify the race committee at the *finish* when they were required to, they filed too late, or the like), then there is **no protest** and you both can be disqualified if the **protest committee** finds out about your contact.

It might happen that the boat you hit will retire or appear to be retiring. USYRU Appeal 210 is clear: "Retirement by itself does not necessarily indicate acknowledgement of an infringement, especially when serious damage has occurred. Without evidence of such acknowledgement the other yacht is obligated to protest under Rule 33 and may not claim lack of knowledge of the facts justifying a protest under Rule 68.4(a) as grounds for being exonerated for failure to display a protest flag. If she is in doubt regarding the significance of the yacht's retiring, she always has the option of displaying a flag and filing a protest."

"What if a boat hits me at the start, but because there was so much going on, I couldn't get the boat's number?"
The problem arises when you know you've touched another boat but because you were capsized or in the act of a difficult *gybe* or in a pile-up at a crowded mark or start, you don't know **which** boat you touched. Rule 33 requires that you **protest,** but can you **protest** an unknown boat?

No. To **protest** you must comply with Rule 68 and any pertinent sailing instructions. Rule 68.5 now requires you to include "the identity of the yacht being protested." However, Rule 68.8 permits you to remedy any defects provided you identify the nature of the incident. It would appear that you could change the protestee's number in a case of mistaken identification.

In reality, if you are capsized or in a jam and get hit, there is a good chance that the contact was minor and unavoidable, rendering Rule 33 inapplicable. But to be safe you or someone in the crew should make a special effort to get some identifying glimpse of any boat that you touch (hull color, name, sailor's clothing) so that you can track them down later.

 ### *"What's a 'third-party' protest?"*
If two (or more) boats touch and a third boat **sees** the contact and does not see either yacht indicate that they will lodge a **protest** or accept a penalty, they can protest on **that fact** alone. This is why Rule 33 is often referred to as the "third-party" rule. This **protest** under Rule 33 must conform to all the requirements of Rule 68, just like any other **protest.** Notice that Rule 68.3 requires the third party to **fly their flag** unless one of the boats that touched flies theirs. In this case, the third party does not have to fly their flag (because they have no reason to in that it appears to them that Rule 33 will be complied with). They can wait until they are ashore to see whether the boats that collided have lodged a valid **protest.** If not, the "third party" can lodge a **protest** under Rule 33 without having flown a flag (see Rule 68.4[b]). In either case, the third party must lodge their written protest properly and try to **inform each yacht** that they intend to protest (Rule 68.2).

One issue is whether a "third-party" **protest** needs to be filed within the time limit for filing **protests.** It could be argued that you will not know whether the yachts involved have filed valid **protests** until the **protest** time limit expires (Rule 68.4[b]), and that Rule 68.6(a) allows the **protest committee** to extend this time when it has a reason. The reason could be that you had to wait until the **protest** time expired before you knew if their **protests** were filed. However, a much safer move is to file your **protest** within the time limit. Then, if the yachts involved do lodge their **protests,** yours becomes immaterial and its purpose is served.

Remember, a "third-party" **protest** can be made only by a yacht directly involved in or witnessing an incident (Rule 68.1), or by the race or **protest committee** (Rule 70.2). If the race or **protest committee** wants to **protest,** they must have learned of your possible rule violation (in this case a collision) in one of the following ways:

70.2(a), they must have **seen** the apparent infringement themselves; or

70.2(b), they must have learned of it "directly from a written or oral statement including one contained in an invalid **protest** by a yacht that she may have infringed a rule" (i.e., self-incrimination); or

70.2(c), they must have "reasonable grounds for believing that an infringement resulted in serious damage"; or

70.2(d), they must have received "a report not later than the same day from a witness who was neither competing in the race nor otherwise an interested party alleging an infringement"; or

70.2(e), they must have "reasonable grounds for supposing from the evidence at the hearing of a **valid protest,** that any yacht involved in the incident may have committed an infringement."

For instance, let's say a *starboard-tack* boat protested you under Rule 36 for hitting them while you were on *port-tack*, and that they flew their flag five minutes after the incident. You both walk into the hearing, sit down, and say nothing. The **protest committee** is sharp and is running the hearing by the rules (71–74 and Appendix 6). Rule 73.2 reads, "When the protest committee decides that the requirements of rule 68, Protest by Yachts, and of the sailing instructions have been met, the protest committee shall proceed with the hearing." Rule 73.2 continues, "When these requirements are not met, the protest is invalid and shall be refused. . . ." Before any of the **protest committee** members have read the form, the chairman asks the protestor why they delayed in raising their flag. If the committee is not satisfied with the answer they should refuse to hear the **protest** (see also Appendix 6,1.3). Because they have not read the protest form nor heard anything from either of you, they do not know that there was contact and you will both escape unpenalized. However, if any member of the committee does read the form before you even come into the room, they would learn from the *starboard-tacker*'s written statement that the *starboard-tack* yacht had contact. Then once they determined that the **protest** was not valid they could call a hearing under 70.2(b) and both of you would be disqualified under Rule 33.

The only exception to all of this is that if the contact is **both** minor **and** unavoidable, Rule 33 does not apply. If two boats have contact each boat can quickly consider if they feel the contact was minor **and** unavoidable. If either boat doesn't think so, they must acknowledge their mistake or protest (by displaying their flag immediately or, if on a sailboard, by hailing the other boat). But if they both feel the contact **was** minor **and** unavoidable, they can choose not to protest. They are not yet off the hook, however.

If, after the race, a third boat or the race or **protest committee** protests them under Rule 33, they will not be penalized if the **protest committee** finds that the contact was indeed minor **and** unavoidable. If, however, the **protest committee** decides that the contact was **not** minor **and** unavoidable, they will both be penalized.

There are definitely people who feel that Rule 33 is offensive to their integrity. Their feeling is that often a collision does not amount to a substantial foul and that each sailor should be able to decide when and for what they want to protest. Rule 68.9 permits a protesting boat to ask the **protest committee** to find that the contact was minor and unavoidable. When the **protest committee** so concludes, the protesting boat may withdraw her **protest** under Rule 68.9. But when it finds that the contact was not minor and unavoidable, the **protest** will be heard and the infringing yacht penalized. This gives a right-of-way boat some latitude when they don't want to press for another boat's penalization.

But remember, if you are protested for any rule other than Rule 33, you cannot use the "minor and unavoidable" protection in Rule 33. You must defend yourself as in a regular **protest** (USYRU Appeal 240). Therefore, if a third yacht witnesses an incident (and a collision is certainly an incident), they can protest under an appropriate rule in Part IV (and not necessarily even the correct rule; see Rule 74.4 and IYRU Case 44) other than Rule 33, provided they display their flag promptly, as in a regular **protest.** Also, the **protest committee,** upon learning of a collision within the regulations of Rule 70.2, can call a hearing based on another rule of Part IV other than Rule 33. At this point the rules and IYRU Cases become very strict. When a **protest committee** has before it an incident involving contact, the contact is "**prima facie** evidence that some rule has been infringed and the protest committee is obliged to disqualify one yacht or the other" (IYRU Case 23). IYRU Case 44 chastises a **protest committee** for failing to "investigate a collision— one of the most obvious and fundamental infringements of the racing rules." And IYRU Case 77 says, "When two yachts collide, there must have been an infringement of a rule. Therefore, when hearing a protest arising from such an incident, the **protest committee** must, under Rules 74.1 and 74.6 [notice the word 'shall' in these rules], find the relevant facts and give a decision on them."

Only in rare circumstances may **protest committees** take exception to this. (See USYRU Appeal 232.)

What is the interpretation of "minor and unavoidable"?
First, the two go together—i.e., the contact must have been **both** "minor" **and** "unavoidable."

- Minor: A minor contact is not tough to judge. A slight bump, a spinnaker touching a shroud, a hand lightly fending off, and the like, are all minor.

- Unavoidable: This is the tough one. USYRU Appeal 240 says, "The test of unavoidability is not to be applied at the instant before contact. In almost all cases a collision is unavoidable at that time. It applies to the events leading up to the contact. If the yachts had steerageway, even a minor contact would have been avoidable."

USYRU Appeal 240 continues, "[Minor and unavoidable] is intended to cover contact at starts and mark roundings when there is very little wind and a concentration of yachts. It is not intended as a reason for exonerating poor seamanship or failure on the part of the obligated yacht to keep clear when there is reasonably good steerageway. The protest committee . . . found that the yachts were able to maneuver themselves in and out of the situation involved and to complete the course shortly thereafter. They obviously had steerageway. This is not the situation that [minor and unavoidable] covers."

It is clear that most collisions are "avoidable," which means that **very few** qualify as "minor" **and** "unavoidable." Based on USYRU Appeal 240, a contact that was "unavoidable" would require that **both** of the boats had little or no steerageway and that the lack of steerageway was caused by the sailing conditions (i.e., wind, current, and the like) as opposed to poor boat handling.

The following are examples that to me would qualify as "minor and unavoidable":

• You're sailing *close-hauled* side by side with another boat just after a *start* in light air, and a motorboat goes bombing by the fleet, its wake causing your boat to bump into the other boat.

• You're in a jam-up at the reach *mark* and the boat next to you shoves you backward into the boat behind you.

The rock-bottom line to all of this is that whenever you touch another boat, either take your penalty or protest them to be safe.

RULE 34   MAINTAINING RIGHTS

Rule 34—When a yacht that may have infringed a rule does not retire or exonerate herself, other yachts shall continue to accord her such rights as she has under the rules of Part IV.

When a yacht **knows** she has infringed a rule she is required by Fundamental Rule D, Accepting Penalties, to take a penalty. But when a yacht is **not sure** whether they were in the right, they may continue to race and then file a **protest.** And while they continue to race they maintain all their rights just as any other boat.

USYRU Appeal 4 reads, "Yachts A and B were involved in a foul early in a race and each protested the other. Later in the same race C, which had observed the incident between A and B and believing A to have been in the wrong, refused to yield to her right-of-way. A altered course and protested C. At the hearing the race committee disqualified A in the first incident and C in the second despite her contention that A, having been disqualified, was no longer entitled to rights under the rules. C appealed. DECISION: The decision of the race committee is confirmed and C is disqualified. Rule 34 . . . specifically relates to the situations in this case."

IYRU Case 2 reads, "Yachts A, B, and C are racing with others. A protests B, which is disqualified after the race. However, B does not retire from the race and protests C in a second incident. Once B has been disqualified, does her protest remain valid?

"ANSWER: In accordance with Rule 34, when a yacht persists in racing after an alleged rule infringement, other yachts shall continue to accord her such rights as she has under the rules of Part IV. Consequently, B's protest is valid and, when the protest committee is satisfied from the evidence that C infringed a rule, she must be disqualified, even though A's protest against B is upheld."

7

Principal Right-of-Way Rules and Their Limitations (Part IV—Section B)

Section B of Part IV contains the following principal right-of-way rules. These rules apply except when overridden by a rule in Section C.

1. *port/starboard*, Rule 36
2. *windward/leeward*, Rule 37.1
3. *clear astern/clear ahead*, Rule 37.2
4. *tacking* or *gybing/on a tack*, Rule 41

The other rules in Section B (35, 37.3, 38, 39, and 40) simply put **limitations** on the actions of the right-of-way boats. They do not **change** the right-of-way.

RULE 35   LIMITATIONS ON ALTERING COURSE

When one yacht is required to keep clear of another, the right-of-way yacht shall not alter course so as to prevent the other yacht from keeping clear; or so as to obstruct her while she is keeping clear.

Rule 35 is an extremely important rule, so we will spend a little extra time studying it.

Rule 35 is talking clearly to right-of-way boats. (See IYRU Case 115/USYRU Appeal 63.) When two boats are about to collide,

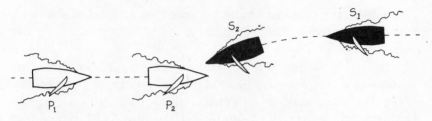

S has the right-of-way over P, but Rule 35 requires that S not alter her course near P in such a way that P is prevented from keeping clear.

the give-way boat has the obligation to keep clear. The only way they can decide how to do this is if they can accurately figure out where the right-of-way boat is going. It would be chaos if just as a *port-tack* boat was reaching by a *starboard-tack* boat, S could suddenly and unexpectedly turn and hit P.

USYRU Appeal 167 reads, "The purpose of Rule 35 is to protect a burdened [give-way] yacht from unpredictable alterations of course by the right-of-way yacht which prevent or obstruct the burdened yacht in fulfilling her obligations of keeping clear."

"If I'm on starboard, doesn't Rule 36 override Rule 35 and allow me to steer any course deliberately to hit a port-tack boat by luffing, or bearing away?"
Absolutely not. That is exactly what Rule 35 is designed to prevent. As IYRU Case 36 says, "Rule 35 always applies." "Tactical desires do not relieve a yacht from her obligations under the racing rules" (IYRU Case 129/USYRU Appeal 178). However, USYRU Appeal 167 points out, "Rule 35 does not shift the basic rights and obligations of the two yachts." It is simply a commonsense restriction requiring the right-of-way boat to hold her course when a give-way boat is close by and trying to keep clear.

"If I'm making a smooth turn toward a give-way boat, do I have to stop turning?"
USYRU Appeal 172 says, "Yes, it is an alteration of course for B [right-of-way boat] to continue the established arc of her circle. The skipper of A [give-way boat] might or might not expect B to continue circling. If B does not alter her helm and bring it amidships, she is altering course. She

must settle on a compass course (straight-line) as soon as she gains right-of-way or risk infringing Rule 35."

Notice that before you become a right-of-way boat you can maneuver as you want, as long as you keep clear of right-of-way boats. But the moment you get the right-of-way, and a give-way boat is nearby and trying to keep clear, you must hold your course (IYRU Case 115/USYRU Appeal 63).

Finally, notice that Rule 35 only prohibits an "alteration" of course. It reads, "The right-of-way yacht shall not **alter course** so as to prevent the other yacht from keeping clear; or so as to obstruct her while she is keeping clear." It in no way applies to a change in your boat's fore or aft speed or its angle of heel. When P reaches by just to windward of S such that S momentarily loses her wind, straightens up, and hits P's mast, P is wrong under Rule 36. Of course, Fundamental Rule C, Fair Sailing, is available to P if they suspect that S deliberately tried to hit her.

"Would you elaborate on the meaning of 'prevent' and 'obstruct'?"

"Prevent" is pretty obvious. If a give-way boat is keeping clear and the right-of-way boat alters course thereby causing a collision, then the give-way boat has been "prevented" from keeping clear. (See USYRU Appeal 71 and IYRU Case 129/USYRU Appeal 178.)

"Obstruct" means to hinder, impede, or interfere with. If the give-way boat is keeping clear and the right-of-way boat alters course such that the give-way boat must immediately alter **her** course to avoid an immediate collision, then she has been "obstructed" while keeping clear.

"Well, if I'm the right-of-way boat, how close to the give-way boat can I be and still alter my course?"

That's the important question to examine. Say P and S are on a beat and on a collision course. When five lengths away from S, P *bears away* in preparation to pass astern of S. Almost immediately, S *luffs* and *tacks*. P heads back up to *close-hauled* and protests under Rule 35 (see illustration). IYRU 10/USYRU Appeal 93 reads, "The action of P, in altering course, did not of itself require the starboard-

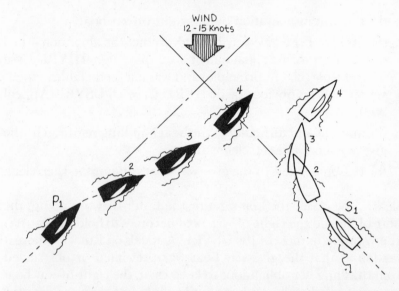

tack yacht to maintain her course. To rule that the right-of-way yacht must do so for this reason alone would seriously and unnecessarily limit her rights under fundamental opposite tack Rule 36. The facts indicate that when S luffed, preparatory to tacking, she did so at a sufficient distance from P so that P did not find it necessary **at that time** to alter course **again** in order to keep clear, and in fact, after bearing away P could not have collided with S while S remained on the starboard tack" (emphasis added). In other words, S's alteration of course four to five lengths away did not require P to alter her course to avoid an immediate collision.

The major considerations are: how predictable the right-of-way boat's alteration was, how accurately the give-way boat could anticipate and plan for it, and how much time and opportunity the give-way boat had to take further evasive action. (See USYRU Appeal 203.)

In judging this you should consider:

1. the distance between the boats;
2. the speeds and sizes of the boats;
3. the angles at which they are converging;
4. the visibility and ability to hail and hear between the boats;

5. the amount of alteration by the right-of-way boat;

6. the ability of the give-way boat to predict the alteration—i.e., did the right-of-way boat hail or attempt to signal (IYRU Case 35 and Rule 32.2 in principle) and was it a predictable maneuver such as an obvious tactic (IYRU Case 86/USYRU Appeal 202);

7. the amount and difficulty of the boat handling required by the give-way boat to keep clear; and

8. the reasonableness of the give-way boat's attempt to keep clear.

Clearly, the closer the boats get or the faster they are going, the more obligated the right-of-way boat becomes to hold her course. Interestingly, in most of the USYRU Appeals on Rule 35 where it was found that the give-way boat was prevented or obstructed from fulfilling her obligations to keep clear, the right-of-way boat was wrong if she altered her course when less than two lengths away from the give-way boat (USYRU Appeals 135, 157, 166, 172, 178 [IYRU Case 129], and 203). However, each incident must be judged on its own, and there are certainly times when a right-of-way boat's alteration when less than two lengths from a give-way boat is not a violation of Rule 35. (See IYRU Case 86/ USYRU Appeal 202, and IYRU Case 35.)

In IYRU Case 35, S and P are running on parallel courses (with S to P's left) less than one length apart. After about two minutes, S **hailed** and began to *luff* and the yachts touched. The USSR Yacht Racing Federation asked, in essence: "Can S luff or otherwise sail where she pleases even though P is less than one length away and keeping clear?" "ANSWER: S . . . was the starboard-tack right-of-way yacht under Rule 36, and P, as the port-tack give-way yacht, was bound to keep clear. In this opposite-tack situation, Rule 38.1 did not apply, so S did not have the right to luff 'as she pleased.' Nevertheless, she was not bound to hold her course and could alter it by luffing in such a way as not to infringe Rule 35."

The message here is clear. A right-of-way boat should not be restricted from sailing where she chooses by a give-way yacht; and it is not simply the physical proximity of the two boats that determines when Rule 35 has been infringed; rather, it is the ability of the give-way boat to anticipate the alteration and take evasive action.

The following USYRU Appeals show the rule in action (emphasis added).

In USYRU Appeal 135, "WP and LS were sailing close-hauled on the port-tack with LS about three lengths ahead and three lengths to leeward of WP. LS tacked to starboard and bore away to pass astern of WP as a result of which WP, who had already borne away somewhat, had to **bear away further** in order to pass to leeward and astern of LS without contact." Had LS remained *close-hauled* after her *tack* she would have been okay, but the Appeals Committee said, "Her bearing away **after** obtaining right-of-way on the starboard-tack was a **dangerous maneuver** and her alteration of course obstructed WP." LS was disqualified.

In USYRU Appeal 150, "Prior to the starting signal, S approached P making her final approach to the line. S slowly altered her course to windward in a long sweeping curve of about 25 degrees. At a point halfway along this curve P **saw** S coming at her. P made **little effort** to keep clear, nor did she hail the other vessels next to her on the same port-tack to yield and S was forced to bear off to avoid a collision." The Appeals Committee decided, "The alteration of course by S was **clearly consistent with making a proper approach to the starting line.** P had **ample time** to avoid her yet made little effort to do so. She could **easily** have borne off and passed astern of S. Since S's alteration of course did not prevent P from keeping clear and her failure to do so was the result of **her own inaction,** the disqualification of P . . . is upheld."

IYRU Case 86/USYRU Appeal 202 reads: "At thirty seconds before the start Yacht A is proceeding slowly toward the starting line on a starboard reach which will clearly enable her to make a proper start. Yacht B is sheeted in and coming up fast astern of A on the same basic course. As B bears off to pass to leeward of A, A also bears off to retain a position dead ahead. B hails A not to bear off and alters course further to leeward. A continues to bear off further and then alters course **radically** to windward for a close-hauled course to the committee boat. As A pivots, her stern swings directly into the path of B who is now very close, and a collision results. . . . B alleges that the maneuver was purely obstructional."

The Appeals Committee said, "As long as Yacht A is clear ahead of Yacht B, she is free to maneuver to protect her position and give her a good start. Bearing down to prevent B from establishing a leeward overlap is consistent with such a tactic and within her rights. Yacht A was **privileged** throughout the maneuvers illustrated and Yacht B was **burdened.** There is no indication that A endeavored to **mislead** B or that she did anything that should not have been **anticipated,** or knowing that A would be altering course to get to the line, that B was prevented from keeping clear or was obstructed while doing so. **Yacht B was in error in not keeping sufficiently clear to fulfill her obligations** and, in an instance such as this, should be penalized." Notice here that even a "radical"—i.e., sharp and sudden—maneuver **before the start** is not a violation of Rule 35 when it is obviously predictable and where the give-way boat could have kept clear.

"I assume from all this that if I get a windshift on a beat, I can't follow the shift and hit a port-tack boat that is just crossing my bow?"
That's absolutely right. In 1965 the rule read, "A yacht is not misleading or balking another if she alters course by *luffing* or *bearing away* to conform to a change in the strength or direction of the wind." But the rule writers realized that (a) it was too difficult for the give-way boat to anticipate how the wind might suddenly shift, and (b) this rule gave the right-of-way boat the ability to misuse the rule too easily. In 1969 the words "mislead" and "balk" were replaced by the word "obstruct," and the permission to respond to a windshift was removed.

IYRU Case 52 and USYRU Appeal 157 address this situation directly. In the U.S. Appeal, "S asked when she may alter her course to windward in response to a windshift. She may do so at any time unless she is so close to an obligated vessel in the act of keeping clear that her course change would prevent the obligated vessel from keeping clear, or obstruct her while so doing. Such a course change less than two boat-lengths from the obligated vessel is too close." By specifying "two boat-lengths," the Appeals Committee is making it clear that when boats are converging at 90 degrees, small course alterations make a big difference and that alterations due to windshifts are difficult to anticipate. (See also USYRU Appeal 166.)

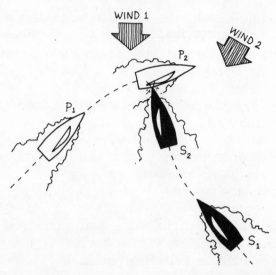

P was safely crossing S. Suddenly the wind shifted to the right, giving S a "lift" and P a "header." In following the "lift," S hit P, who was unable to keep clear after S altered her course. S infringed Rule 35.

"Does this mean that I can never alter my course when a give-way boat is nearby and keeping clear?"

Not at all. USYRU Appeal 172 says, "B is not required to sail a straight course once she becomes a right-of-way yacht. She may continue to circle or otherwise alter course as long as she does not thereby prevent A from keeping clear (or obstruct her while she is keeping clear)." For instance, if P is crossing you on a beat and you get a favorable windshift, you can head up and pass within inches of their transom. But if they don't understand **your intentions** they may *tack* or *bear away* to miss you and protest under Rule 35. So it's a good idea to hail so they know exactly what you're doing. (See IYRU Case 52 and USYRU Appeal 157.)

"Who has the 'onus of proof' when a give-way boat claims a right-of-way boat infringed Rule 35?"

There is no specific "onus of proof" in this situation, so the benefit of the doubt properly goes to the right-of-way boat. IYRU Case 36 states, "The protest committee must be satisfied from the weight of the evidence that a right-of-way yacht infringed Rule 35."

There are three specific times when Rule 35 does not apply to a right-of-way boat. As USYRU Appeal 203 explains, "These alterations are so predictable, a [give-way] yacht has ample time to anticipate them and to keep clear." They are:

Rule 35(a) to the extent permitted by Rule 38.1, Luffing Rights, and

    (b) when assuming a *proper course:* either

        (i) to start, unless subject to Rule 40, Same Tack, Luffing before Clearing the Starting Line, or to the second part of Rule 44.1(b), Returning to Start, or

        (ii) when rounding a *mark.*

Rule 35(a) gives L (a right-of-way boat) permission to *luff*, to the extent allowed by Rule 38.1, as fast and as suddenly as she wants **after starting and clearing** the starting line provided the *luff* is not likely to cause serious damage to any yacht (Rule 32.1). W (the give-way boat) is thus warned to stay far enough away from L so she can keep clear if L decides to *luff* quickly and unexpectedly. IYRU Case 3 and USYRU Appeal 20 make it clear that after *luffing* L may *bear away* sharply, and W must continue to keep clear. (See the discussion of Rule 37.1.)

Rule 35(b)(i) gives a right-of-way boat permission to assume a *proper course* to *start*. USYRU Appeal 227 points out, "The definition of 'proper course' is explicit as to the time when a yacht starts to have a proper course. The first sentence begins, 'A **proper course** is any course which a yacht might sail after the starting signal. . . .' "

Therefore, **after** the starting signal, a right-of-way boat can suddenly and quickly alter her course to assume a *proper course*. But **before** the starting signal, she is bound by the primary restrictions in Rule 35. (See also USYRU Appeal 203 and IYRU Case 86/USYRU Appeal 202.)

The most common situation is where S is reaching down the line prior to an upwind start and P is keeping clear by crossing her bow. The starting signal goes off, and S *luffs* sharply to *close-hauled*, hitting P. *Close-hauled* is clearly S's *proper course* and P knows **exactly** when S is allowed to *luff* up to it—i.e., as soon as the gun goes off.

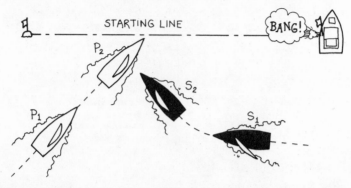

In position 1, P was safely crossing S. Then the starting signal was made. Rule 35(b)(i) permits S to luff up to her proper course, which in an upwind start is usually a close-hauled course.

Notice also that when a right-of-way boat is subject to Rule 40, Rule 35(b)(i) does **not** override it. Rule 40 requires L to *luff* **slowly** and initially with room and opportunity for W to keep clear before *starting,* and Rule 35(b)(i) does not change this in any way.

Rule 35(b)(ii) applies when rounding a *mark,* which implies that a right-of-way boat is actually turning **around** the *mark* as opposed to simply sailing past it. In most cases the right-of-way boat will be altering course to a new *proper course* when rounding the *mark* (USYRU Appeal 167).

A common situation is at windward *marks* that are to be left to port, where *close-hauled* **starboard-tack** boats are *bearing away* onto a run. As S rounds the *mark,* she is permitted to *bear away* immediately to a downwind course. If she hits P, who is approaching the *mark close-hauled,* P is wrong. P must anticipate S's very predictable alteration of course.

"Does that mean that going onto a beat, I can tack immediately onto starboard around a leeward mark even when port-tack boats coming downwind might not be able to keep clear?"
No. Rule 35(b) allows you to assume **"a"** *proper course,* which you did when you *luffed* up to *close-hauled* on *port-tack.* If you decide to

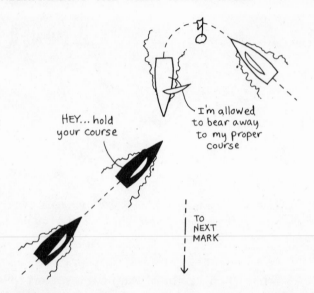

tack to a **different** *proper course,* you are subject to Rules 41.1 and 41.2 (*tacking* too close).

RULE 36   OPPOSITE TACKS—BASIC RULE

A *port-tack* yacht shall keep clear of a *starboard-tack* yacht.

This basic rule applies to boats that are on **opposite** *tacks.* When boats are on the **same** *tack,* Rules 37.1 (*windward/leeward*) and 37.2 (*clear astern/clear ahead*) apply. Thus, if on a run a *starboard-tack* boat comes up from *clear astern* and runs into a *port-tack* boat, who is disqualified? The *port-tack* boat, because the two boats are on **opposite** *tacks.*

The common *port/starboard* incidents happen on a beat when a *port-tack* boat tries to cross in front of a *starboard-tack* boat. The common questions are: If the *port-tacker* hails "Hold your course," is that hail binding; does the *starboard-tacker* have to hit the *port-tacker* to prove there was a foul; and if there is no contact, whom is the "onus of proof" on?

USYRU Appeal 137 reads, "In response to the question regarding a yacht that has been hailed to hold course, it is permissible to hail but the rules do not recognize such a hail as binding on the other yacht. S can

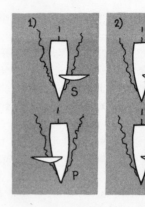

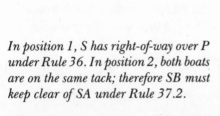

In position 1, S has right-of-way over P under Rule 36. In position 2, both boats are on the same tack; therefore SB must keep clear of SA under Rule 37.2.

tack [or *bear away*] at any time she is satisfied that an alteration of course will be necessary to avoid a collision."

USYRU Appeal 157 continues, "However, in order for the port-tack yacht to be liable for failure to keep clear, it is essential that as they approach each other the starboard-tack yacht **hold her course** [emphasis in the appeal] as long as she can do so with safety." I recommend that a *port-tack* yacht always hail "Hold your course" to the *starboard-tack* yacht to alert them that P is there, that she realizes it will be close, and that she wants S to hold her course for as long as possible.

"Does S have to hit P to prove P is wrong?"
Absolutely not. IYRU case 113 discusses the whole issue, including the question of "onus of proof": "It is not necessary for a starboard-tack yacht to hold her course to prove conclusively, by hitting a port-tack yacht, that a collision was inevitable. S is entitled to bear away and protest. At a protest hearing, the initial responsibility is on S to establish either that contact would have occurred if she had held her course, or that there was such doubt that P could safely cross ahead as to create a reasonable apprehension of contact.

"Once S meets this responsibility, P must present adequate evidence to establish either that S did not alter course or that P would have safely crossed ahead of S if S had held her course. When, on all the evidence, the protest committee finds that S did not alter course or that there was not a genuine and reasonable apprehension of collision on her part, it should disallow the protest. When, however, it is satisfied that S did alter course and that there was reasonable doubt that P could have crossed ahead if S had not so altered course, then P should be disqualified.

"DISCUSSION ON RULE 36 PROTESTS: Rule 36 protests involving no contact are very common and protest committees tend to handle them in a most disparate manner. Some place an onus on the port-tack yacht to prove conclusively that she would have cleared the starboard-tack yacht, even when the latter's evidence is barely worthy of credibility. No such onus appears in Rule 36 [unlike Rules 41.3, and 42.1(c) and (d)]. Other protest committees appear reluctant to allow any Rule 36 protest in the absence of contact, unless the starboard-tack yacht proves conclusively that contact would have occurred, had she not altered course.

"Both approaches are incorrect: the first places an improper and undue onus on a port-tack yacht, and the second places too great a responsibility on the starboard-tack yacht and encourages collisions, which the rules are intended to prevent. This appeal presents a proper guideline for protest committees and is consistent with USYRU Appeal 32." (See also USYRU Appeal 137.)

RULE 37   SAME TACK—BASIC RULES

Rule 37 gives the basic rules for boats on the **same** *tack*. When boats are on the same *tack* they can either be *overlapped* or **not** *overlapped*. If they are **not** *overlapped*, they are either *clear ahead* or *clear astern*. (See definitions of *Clear Astern* and *Clear Ahead; Overlap*.)

Rule 37.1   When Overlapped

A *windward yacht* shall keep clear of a *leeward yacht*.

When the boats are *overlapped*, Rule 37.1 applies. When boats are on much different angles of sail, it is often difficult to know which is the *leeward* boat. The boat that will hit the other's *leeward* side or be hit on her own *windward* side is the *leeward* boat. As a good rule of thumb, the boat that is on the point of sail closer to the wind is the *leeward* boat—i.e., between a boat sailing downwind and a boat sailing *close-hauled*, the *close-hauled* boat is the *leeward* boat.

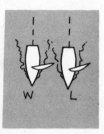

The question is: How clear does the *windward* boat (W) have to be? While the *leeward* boat (L) is sailing on a straight line, W simply must not hit L or force L to take any avoiding action to miss W—i.e., alter course, ease the spinnaker pole forward, or require any of the crew to duck or move to avoid being hit.

But Rules 40 and 38.1 permit L to *luff* before and after clearing the starting line, respectively. Knowing this, W must keep clear enough to respond to L's *luff*. **Before** L has *started* **and** cleared the starting line, Rule 40 requires her to *luff* **slowly** and initially in such a way as to give W room and opportunity to keep clear. Therefore W can comfortably sail a little closer to L.

But **after** L has *started* **and** cleared the starting line, she can *luff* "as she pleases"—i.e., fast and suddenly. This is supported by Rules 35(a) and 32.2. (See Chapter 3, Principles—The Sharp Luff.) Therefore, W is well advised to keep farther away from L so that they will have no trouble in responding if L *luffs* (USYRU Appeal 42). Rule 38.2(d) also requires W to stay far enough away from L so that L does not have to curtail—i.e. stop—her *luff.*

"Can L bear away and hit W with her transom?"
USYRU Appeal 20 reads, "W overtook L to windward and L luffed suddenly, head to wind. When L bore away her stern swung into W. W protested L for bearing away 'suddenly' and in such a manner as to prevent her from keeping clear in violation of Rule 35." The Appeals Committee stated, "A leeward yacht that has luffed a windward yacht as permitted by Rule 38.1, may bear away suddenly. In responding to L's luff W was obligated to keep far enough away from L so as to give her room to bear away both 'suddenly' and rapidly. Rule 35 . . . cannot properly be applied in this situation since L's right to maneuver under Rule 38.1 is an exception to the limitations of Rule 35." (See also IYRU Case 3.)

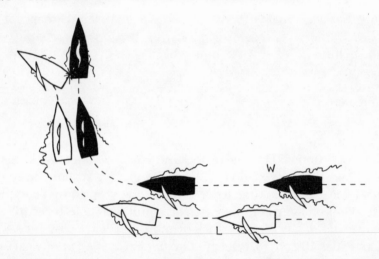

By applying the same logic to the similar situation **before** *starting* **and** clearing the starting line, W must keep clear of L's stern, but L must *bear away* slowly so as not to risk violating Rule 35. Note, however, that Rule 35 does not apply when L is assuming a *proper course* to *start* such that L is permitted to *bear away* rapidly to a *proper course* **after** the starting signal. (See IYRU Case 86/USYRU Appeal 202 and the discussion of Rule 35.)

Notice also that when L is permitted to *luff* to head to wind, it is quite possible that W will be required to go **beyond** head to wind (i.e., *tack*) in order to keep clear. If this be the case, she must do so. Also, W has not kept clear if any part of W touches L's hull, crew, or equipment in *normal position*. If L suddenly extends her extendable hiking stick in light air and hits W with it, L must explain to the **protest committee,** if protested, why she extended her stick, why it swung out and hit W, and why she considers that "normal." (See USYRU Appeal 232 and the discussion of Fundamental Rule C, Fair Sailing.)

Rule 37.2   When Not Overlapped

A yacht *clear astern* shall keep clear of a yacht *clear ahead*.

In 1949 the rule read, "A yacht Overtaking another shall keep clear while she is Clear Astern". Now the rules only talk about boats that are *clear ahead* or *clear astern;* however, the concept is still the same. A boat, just like a car on the highway, coming up from behind another boat, must not hit her.

Technically, a boat *clear astern* cannot "hit" a boat *clear ahead.* The definition tells us that a boat is *clear astern* of another when she is **behind** the imaginary line drawn through the aftermost point on the other boat. If she is not *clear astern,* then she is *overlapped.* So if her bow just hits the other's stern, she is "on" that line and therefore *overlapped* and governed by Rule 37.1. (She would be a *windward* or *leeward yacht* depending on which side of the other's centerline she was on. If she were exactly on centerline she could be one or the other, but the point is moot, as she would be wrong under either Rule 37.1 or 37.3.) (See also USYRU Appeal 232.)

So a yacht *clear astern* can only be penalized under Rule 37.2 when the yacht *clear ahead* claims she had to alter course to avoid being hit by the yacht coming up from *clear astern.*

However, Rule 37.2 clearly identifies a yacht or yachts *clear ahead* as right-of-way boats, therefore making them *obstructions* to boats coming up from behind. IYRU Case 91 reads, "With respect to A [*clear ahead*], both yachts astern are subject to Rule 37.2. A thus ranks as an obstruction to both. When they come within two lengths of A, still overlapped, Rule 42.1(a) will come into effect."

Rule 37.3   Transitional

A yacht that establishes an *overlap* to *leeward* from *clear astern* shall initially allow the *windward yacht* ample room and opportunity to keep clear.

Actually, Rule 37.2 is a foreshadowing of this rule. While a boat *clear astern* is approaching a boat *clear ahead* **on the same** *tack,* she must keep clear. When she establishes the *overlap* to *windward* of the other boat, Rule 37.2 ceases to apply and she is required to keep clear under Rule 37.1.

When she establishes the *overlap* to *leeward,* Rule 37.2 ceases to apply and she **instantly** has the right-of-way under Rule 37.1. However, she has a **temporary obligation** under Rule 37.3 to give the *windward* boat **ample** room and opportunity to keep clear.

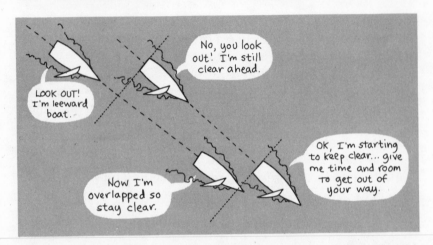

Notice the insertion of the word "initially." This clarifies that the protection of "ample room and opportunity" is available to W only at the outset of the *overlap*. Once the yachts have been *overlapped* for a time sufficient for W to have kept clear, the protection of Rule 37.3 ceases. (See Chapter 3, Principles—When the right-of-way shifts . . . , and IYRU Cases 11, 46, and 116/USYRU Appeal 126.)

"Is it true that a boat sailing backward has no right-of-way?"
Absolutely not, except in **sailboard racing** when near the starting line. Appendix 2—Sailboard Racing Rules, 3.4 reads, "When approaching the starting line to *start* or when returning to the pre-start side of the starting line, a sailboard sailing or drifting backward shall keep clear of other sailboards or yachts that are *starting* or have *started* correctly."

Otherwise the rules make no distinction between whether the boats are moving forward, are stopped, or are moving backward. IYRU Case 132/USYRU Question 256 says, "While B was stationary and A was sailing backward with respect to the bottom, both yachts were sailing forward through the water, B at about 1½ knots and A at somewhat less speed, so that they both had some steerageway. B could and should have kept clear by bearing away when she found her distance from A was narrowing. When instead she became overlapped to windward of A, but was unable to keep clear, she infringed Rule 37.1."

RULE 38   SAME TACK—LUFFING AFTER CLEARING THE STARTING LINE

This rule discusses the *luffing* rights of a right-of-way boat **after** she has *started* **and** cleared the starting line. Remember, a *luff* is defined as "altering course towards the wind." If a boat isn't **turning,** it is not *luffing*. Rule 40 covers *luffing* **before** *starting* and clearing the starting line. "Clearing the starting line" is defined by USYRU Appeal 99: "When no part of a yacht's hull, equipment, or crew is still on the . . . line she has cleared it."

Rule 38 only applies to a yacht *clear ahead* or a *leeward yacht*. It is telling **them** (the right-of-way boats) what they can and cannot do. It does not shift any right-of-way to a *windward* boat. Also, Rule 38 only applies when the *luff* of the right-of-way boat will affect other boats **on the same** *tack*. A *starboard-tack* boat cannot *luff* as she pleases and smash into a *port-tack* boat sailing next to her. (See IYRU Case 35.)

Rule 38.1   Luffing Rights

After she has *started* and cleared the starting line, a yacht *clear ahead* or a *leeward yacht* may *luff* as she pleases, subject to the following limitations of this rule. (The limitations are discussed under Rule 38.2, Limitations.)

USYRU Appeal 42 reads, "Rule 38.1 contemplates that a yacht which attempts to pass on the windward side of another yacht on the same tack assumes an obligation to be prepared for the possibility that the leeward yacht will luff sharply, head to wind if she pleases, and therefore should establish and maintain her overlap at a sufficient distance so as to be able to respond to a luff and keep clear."

USYRU Appeal 102 says, "It is ruled that head to wind is when the long axis or centerline of a yacht's hull is parallel to, and her bow is facing, the wind, irrespective of the position of the sails." This clarification is helpful because often when a boat is head to wind her sails will blow momentarily to the other side giving the **illusion** that she is *tacking*.

Remember, under the rules L does not "luff" W. L simply *luffs*

L is luffing up to a new proper course in order to get to a puff of wind. Because she is not luffing or sailing above her proper course, she is not infringing Rule 38.2(a), and W must keep clear under Rule 37.1.

(alters her course toward the wind), and W must keep clear even if it means by *tacking*. If W fails to keep clear, she infringes Rule 37.1. Notice that L may not *luff* "as she pleases" when any of the limitations in Rule 38.2 apply.

Rule 38.2   Limitations

(a) Proper Course Limitations:

A *leeward yacht* shall not **sail** above her *proper course* while an *overlap* exists, if when the *overlap* began or at any time during its existence, the helmsman of the *windward yacht* (when sighting abeam from his normal station and **sailing** no higher than the *leeward yacht*) has been abreast or forward of the mainmast of the *leeward yacht*.

Rule 38.1 gives the *leeward* boat the right to *luff* "as she pleases." A *windward* boat can take away that right by getting "mast abeam" on the *leeward* boat. Here's how to get "mast abeam."

First, the *windward* boat must be sailing on a course no higher than the *leeward* boat.

Second, the helmsman of the *windward* boat must be sitting in their **normal position. Normal position** is where the helmsman

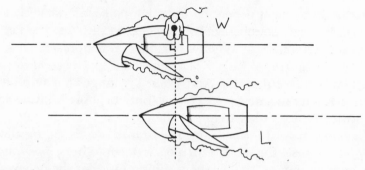

W is in the "mast abeam" position.

normally sits on that point of sail and in those wind and wave conditions. IYRU Case 101 says, "The helmsman's normal position may vary in yachts of the same class, depending on the strength of the wind, sea conditions, and other factors, provided always that he does not move to a position in order to justify a mast-abeam hail."

Third, the helmsman must look directly to leeward on a "line of sight" perpendicular with the centerline of the boat.

If their "line of sight" is **at** or **ahead** of the mainmast of the *leeward* boat, they have "mast abeam." Obviously, for most racing boats "mainmast" means "the mast." On a sailboard, "mainmast" means "foot of the mast"—i.e., the base of the mast (Appendix 2,3.2).

Once you get "mast abeam" on a *leeward* boat, you instantly put this **limitation** on their action: For as long as you two remain *overlapped,* the *leeward* boat can not sail **above her** (the *leeward* boat's) *proper course.* Notice you don't have to **stay** in the "mast abeam" position. If at some point during the *overlap* of two boats the *windward* boat gets "mast abeam" then the limitation sticks for as long as the boats stay *overlapped.*

A firm understanding of the concept of "proper course" is required to fully understand Rule 38.2(a). Remember that a *proper course* is any course a boat chooses to sail in order to get to the next *mark* and ultimately to *finish* as quickly as possible. (See the definition and discussion of *Proper Course.*) USYRU Appeal 127 reads, "It is possible therefore that there may be several proper courses at any given moment depending upon the particular circumstances involved. It is also obvious that two overlapping yachts sailing for the same mark will converge." When L is sailing on her *proper course*, W must keep clear under Rule 37.1, even when W's *proper course* may be a lower course than L's. And when L changes her mind and wants to *luff* up to a **new** *proper course* (but not above it), Rule 38.1 and Rule 35 permit her to *luff* as she pleases.

If when you get "mast abeam" the *leeward* boat is sailing **above her** *proper course,* she must return back down to **her** *proper course* immediately; but as long as she is sailing on what she believes **is her** *proper course,* she is not in violation of Rule 38.2, and you must stay clear under Rule 37.1 even when you might want to sail a lower *proper course.* (See IYRU Case 25.) IYRU Case 62 defines "above her *proper course*" as "on the same side of a yacht's *proper course* as her *windward* side." USYRU Appeal 6 says, "When there is doubt that a yacht is sailing above her proper course, she should be given the benefit of the doubt." And IYRU Case 11 continues, "It is L's proper course that is the criterion for deciding whether Rules 37.1 and 38.2 have been infringed."

In IYRU Case 106/USYRU Appeal 224 two yachts were approaching a downwind finish. The boats were *overlapped* and the *leeward* boat had established the *overlap* from *clear astern.* Therefore there was no doubt that at some point during the *overlap* the *windward* boat had "mast abeam." As they got nearer to the line, L decided that she wanted to sail a higher *proper course* in order to *finish* faster. She hailed W of her intention but got no reply. Does anything in the rules prohibit L from sailing **her** proper course? No. The decision in IYRU Case 106 reads, "Basic Rule 37.1 says that, when two yachts on the same tack are overlapped, the windward yacht shall keep clear. A leeward yacht's actions, however, are limited by Rules 37.3 and 38.2 L, in this case, by hailing twice before luffing, gave W room and opportunity to keep clear, as required by Rule 37.3. The protest committee, although it did not say so explicitly, recognised that L's proper course was directly towards the finishing line. A direct course to the line was not only closer but would also have put both yachts on a faster point of sailing. While L was not entitled to luff above her proper course, she **was** entitled to sail up to it. Accordingly, she did not exceed the limitation to which rule 38.2 subjected her."

(b) Overlap Limitations:

For the purpose of Rule 38 only: An *overlap* does not exist unless the yachts are clearly within two overall lengths of the longer yacht; and an *overlap* that exists between two yachts when the leading yacht *starts,* or when one or both of them completes a *tack* or *gybe,* shall be regarded as a new *overlap* beginning at that time.

In Rule 38.2(a) we see that once the *windward* boat gets "mast abeam," the *leeward* boat has a limitation on her—she cannot sail above her *proper course* for as long as the boats remain *overlapped.* How does the *leeward* boat get back her right to *luff* "as she pleases"—i.e., get rid of her limitation? She must **break** the *overlap* with the *windward* boat.

We've read the definition of *overlap* in Part I. But Rule 38.2(b) puts some restrictions on this definition for the purpose of applying Rule 38 **only:**

1. If the boats are not "clearly" within two overall lengths of the longer boat, they are **not** *overlapped* (even though the bow of one is over the imaginary line drawn through the aftermost part of the other). This is intended to permit L to sail where she pleases until she is **within** two lengths of W. At that moment, Rule 38.2 begins to apply. In addition, as L and W converge, "two lengths" builds in time for W to hail if necessary and for L to return to her *proper course.*

2. When one or both of them completes a *tack* or *gybe* it shall be regarded as a new *overlap* beginning at that time.

3. Between two *overlapped* yachts, when the leading one *starts*—i.e., her bow crosses the starting line after the starting signal—their *overlap* shall be regarded as a new one at that time.

So when W has reached "mast abeam," the common ways for L to break the overlap are: (a) by pulling *clear ahead* of W; (b) by moving more than two boat-lengths to *leeward* of W; or (c) by *gybing* twice (to end up on the same *tack* again).

In handicap racing, when the smaller classes start first, at some point the larger boats will sail by the smaller ones. Let's say a fifty-foot boat is passing a thirty-foot boat to *leeward* on a reach. As the fifty-foot boat pulls in to *leeward* some 150 feet away from the

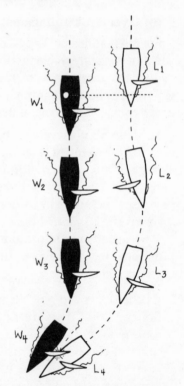

In position 1, W has "mast abeam" and L must not sail above L's proper course. In position 2, L gybes, so that the two boats are on opposite tacks and Rule 38 no longer applies. In position 3, L gybes back, establishing a new overlap on W in which W does not have "mast abeam." In position 4, L luffs sharply, as permitted by Rule 38.1, and W is wrong under Rule 37.1 for not keeping clear.

windward boat, the helmsman of W hails "mast abeam." L then *luffs* and sails above her *proper course,* converging with W. When L gets clearly within 100 feet of W, the two boats are bow to bow. L continues to *luff* and to sail above her *proper course* and hits W. In this example, who is wrong? Before the boats were clearly within two lengths of the longer boat, they were **not** *overlapped* for the purpose of Rule 38. Therefore, the helmsman of the *windward* boat was premature in hailing "mast abeam." When L got within 100 feet (two of her lengths) and the *overlap* **began,** W did not have "mast abeam"; therefore, the limitation of Rule 38.2(a) did not apply and L could *luff* as she pleased. W is wrong.

(c) Hailing to Stop or Prevent a Luff:

When there is doubt, the *leeward* yacht may assume that she has the right to *luff* or *sail* above her *proper course* unless the helmsman of the *windward* yacht has hailed either:

(i) "Mast abeam" or words to that effect;

(ii) "Obstruction" or words to that effect.

The *leeward* yacht shall be governed by such hail and curtail her *luff*. When she deems it improper, her only remedy is to protest.

When the *windward* boat gets "mast abeam" on an *overlapped leeward* boat, the *leeward* boat is required not to sail above her *proper course*. But how does the *leeward* boat know when the *windward* boat gets "mast abeam"? Well, sometimes it's obvious, as when the *leeward* boat establishes the *overlap* from *clear astern*. But other times it's not so obvious.

USYRU Appeal 78 reads, "The hailing provisions in Rule 38.2(c) were included in the 'luffing rule' to reduce arguments and protests and they should be so interpreted. The helmsman of a windward yacht who fails to protect his rights by hailing in proper time is entitled to little consideration. It is easy for him to see when he attains the 'mast abeam' position. On the other hand, the helmsman of the leeward yacht is, as a rule, in no position to determine 'mast abeam.' Hence he must rely on, and be governed by, a hail to know when he has lost his luffing rights.

"A hail should, as a rule, be unnecessary when the leeward yacht established her overlap from clear astern. But when an overlap results from convergence, or the completion of a tack or jibe, the leeward yacht should be held blameless if the helmsman of the windward yacht:

a. that attains the 'mast abeam' position fails to hail either before the leeward yacht begins to luff or the instant she begins to luff. Failure to notice a luff is no excuse for not responding to it or for not hailing.

b. that attains the 'mast abeam' position during a luff, fails to hail in time to enable the leeward yacht to bear away before contact."

Notice that the *leeward* boat can continue to *luff* until either she is sure the *windward* boat has "mast abeam" or until the *windward* boat hails "mast abeam." When L hears the hail, USYRU Appeal 151 states, "Rule 38.2(c) requires L to be governed by such hail and if she deems it improper [i.e., she doesn't believe the *windward* boat has reached "mast abeam"], her only remedy is to protest." In other words, when she hears the hail she must immediately **begin** to stop her *luff* and make every attempt to return back down to her *proper course,* even when she thinks the hail was premature.

In USYRU Appeal 78 the race committee found as fact that the helmsman of W hailed "Mast Abeam" either immediately before or at the moment of contact and that at the moment of contact the helmsman of W was three feet forward of the "mast abeam" position. The Appeals Committee said, "Since the helmsman of W . . . failed to hail in time to enable L to bear away before contact . . . L is absolved from blame, and W is disqualified for infringing Rules 37.1 and 38.2(d) in not keeping sufficiently clear of L to enable her to avoid contact by curtailing her luff as soon as she was obligated to begin doing so by the hail of 'Mast Abeam.' ". Thus it's clear that there might be a few seconds between the hail and when L bears away, during which time W must continue to keep clear.

Remember that IYRU Case 101 states, "Rule 38.2(c) is not satisfied by a hail that is not loud enough to be heard. In this case, while L is still in doubt, she has a right to luff until W succeeds in informing her that she has attained 'mast abeam.' If W's first hail was inadequate, a second louder hail was required." Also notice that other phrases such as "mast line" are acceptable, though it is best when you use "mast abeam."

Notice also that the moment L **knows** W has "mast abeam," L must stop *luffing* and return to her *proper course*. Only when there is any **doubt** in her mind can she continue to *luff* or sail above her *proper course* until she hears a hail.

IYRU Case 99/USYRU Appeal 220 is clear: "Rule 38.2(c) operates only when there is doubt as to whether that point has been reached. Where the facts permit no reasonable doubt and establish that the windward yacht actually has achieved 'mast abeam,' Rule 38.2(c) does not become operative and the absence (or lateness) of a hail by the windward yacht is of no consequence.

"That is the situation here. Based upon the point of contact (L's pulpit striking W near the forward end of her cockpit which in W is close to her helmsman's normal station), it is clear that W had reached a position well ahead of 'mast abeam' prior to the time of contact, indeed by a sufficient distance that it should have been obvious to L. There being no doubt that L's luffing rights had been terminated under Rule 38.2(a), she infringed that rule by failing to bear away to her proper course." The point here is not that at the moment of contact W was ahead of "mast abeam," but that W was **so far** ahead that "mast abeam" had undoubtedly been reached in plenty of time for L to have *borne away* and avoided the collision.

Notice the addition of the hail "obstruction" into the rule. The reason is one of safety. It arises that W cannot respond to L's *luff* because of an *obstruction* to *windward* of her, and often L will not realize the *obstruction* is there. W may now hail "obstruction," thereby causing L to stop ("curtail") her *luff* (see Rule 38.2[d]) when a collision would result otherwise.

(d) Curtailing a Luff:

The windward yacht shall not cause a *luff* to be curtailed because of her proximity to the *leeward yacht* unless an *obstruction,* a third yacht or other object restricts her ability to respond.

Any time a *windward* boat is so close to a *leeward* boat that L cannot legally *luff* without hitting her, W has infringed this rule. (See USYRU Appeal 78 and IYRU Case 106/USYRU Appeal 224.) But USYRU Appeal 44 continues, "It is to be noted also, in accordance with Rule 38.2(d) that a windward yacht is not subject to disqualification when her ability to respond to an otherwise legitimate luff of a leeward yacht is restricted by an obstruction."

So if you are W and cannot respond to L's *luff* because of your proximity to a right-of-way boat, the stern of the race committee boat, a log, or **anything,** you should inform L immediately. This

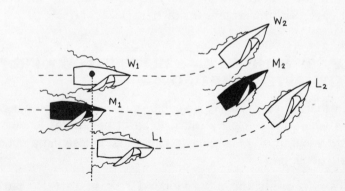

Neither W nor M has "mast abeam" on L; therefore L is permitted to luff as she pleases. W has "mast abeam" on M. However, Rule 38.2(e) requires W to keep clear of M when M is merely luffing to keep clear of L.

hail is anticipated in Rule 38.2(c), Hailing to Stop or Prevent a Luff. If L does continue to *luff* and hit you, they have infringed Rule 35. Furthermore, if you have hailed "obstruction" or similar words, L has also infringed Rule 38.2(c).

(e) Luffing Rights over Two or More Yachts:

A yacht shall not *luff* unless she has the right to *luff* all yachts that would be affected by her *luff,* in which case they shall all respond, even when an intervening yacht or yachts would not otherwise have the right to *luff.*

If you are sailing down a reach and have three boats to *windward* of you, you are allowed to *luff* as long as none of the boats that might get hit have ever had "mast abeam" on **you** during their *overlap* with you. Assuming they haven't, you may *luff,* and they all must *luff* to stay clear of you. It might be that the third boat to *windward* has "mast abeam" on the second. Thus, in your absence, the second boat would not be allowed to *luff* or sail above her *proper course.* But you **are** there and you **do** have *luffing* rights over the third boat, so she must keep clear of the second boat, which is keeping clear of you. (See IYRU Case 48/USYRU Appeal 130.)

Notice that in a big group any *windward* boat that is not clearly within two boat-lengths of the *leeward* boat is **not** *overlapped* and therefore it is immaterial that she may have "mast abeam" until L gets clearly within two lengths of her.

RULE 39   SAME TACK—SAILING BELOW A PROPER COURSE AFTER STARTING

A yacht that is on a free leg of the course shall not *sail* below her *proper course* when she is clearly within three of her overall lengths of a *leeward* yacht or of a yacht *clear astern* that is steering a course to *leeward* of her own.

This is possibly the most violated rule in Part IV, partially because many sailors don't know it and partially because it is very difficult to prove an infraction.

This rule applies only to a boat that is on a "free leg" of the

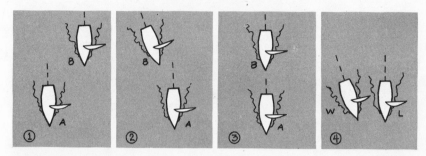

Rule 39 applies to A in positions 1 and 2, but not to A in position 3. It applies to W in position 4.

course. Though "free leg" has never been interpreted by an appeal, my opinion is that a "free leg" of the course is any leg that is not a "windward leg" for the boat in question. On a "windward leg" you must sail *close-hauled*. (See definition of *Close-hauled*.) So any leg on which **you** do not have to sail *close-hauled* to reach the next *mark* is a "free leg" for you. Interestingly, the 1930 NAYRU rules in effect read, "A yacht not sailing close-hauled and not head to wind is sailing free."

If you are on a beat sailing *close-hauled* near the *starboard-tack* layline and the wind shifts 20 degrees to the right such that now you can get to the *mark* by sailing a lower than *close-hauled* course, **you** are on a "free leg," whereas the boats on the left side of the beat may still be on a "windward leg."

The same logic applies to an offwind leg. If you can get to the next *mark* by sailing a course lower than *close-hauled*, it is a "free leg" for you. But if the wind shifts such that you must now sail *close-hauled* to get there, the leg is no longer "free" for you.

Notice the new phrase "steering a course to *leeward* of her own." This is a clarification of the similar phrase in the previous Rule 39. In the previous rule, the word "passing" led some to factor in the speed of the boat *clear astern*—i.e., if she was capable of "passing" the boat *clear ahead*. The change clarifies that it is only the **course** being steered by the boat *clear astern* that applies. A boat *clear astern* is considered to be steering a course to *leeward* of the *clear ahead* boat's course anytime her course is aiming to the *leeward* side of the boat *clear ahead,* or anytime she is steering a

In position 2, W sailed below her proper course in order to get closer to L and slow her down. This is a common infringement of Rule 39.

lower (more *leeward*) course than the boat *clear ahead*. This includes a boat *clear astern* that is up to *windward* of the boat *clear ahead*'s wake. An example of a boat *clear astern* **not** "steering a course to *leeward*" is when the boat *clear astern* is sailing a course parallel to or higher than the boat *clear ahead* while aiming at, or to *windward* of, her transom.

The rule is clear: When you are to *leeward* or *clear astern* and "steering a course to *leeward*," the boat *clear ahead* or to *windward* **cannot** sail below **their** *proper course* when they are on your *tack*, on a "free leg" of the course, and when they are clearly within three of **their** overall lengths from you. This is only fair, because when you try to pass a boat to *windward*, she can prevent you by *luffing*. It would give that boat too much of an advantage if, when you tried to pass her to *leeward*, she could *bear away* on your wind too. This rule is commonly violated as boats near *marks* and boats ahead are trying to prevent or discourage boats behind from getting an inside *overlap*.

Notice that on a "windward leg" it **is** legal to *bear off* to get closer to a boat to *leeward* or *clear astern* of you.

RULE 40   SAME TACK—LUFFING BEFORE CLEARING THE STARTING LINE

Before a yacht *clear ahead* or a *leeward* yacht has *started* and cleared the starting line, any *luff* on her part that causes another yacht to have to alter course to avoid a collision shall be carried out slowly and initially in such a way as to give a *windward yacht* room and opportunity to keep clear. Furthermore, the *leeward yacht* shall not so *luff* above a *close-hauled* course while the helmsman of the *windward yacht* (sighting abeam from his normal station) is abreast or forward of the mainmast of the *leeward* yacht. Rules 38.2(c), Hailing to Stop or Prevent a Luff; 38.2(d), Curtailing a Luff; and 38.2(e), Luffing Two or more Yachts, also apply.

This rule governs the *luffing* of a boat **before** it has *started* **and** cleared the starting line. It makes several points, some of which are different from *luffing* **after** *starting* **and** clearing the starting line.

1. This rule governs until the boat has "**cleared** the starting line" (see the discussion of Rule 38), so it definitely applies after the starting gun has gone off.

2. This rule is only talking about a *luff* that will directly cause another boat to have to alter their course to avoid a collision. Any other *luff* can be as fast or sudden as the right-of-way boat wants.

3. When a *windward* boat or a boat *clear astern* will be directly affected, the right-of-way boat must *luff* (alter her course toward the wind) **slowly.** There is never a time when she can *luff* other than slowly. Of course, "slowly" may be tough to absolutely define, but in principle it means "not quickly," "smoothly."

4. When there is a boat directly to *windward*, L must begin her *luff* (initially) in such a way that W has "**room**" (space) and "**opportunity**" (the time necessary to get clear, including picking up enough speed to get steerageway when necessary) to keep clear. Remember, this is a **temporary obligation** on L. Once she has given W "room and opportunity," she can continue with her slow *luff*. (See Chapter 3, Principles—When the right-of-way shifts. . . .)

"Who has 'onus' to prove there was or wasn't enough 'room and opportunity'?"

In an argument over whether L provided enough "room and opportunity," neither the rule nor the appeals place an "onus" on either boat. However, USYRU Appeal 233 reminds us "that a windward yacht's right to 'room and opportunity to keep clear' under both Rule 37.3 and Rule 40 is a shield and not a sword for W." Also, in USYRU Appeal 233 W was disqualified for responding with an "unnecessarily extreme luff," the reasoning including the fact that L, before the start, is only permitted to *luff* slowly. Therefore, to be entitled to the protection, W must respond **as soon as she can** to the *luff* and in a **reasonable** attempt to get clear. From there it will be up to the **protest committee** to decide from the weight of the evidence on (a) the wind and sea conditions, (b) the nature of the incident, and (c) the exact actions of both boats, whether or not W had "room and opportunity." In this case, hails by both boats will help their claims in a **protest.** (See USYRU Appeals 204, 227, and 233.)

Notice also that when L establishes an *overlap* to *leeward* of W, she is required by Rule 37.3 to initially give W "**ample** 'room and opportunity' to keep clear." It is only when L *luffs* (alters her course toward the wind) that Rule 40 comes into effect. When L does *luff* properly W must keep clear, which includes leaving room enough for L's stern to swing when she *bears away* after the *luff.* (See the discussion of Rules 35 and 37.1.)

"Is there 'mast abeam' before the start?"
Yes. It is a common misconception that there is no such thing as "mast abeam" before the start. There is, but it works a little differently from **after** the start. (See Rule 38.2[a].)

1. There is no *proper course* before the starting signal. (See Part 1, Definitions—*Proper Course.*)

2. The *windward* boat gets "mast abeam" in the same way as described in the discussion of Rule 38.2(a), **except** that the *windward* boat is allowed to be sailing on a **higher course** than the *leeward* boat. This makes it a lot easier for W to get "mast abeam."

3. In Rule 40 "mast abeam" doesn't last for the entire *overlap.* You either physically have "mast abeam" or you don't. A *wind-*

ward boat that has "mast abeam" can drop back five feet and no longer have it. It is the simple relationship between the two boats **at the time** that determines "mast abeam."

Before L has *started* **and** cleared the starting line, when W has "mast abeam" L cannot *luff* above L's *close-hauled* course. Rule 38.2(c) also applies, so when there is doubt, L may assume she has the right to *luff* unless the helmsman of W has hailed "mast abeam."

Remember that a *luff* is an alteration of course toward the wind. If two boats are sitting almost head to wind and then W gets "mast abeam," L is **not required** to *bear away* back down to *close-hauled*. L just must not *luff* anymore, because she is already above *close-hauled*. In Rule 38.2(a), when W gets "mast abeam," L is required not to **sail** above her *proper course*, which is why she must *bear away* back down to it **after** *starting* and clearing the starting line (USYRU Appeal 227).

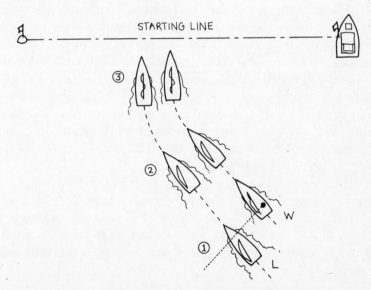

In position 1, W has "mast abeam" on L; therefore L cannot luff higher than a close-hauled course. In position 2, L has moved forward and W no longer has "mast abeam." Now L is permitted to luff slowly up to head-to-wind, and W must keep clear.

Also, notice that though W may have "mast abeam" momentarily, as soon as L pulls forward a few feet so that W no longer has "mast abeam," L can *luff* slowly to head to wind and W must keep clear if she can. If boats to *windward* of her restrict her ability to respond (as they commonly will in a crowded start), Rule 38.2(d) applies, and W should hail L to the effect, "I am trying to keep clear but I have these other boats to *windward* that are slowly responding." And under Rule 38.2(e) no boat that will be affected by L's *luff* can have "mast abeam" on L if L wants to *luff* above *close-hauled*.

RULE 41 CHANGING TACKS—TACKING AND GYBING

Rule 41.1 Basic Rule

A yacht that is either *tacking* or *gybing* shall keep clear of a yacht *on a tack.*

Remember that under the Definitions (Part I) you are technically *tacking* from the moment you pass head to wind until you *bear away* to your *close-hauled* course, regardless of whether your sails are full or your boat is moving. (See IYRU Case 32.) Prior to *tacking,* as you are turning toward the wind you are merely *luffing on a tack.*

You are *gybing* from the moment the boom crosses the centerline (with the wind behind you) until it fills on the other side. As it will fill well before it has gone all the way out, you are only *gybing* for a few seconds **at the most.**

If, while you are *tacking* or *gybing,* a boat *on a tack* hits you or has to alter her course to miss you, you have not kept clear and are in the wrong. In IYRU Case 23, P bore off to pass astern of S but S suddenly *tacked,* forcing P to *bear away* **farther** to avoid the collision. Because P would have hit S while S was *tacking,* S was disqualified under Rule 41.1.

Rule 41.2 Transitional

A yacht shall neither *tack* nor *gybe* into a position that will give her right of way unless she does so far enough from a yacht *on a tack* to enable

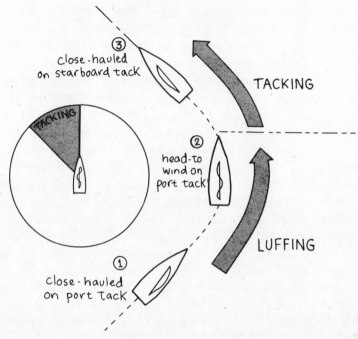

From positions 1 to 2, A is luffing and has not begun to tack. From positions 2 to 3, A is past head-to-wind but not yet close-hauled; therefore she is tacking. In position 3, A is on a close-hauled course. Her tack is completed, regardless of whether her sails are not full or she has no speed on.

this yacht to keep clear without having to begin to alter her course until after the *tack* or *gybe* has been completed.

Rule 41.2 is the rule at the bottom of all the "*tacking* too close" arguments. For a good analogy (though this may not be the actual highway law), picture yourself coming up the entrance ramp to a three-lane highway. Cars driving down the right-hand lane must stay clear of other cars in the right-hand lane in front of them. While you're on the ramp you cannot interfere with cars driving in the right-hand lane. If, while you are moving across the white line into the right-hand lane, a car hits you or swerves to miss you, you are in the wrong. But once you get **all four wheels** across the line, you are now technically in the right-hand lane yourself, and cars coming up from behind have to keep clear of you. However, these cars are not required to begin to avoid you or even to **anticipate** avoiding you until you are completely in the lane. Once you are in the lane they have to try reasonably hard to miss you. If they can't, then you've moved on too close in front of them.

The same is true in sailboats. Let's say I'm on *starboard-tack* and you want to *tack* on my lee-bow or in front of me. If I could hit you before you passed head to wind (i.e., before you began to cross the white line), you'd be wrong under Rule 36 (*port/starboard*). If I could hit you after you'd passed head to wind but before you were **aiming** on your *close-hauled* course (i.e., while you were crossing the line), you'd be wrong under Rule 41.1 (a *tacking* boat must keep clear). However, the moment you get to your *close-hauled* course (i.e., completely in my lane) and you are either *clear ahead* or to *leeward* of me, you have the right-of-way under either Rule 37.2 or Rule 37.1, and I have to try reasonably hard to keep clear. I say "reasonably" because I don't have to go to the extreme of "crash-*tacking*" and capsizing to avoid you. (See Chapter 3, Principles—When the right-of-way shifts. . . .) But the moment you are on your *close-hauled* course (which will usually be close to **parallel** with the course I'm sailing), I must **begin** to try to keep clear of you. Of course, in most situations it will take me only a second or two to react enough to *luff* or *bear away* slightly to avoid a collision.

The same is true when *gybing*. If two boats are running side by side on *port-tack* and the *windward* boat throws her boom over, the **moment** the sail fills on the new side she is on starboard and the

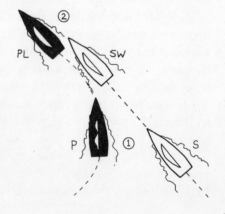

In position 1, P is past head-to-wind; therefore she is tacking. If S has to alter course to avoid hitting P, P is wrong under Rule 41.1. In position 2, P is on a close-hauled course; therefore her tack is completed. Now, as leeward boat, PL has the right of way, and S must immediately try to avoid hitting PL.

other boat (P) must begin to get clear immediately. However, S must plan to initially give P "room and opportunity" to keep clear.

Rule 41.3 Onus

A yacht that *tacks* or *gybes* has the onus of satisfying the **protest committee** that she completed her *tack* or *gybe* in accordance with Rule 41.2.

"Can the onus be applied in determining whether a yacht actually completed her tack or not before the other yacht had to alter course?"

No. The onus applies only when the incident occurs, or would have occurred, **after** the *tack* has been **completed.** One of the most common scenarios involving *tacking* is when P chooses to *tack* either directly in front of or on the "lee-bow" of S. In the protest hearing S claims that she *luffed* to avoid P while P was in the act of *tacking*. P claims that she completed her *tack* and that S thereafter *luffed,* thereby proving P's innocence. The issue before the committee is: Was P or was P not in the act of *tacking* when S altered course? In this issue, neither boat has any "onus" under the rules. In resolving this dispute, many protest committees apply the principle in IYRU Case 113 (see Rule 36 discussion), which first puts responsibility on S to satisfy the committee that the yachts were close together, and then puts the responsibility on P to satisfy them that P would have kept clear had S held her course.

A similar scenario in which neither yacht has an "onus" under the rules is when L *luffs* to "shoot" around a windward *mark*. L and W collide, with L claiming she was head-to-wind and W claiming that L went beyond head-to-wind and therefore was *tacking*. (See IYRU Case 77.) Furthermore, the "onus" in Rule 41.3 does not apply to a boat that crosses another and *tacks* to *windward* of her, because she has not *tacked* into a right-of-way position.

The "onus" in Rule 41.3 applies only in one specific type of incident: when the fact is found that the collision took place or would have taken place **after** the *tack* was completed. If there was no contact and S held her course until P completed her *tack,* then P has not infringed Rule 41.2. But when there is contact, or when S alters course while P is in the act of *tacking* for fear that she will collide with P **after** P completes her *tack,* Rule 41.3 puts the "onus" on P to satisfy the protest committee that S did in fact have enough time and distance to avoid her without needing to alter course before P's *tack* was completed. This "onus" is very difficult to win against. Hails to the effect of "my tack is completed 2–3–4, now you're altering course" and a witness are very helpful in satisfying the "onus."

In USYRU Appeal 153, two boats were sailing *close-hauled* on *port-tack.* When PL reached the *starboard-tack* layline she *tacked* without hail or warning. Seconds later, PW collided with her amidships despite attempting to *bear away,* and protested. The Appeals Committee said that "the onus is on the protested yacht [PL] to satisfy the protest committee that the tack was completed in accordance with Rule 41.2 and they did not feel that [she] was able to do this. The committee also felt that the timing of the chain of events and resulting courses of action to avoid collision might have been somewhat different under lower wind conditions. Considering the wind conditions of 15 to 18 knots, gusting to 25, and resulting boat speeds, the reaction times under Rule 41.2 must be extended somewhat. They felt that in a 6 knot wind [PW] might have been able to bear off and avoid collision, but not in the conditions existing."

In USYRU Appeal 50, "Two yachts, about seventeen feet overall, were beating on opposite tacks. After completing a tack from port to starboard, A was between six and ten feet directly ahead of B who thereupon gained and narrowed the interval between them to two or three feet. B then tacked and duly submitted a protest claiming that A had infringed Rule 41.2 by tacking too close.

"DECISION: The important consideration here is that the yacht that will have to take steps to keep clear after another yacht's tack has been completed is not obligated to begin to alter her course prior to the completion of the tack, that is, until the other yacht has borne away to a close-hauled course. The facts found by the race committee indicate clearly that B held her course for about three seconds after A's tack had been completed and then was able to tack without interfering with A.

This information confirms by actual performance that the requirements of the rule were complied with and that A's tack was made properly and at sufficient distance from B."

When a boat *tacks* into a right-of-way position, she has every right to assume that the new give-way boat will make a reasonable attempt to keep clear. In USYRU Appeal 173, two *port-tackers* were sailing *close-hauled.* The *leeward* boat (LS) *tacked* to *starboard* and the *windward* boat (WP) hit her after first starting to *bear away,* then deciding to try and *tack.* The Appeals Committee disqualified her, saying, "WP, however, followed neither course of action decisively but vacillated between them and when she abandoned her initial remedial action and altered her course to weather, she created the very situation which precipitated the collision. This miscalculation on the part of WP was not an assumption that was required of LS under Rule 41.2."

Finally, IYRU Case 10/USYRU Appeal 93 discusses a common tactic where P starts to *bear away* to duck S and S quickly *tacks* to *leeward* of P. The decision reads, "The facts indicate that when S luffed, preparatory to tacking, she did so at a sufficient distance from P so that P did not find it necessary at that time to alter course again in order to keep clear, and in fact, after bearing away P could not have collided with S while S remained on the starboard tack. When S began to tack by passing beyond head to the wind, she became obligated by Rule 41 to keep clear of P, a yacht on a tack, and on completion of her tack she became a leeward yacht with the right to luff P, a windward yacht, under Rule 38.1. There is nothing in the facts presented to indicate that S infringed Rule 35, either by so altering course as to prevent P from keeping clear or so as to obstruct her while she was doing so. In view of the foregoing, it is ruled that S luffed and tacked at a sufficient distance from P so that she infringed neither Rule 35 nor Rule 41."

Rule 41.4   When Simultaneous

When two yachts are both *tacking* or both *gybing* at the same time, the one on the other's port side shall keep clear.

This rule can be applied only if the incident happens when **both** boats are *tacking* or **both** are *gybing* at the same time. If one boat is *tacking* or *gybing* and the other is *on a tack,* then Rules 41.1

and 41.2 apply. Rule 41.4 does not specify that the boats must "begin" their *tacks* or *gybes* simultaneously. But for there to be contact in the case where one boat began to *tack* before the other, it implies that when one boat was *tacking*, the other was *on a tack* (i.e., not *tacking*). In this case the boat *on a tack* is a right-of-way boat and is governed by Rule 35 not to alter course in such a way as to prevent or obstruct the give-way (*tacking*) boat. Furthermore,

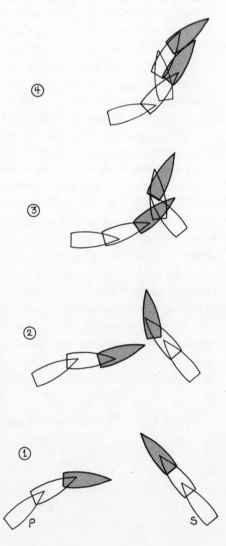

THE SLAM DUNK. In position 1, P has borne away to pass astern of S. The moment P is steering a course to clear S's transom, S luffs preparatory to tacking. In position 2, if P luffs she will hit S's transom. Because S is not past head-to-wind, she is still on starboard-tack with the right-of-way. In position 3, S has passed head-to-wind; therefore she is tacking. P is now the right-of-way boat because she is on a tack. Rule 35 requires that P not alter course so as to obstruct S or prevent her from keeping clear. In position 4, throughout S's tack, P continues to alter course toward S, eventually hitting her. P has infringed Rule 35.

when **both** boats are in the act of *tacking* or *gybing,* the one on the other's right has the right-of-way and is therefore similarly governed by Rule 35 not to alter course toward the other boat if it will obstruct or prevent the other boat from keeping clear.

USYRU Appeal 129 reads, "While beating, . . . [P] on the port tack passed close astern of . . . [S] on the starboard tack. . . . After P's bow passed astern of S, S proceeded approximately one length and then put her helm down preparatory to tacking. Immediately after P saw S alter course to tack, she also put her helm down and tacked. Both yachts were tacking at the same time about three lengths apart. S started to tack [passed head to wind] before P and also completed her tack while P was still tacking. . . . Shortly thereafter, a collision would have resulted had not both yachts tacked back again to their original tacks.

"DECISION: Rule 41.4 says that 'When two yachts are both tacking . . . at the same time, the one on the other's port side shall keep clear.' During the period when S and P were both tacking at the same time, there was no contact between them, S being approximately three lengths from P, so that S did not infringe Rule 41.4.

"Inasmuch as S completed her tack onto the port-tack while P was still tacking, P, even though she 'tacked into a position that gave her right of way' did not 'do so far enough from a yacht on a tack to enable this yacht to keep clear.' P accordingly infringed Rule 41.2.

"Also it is to be noted that when S started to tack by passing head to wind, she became the obligated yacht, and that P, as she altered course, held right of way first briefly under Rule 41.1, while still on a tack, then under Rule 41.4 when on the starboard side of S while both yachts were tacking—during both of which time S kept clear—and finally under Rule 36, after completing her tack. This persistent alteration of course by P in contravention of Rule 35 put S in a position from which she was unable to keep clear by her own efforts alone."

This is close to what some sailors call a "slam dunk"—i.e., a tactic common in match racing where a *starboard-tack* boat *tacks* to *windward* of a *port-tack* boat that is ducking her transom (see diagram). Notice that the "onus" in Rule 41.3 does not apply to S here.

8

Rules that Apply at Marks and Obstructions and Other Exceptions to the Rules of Section B (Part IV—Section C)

(Preamble) When a rule of this section applies, to the extent to which it explicitly provides rights and obligations, it over-rides any conflicting rule of Section B, Principal Right of Way Rules and their Limitations, except Rule 35, Limitations on Altering Course.

Section C contains the following rules:

- Rule 42, "room" at *marks* and *obstructions*.
- Rule 43, calling for "room to *tack*" at an *obstruction*.
- Rule 44, your rights and obligations when you are a premature starter.
- Rule 45, your rights and obligations when you have touched a *mark*.
- Rule 46, your rights and obligations when you are anchored, aground, capsized, or rescuing a person overboard.

When any of these rules explicitly provides a right **or** obligation that may be in conflict with a rule in Section B, the rule in Section C overrides it. For instance, if you are on *port-tack* shortly after the start and a *starboard-tack* boat is reaching back to the line because they were over early, Rule 44 (Section C) requires them to keep clear of you because you have *started* correctly, even though they are on *starboard* and you are on *port* (Rule 36—Section B). In this case you become the right-of-way boat and they are the give-way boat for as long as the rule requires them to keep clear. But also notice that Rule 35 **always** applies. So as the right-of-way boat in this situation, **you** are bound by Rule 35 not to prevent or obstruct them while they are fulfilling their obligation to keep clear.

RULE 42   ROUNDING OR PASSING MARKS AND OBSTRUCTIONS

Rule 42 applies when yachts are about to round or pass a *mark* on the same required side or an *obstruction* on the same side. . . .

This is the rule that governs boats at *marks* or *obstructions*. It is commonly called the "buoy room" rule, but that is only **half** right. Rule 42 applies whether we're rounding **or** passing a racing *mark,* a breakwater, a right-of-way boat in our race such as a *starboard-tack* boat or a boat that is capsized, a large clump of seaweed, or even an iceberg that has floated onto the course. (See IYRU Cases 20 and 91 and USYRU Appeals 44, 57, and 192.)

Now, Rule 42 can appear overwhelming on a first casual read-through, but it is in fact very clearly written and fits very sensibly with the basic right-of-way rules in Section B. Again, the key to understanding it is not to try to memorize its every detail, but to stand back and see what the rule is **trying to have happen** when boats converge at *marks* and *obstructions.*

As IYRU Case 55/USYRU Appeal 145 says, "The important thing to keep in mind is that the rights and obligations of Rule 42 are designed to bring about a consistent rounding with equity to all yachts concerned, and when such a rounding is made problems do not arise."

Rule 42 is broken into four distinct sections:

42.1 When the boats are *overlapped* at the *mark* or *obstruction.*

42.2 When the boats are **not** *overlapped* at the *mark* or *obstruction.*

42.3 How to establish a proper *overlap* before getting to the *mark* or *obstruction.*

42.4 A special rule at a starting *mark* that you can sail completely around (as opposed to when the starting *mark* is the end of a dock). This is commonly called the "anti-barging" rule.

"To whom is rule 42 talking?"
Rule 42 is "talking" to both the inside and the outside boats, but fundamentally it is talking to the outside boats. As boats get closer to a *mark* or *obstruction,* the "force" of Rule 42 begins to reach out to them, and outside boats, whether on *port-tack* or *starboard-tack* and whether *leeward* or *windward* boats, must start preparing for their upcoming temporary obligation—to give the inside boats "room" to round or pass the *mark* or *obstruction.*

USYRU Appeal 195 says, "Rule 42 is a rule of exception. In some situations at marks and obstructions outside yachts otherwise holding right of way must nonetheless yield to a yacht inside and even alter course to move far enough away from the mark or obstruction to give the otherwise obligated inside yacht the room she needs to pass or round it. A starboard-tack yacht with a port-tack yacht inside and a leeward yacht with a windward yacht inside are examples of this sort of situation which provide limited exceptions to earlier rules."

As the preamble to Section C says, "When a rule of this section applies, to the extent to which it explicitly provides rights and obligations, it over-rides any conflicting rule of Section B. . . . So even if you are the right-of-way boat approaching a *mark* or *obstruction,* when the "force" of Rule 42 begins to reach you, your right of way may momentarily shift to the inside boat.

"As I approach a mark or obstruction, when does the 'force' of Rule 42 begin to apply to me?"
The "force" of Rule 42 begins to apply when you are "about to round or pass the *mark* or *obstruction.*" IYRU Case 55/USYRU Appeal 145 reads, " 'When does a yacht become about to round a mark?' has been a perennial question although not one which has caused real complications by not being answered by a precise determination. Clearly, a yacht two lengths from a mark and steering a course

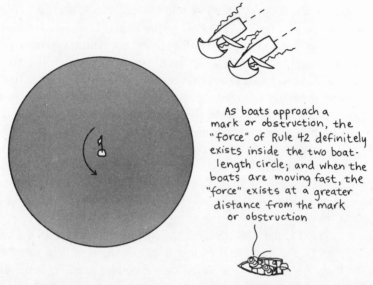

As boats approach a mark or obstruction, the "force" of Rule 42 definitely exists inside the two boat-length circle; and when the boats are moving fast, the "force" exists at a greater distance from the mark or obstruction

to round it on the required side is 'about to round' it within the meaning of Rule 42, and this could be true at a somewhat greater distance as well. Equally clearly, a yacht a quarter of a mile from a mark is not 'about to round' it. In approaching a mark there is no exact point at which a yacht becomes a yacht 'about to round.' The distance varies, too, with such factors as the speed of the yachts, the size of the yachts, and the amount of sail handling to be carried out just before or after rounding. In any event, the transition is gradual; the nearer a yacht is to a mark, the more definitely she is about to round it, the more she is committed to do so, and the more her competitors expect her to do so and plan their own courses accordingly.

So the "force" of Rule 42 is "on you" when you are at least two of your boat's lengths from the *mark* or *obstruction*. Outside of two boat-lengths you have your basic right-of-way rights, so if you are a *leeward* boat, a *windward* boat must keep clear.

But if you are on a catamaran going 20 miles per hour, or on an IOR boat with a huge spinnaker to get down, the "force" of Rule 42 would begin to apply to you sooner. IYRU Case 128/USYRU Appeal 160 reads, "As another example, wind, sea, or current conditions may be such that a luff somewhat more than two lengths from a mark, for the purpose of breaking an overlap, would put L in a position where she could not give the room required by rule 42.1(a), should she fail to break the overlap." Furthermore, I would argue that if L was successful in breaking the *overlap* immediately prior to coming within two lengths of the *mark*, but W, as a direct result of responding to the *luff*, was unable to round the *mark* on the required side because of such wind, sea, or current conditions, L would have similarly infringed Rule 42.1(a). (Note the need for this interpretation now that Rule 42.3(c) has been deleted.) In other words, if the boats are going so fast, because of their hull speed or the fact that the current is behind them, that when L *luffed* at four boat-lengths away from the *mark*, W could not turn back fast enough to get on the required side of the *mark*, L's *luff* effectively denied W of room at the *mark*.

Back to IYRU Case 128/USYRU Appeal 160: "In this case, the wind was light and L still had the right to luff as she pleased (she was three lengths from the *mark*). W's disqualification under Rule 37.1 is upheld."

IYRU Case 55/USYRU Appeal 145 says, "A dinghy six lengths from a mark in a moderate breeze is not about to round, and L was within her rights . . . to luff as permitted by Rule 38 with the intention of breaking an overlap."

Though a boat is "about to pass an *obstruction*" when two boat-lengths away, the "force" of Rule 42 does not grow strong until it is obvious on which **side** of the *obstruction* the right-of-way boat chooses to go. So on a starting line, as two *overlapped* boats approach a boat *clear ahead*, Rule 42 begins to apply at two boat-lengths to the extent that the "inside" boat needs to be *overlapped*. But the *leeward* boat, as right-of-way boat, gets to choose on which side she wants to pass the *obstruction*. The moment it's obvious that L will pass to leeward of the *obstruction*, the full force of Rule 42 is on them and W is entitled to "room" to pass to leeward also, if she chooses. (See USYRU Appeal 192 and IYRU Case 91.)

 "When the 'force' is on the boats, what rights do the inside boats have?" Rule 42.1(a) reads, "WHEN OVERLAPPED, an outside yacht shall give each inside *overlapping* yacht room to round or pass the *mark* or *obstruction*, except as provided in rule 42.3." (Rule 42.3 explains how and when a boat can establish a proper *overlap*, which we will discuss soon.) So the "force" puts an obligation on the outside

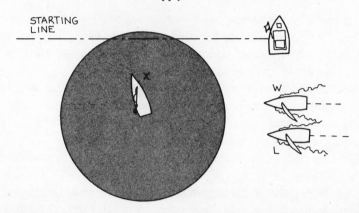

X is clear ahead of W and L, and so, as right-of-way boat, is an obstruction to both. The "force" of Rule 42 exists within the "two boat-length circle" around X, but it is L who gets to choose on which side she will pass. If she chooses to pass to leeward of X, the "force" of Rule 42 requires her to give W room to do likewise if W also chooses to pass to leeward of X.

boats to give the inside boats "room" if they need it, and the inside boats are entitled to the protection of that "room."

Note that the mere fact of being within two lengths of the *mark* or *obstruction* doesn't shift the right-of-way to the inside boat. Approaching the *mark* or *obstruction*, W must keep clear of L; and LO is obligated to provide room under Rule 42.1(a) only if WI needs the room. USYRU Appeal 273 reads, "In this incident rule 37.1 did not cease to apply; it continued to obligate W to keep clear of L unless rule 42.1(a) gave W conflicting rights. Although rule 42 did apply, because the yachts were 'about to round or pass' the mark, and rule 42.1(a) therefore gave W the right to the room she needed to round the mark, the fact was that she already had this room before and at the time of contact. The fact that the yachts were within the two-length circle did not give W any additional rights. She therefore infringed rule 37.1 by failing to keep clear of L."

"When they do need the 'room' and are entitled to have it, how much 'room' can they have?"

Rule 42.1(a) continues, "Room is the space needed by an inside *over-*

lapping yacht that is handled in a seamanlike manner in the prevailing conditions, to pass in safety between an outside yacht and a *mark* or *obstruction,* and includes space to *tack* or *gybe* when either is an integral part of the rounding or passing manoeuvre."

IYRU Case 126/USYRU Appeal 245 reads, "According to the dictionary 'integral' means 'essential to completeness.' " When a yacht can round a mark onto a proper course to the next mark without a tack or a jibe, a tack or jibe is not 'essential to completeness.' "

IYRU Case 40 gives the definitive interpretation of the word and concept of "room."

"QUESTION: What is the maximum amount of room an inside yacht is entitled to take in rounding or passing a mark or obstruction? What is the minimum amount that an outside yacht is required to give? The possible answers vary widely. To suggest the extremes, they might be:

1. as a minimum, enough room with sails and spars sheeted inboard, for the hull to clear by centimetres both the mark and the outside yacht;

2. as a maximum, all the room the inside yacht takes, setting her course as far abeam of the mark as she wishes.

"Between these extremes are two more moderate possibilities: next to the minimum enough extra clearance to allow for some error of judgment or execution; or, next to the maximum, enough room to make a tactically desirable rounding. Perhaps the most reasonable answer would fall roughly between these two.

"ANSWER: The word 'room' in Rule 42.1(a) means the space needed by an inside yacht, which, in the prevailing conditions, is handled in a seamanlike manner, to pass in safety between an outside yacht and a mark or obstruction.

"The term 'prevailing conditions' deserves some consideration. For example, the inside one of two dinghies approaching a mark on a placid lake in light air will need and can be satisfied with relatively little space beyond her own beam. Contrariwise, when two keel sloops, on open water with steep seas, are approaching a mark that is being tossed about widely and unpredictably, the inside yacht may need a full boat-length's room or even more to ensure safety.

"The phrase 'in a seamanlike manner' applies in two directions. First, it addresses the outside yacht, saying that she must provide enough room

so that the inside yacht need not make extraordinary or abnormal ma-
noeuvres to keep clear of her and the mark. It also addresses the inside
yacht. She is not entitled to complain of insufficient room when she fails
to execute with reasonably expected efficiency the handling of her helm,
sheets and sails during a rounding."

USYRU Appeal 64 continues, "A was required to give B room to round
or pass the mark in a normal manner and B was under no obligation to
alter the trim of her sails in order to avoid a collision with either A or the
mark."

USYRU Appeal 119 talks about tactical roundings: "Room means the
room needed to round or pass in a safe and seamanlike manner in the
prevailing conditions, and not all the room the inside yacht might like to
take to make a tactically desirable rounding. In this case [wind, 10 knots],
when the bow of the inside/windward yacht [24 feet in length] came
abreast of the mark, she was fifteen feet [just over half a boat-length]
from it, which is room enough for another yacht of the same class with its
mainsail fully out to be inside of her without contacting either her or the

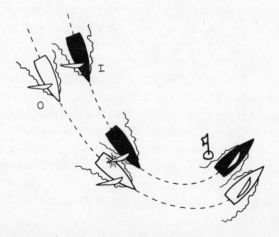

I, by swinging wide and then cutting close, has made a "tactical rounding."
When rounding the mark alone, this is desired. However, the situation changes
when O is to leeward. Now I, as an inside overlapped boat, is only permitted to
take just enough room needed to round in a "seamanlike manner in the prevail-
ing conditions." By making a tactical rounding, I has taken too much room, and
by hitting the leeward boat she has infringed Rule 37.1.

mark. Since this is clearly more room than needed by the inside boat—after turning she passed within five feet of the mark—we . . . disqualify the inside/windward boat under Rule 37.1 [for touching the outside/leeward boat and thereby failing to keep clear]."

The message here is clear: The inside boat has the protection of "room" only while she is taking just enough "room" to round the *mark* or pass the *obstruction* in a safe and normal way. She is not permitted to take enough "room" to do the conventional "swing wide-cut close" type of tactical rounding, though in actual practice most outside boats are a little more forgiving. USYRU Appeal 195 makes it clear that "if the inside yacht takes more room than she needs, the basic rule rather than Rule 42 is the one which applies."

"Does the inside boat have to call for 'room'?"

No. When you are on the inside while passing an *obstruction* or rounding a *mark*, you are **not required** to call for "room." In IYRU Case 112 a *windward*/inside yacht and a *leeward*/outside yacht both on *port-tack* were passing a *starboard-tack* yacht (therefore an *obstruction*) on the same side. Though PW claimed to have hailed twice and PL did not admit to hearing the hail, the Appeals Committee stated that "whatever the truth of that argument . . . the inside yacht is not required to hail." (See also IYRU Case 91.) In USYRU Appeal 46, SL and SW were passing astern of another *starboard-tacker* that had been *clear ahead.* In this case SW didn't know SL was there or that she was even entitled to "room" at the *obstruction.* She *bore off* inadvertently and hit SL. The Appeals Committee stated, "The fact that [SW] was unaware of the presence of [SL] in no way alters [SL's] obligations under the rules or justifies her in not giving [SW] room to clear the obstruction." Clearly, in cases where there is no dispute over the *overlap,* the outside boat must be aware at all times to be sure they give each inside boat enough "room."

And if the inside boat feels she needs more "room" than the outside boat is giving, Rule 42.1(f) says that "a yacht that hails when claiming . . . insufficiency of room at a *mark* or *obstruction* thereby helps to support her claim." USYRU Appeal 22 continues, "While not specifically required by the rules it is customary for a yacht when in doubt as to the sufficiency of the room being accorded her to hail to that effect as a precaution."

"Does the inside boat ever have the right not to round the mark?"
Rule 42.1(e) reads, "When an inside yacht of two or more *overlapped* yachts, either on opposite *tacks* or on the same tack without luffing rights, will have to *gybe* in order most directly to assume a *proper course* to the next *mark,* she shall *gybe* at the first reasonable opportunity."

The protection of "room" includes the "room" necessary to *tack* or *gybe* if either is essential to getting onto a *proper course* to the next *mark.* Rule 42.1(e) goes one step further. If the outside boat is on the same *tack* and had "mast abeam" at some point during the *overlap,* or is on the opposite *tack,* and a *gybe* is necessary to get onto the *proper course* to the next *mark,* the inside boat **is required** to *gybe* at the first reasonable opportunity.

So at a gybe *mark,* if you're on the inside and on *starboard-tack* and the outside boat is on *port-tack,* you must *gybe* immediately, even though you otherwise have right-of-way under Rule 36; and the outside/*port-tack* boat is only required to give you just enough "room" to complete your *gybe.*

In USYRU Appeal 164, "While approaching [the gybe *mark*], both outside and inside the two boat-length circle, IS [inside/*starboard*] hailed OP [outside/*port*] several times saying 'Starboard,' and OP finally responded by asserting that IS was not entitled to rights by reason of

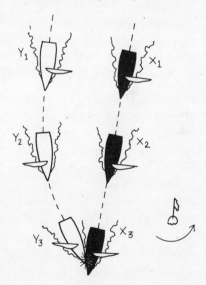

Because X is on the opposite tack from Y, X must gybe at the first reasonable opportunity and sail a proper course to the next mark (position 2). However, X continues on starboard-tack and hits Y (position 3), infringing Rule 42.1(e). If Y had remained on starboard-tack as in position 1, X would have been permitted to continue on starboard-tack past the mark, provided she had luffing rights.

being on starboard, but asked whether IS had sufficient room. . . . When the mark was one boat-length to port of IS at a point between her bow and mast, the starboard foot of IS's spinnaker hit OP's permanent backstay.

"DECISION: Inasmuch as OP had allowed enough room so that IS had 38 feet clear between her and the mark, and the protest committee found that 'just adequate room to jibe' had been given, OP had discharged her obligations under Rule 42.1(a) and it was the responsibility of IS to keep clear, and jibe, if necessary. Rule 36 is clearly over-ridden by Rule 42 at this point. Therefore . . . IS is disqualified under Rule 42.1(e) for failing to keep clear by jibing at the first reasonable opportunity when adequate room had been given."

So clearly, under Rule 42.1(e) the "force" of Rule 42 dissolves Rule 36. If, coming into a *mark* where a *gybe* is required, you are on the outside on the same *tack,* you can require the inside boat to *gybe* immediately simply by throwing your boom over and *gybing* to put you on the opposite *tack.* Also, if you are on the outside on the same *tack* but you've had "mast abeam" on the inside boat at some point during the *overlap,* L has no "luffing rights" and so she is also **required** to *gybe* immediately.

The only time a boat does **not** have to *gybe* (assuming that a *gybe* is required to sail the *proper course* on the next leg) is when L has "luffing rights" under Rule 38.1. In that one situation, the "force" of Rule 42 does not override the *leeward* boat's rights to continue sailing straight by the *mark* if she chooses. (See IYRU Case 62 and USYRU Appeal 195.)

"How long does the force of Rule 42 last?"
Remember what the whole purpose of Rule 42 is. It's so that when boats are rounding or passing a *mark* or *obstruction,* the boats on the inside won't get wedged in between the outside boat(s) and the *mark* or *obstruction,* or get forced onto the wrong side of the *mark.* Now, sometimes these outside boats are going to otherwise have the right-of-way—i.e., a *leeward* boat or a *starboard-tack* boat. The "force" of Rule 42 requires them to give only enough "room" for the inside boat to normally round or pass the *mark* or *obstruction,* and then to **clear it** on the other side. The moment an inside boat, which otherwise does not have the right-

of-way—i.e., a *windward* boat or a *port-tack* boat— can respond to their obligation to keep clear of the outside/right-of-way boat **without** hitting the *mark* or *obstruction,* the purpose of Rule 42 has been served and the "force" shuts off. At that moment the right-of-way shifts back to the outside boat, and the inside/give-way boat must **begin** to keep clear, though the new right-of-way boat must give her the momentary "shield" of "room and opportunity" to respond to her new obligation. (See Chapter 3, Principles—When the right-of-way shifts. . . .)

Let's say that two *overlapped* boats on *port-tack* are rounding the leeward *mark* onto a beat. The outside/*leeward* boat is allowing just enough "room" for the inside/*windward* boat to round, but OL is trying to keep her bow just ahead of IW. As IW comes up to *close-hauled* and her centerboard (i.e., the middle of her boat) just passes the *mark,* OL *luffs* fairly sharply. IW responds by *luffing* and *tacking* onto *starboard.* She keeps clear of OL and does not hit the *mark* nor *tack* too close to any boat about to round the *mark.* No foul. OL gave IW just enough "room" to round the *mark,* and when OL asserted her rights to *luff,* IW was able to keep clear without hitting the *mark*—i.e., she was not prevented from keeping clear of OL because of her proximity to the *mark.* The same would be true if IW were slow in coming up to *close-hauled* around the *mark* and hit OL. (See IYRU Case 50 and USYRU Appeal 12.)

The circumstances would weigh heavily in determining exactly when the outside boat can assert her rights. If there were a lot of boats near the *mark* such that IW could not *tack* without fouling them under Rule 41.2, OL would have to be careful to allow IW the "room" to keep clear without *tacking.* If there were current or strong wind or waves, OL would have to wait until IW could keep clear without risk of losing speed and being pushed back into the *mark.*

But, for instance, when two *close-hauled port-tackers* are ducking a *starboard-tacker,* the *port/leeward* boat can "luff" the *port/windward* boat the moment PW can respond to the *luff* without hitting the *obstruction* (S).

So the "force" of Rule 42 shuts off when the inside boat no longer needs "room" to round or pass the *mark* or *obstruction.* At

As the boats are rounding or passing the mark or obstruction, the "force" of rule 42 shuts off at the moment an inside boat can respond and keep clear of a maneuver by an outside boat which has r-o-w. In some cases, the inside boat will still be overlapped with the mark yet be able to luff to keep clear of a leeward/outside boat.

that moment an outside boat with the right-of-way can assert that right-of-way, including *luffing*, though the inside/new–give-way boat is entitled to the momentary "shield" of "room and opportunity" as long as she legitimately tries to get clear immediately. In most cases an inside boat should be able to respond while still within one length of the *mark* or *obstruction* after rounding or passing, and often well before that.

"How do I become one of these inside boats that are entitled to the protection of 'room'?"
Rule 42.1(a) requires an outside boat to give each inside *overlapping* yacht "room." Rule 42.2(d) re-states this by ruling, "A yacht clear ahead shall be under no obligation to give room to a yacht clear astern **before** an *overlap* is established."

So the magic to getting the "protection" is in getting an inside *overlap,* and the question is: "How do I get a legal (proper) inside *overlap*?"

Up to 1965 a yacht *clear astern* could get a legal *overlap* as long as it was (a) in time to enable the outside yacht(s) to give room; (b) before the yacht ahead altered her course in the act of rounding; and (c) before any part of the yacht ahead came abreast of the *mark* or *obstruction*. Things were often a tad out of control as boats came barreling up from astern yelling for "room" at the last second.

In 1965 the rule writers took a creative step. Realizing that there ought to be some cutoff "point" after which a boat *clear astern* could not establish an inside *overlap,* they devised the "two boat-length circle," which has proved to work very effectively. And because the "point" can be in any direction from the *mark* or *obstruction,* the "two boat-length circle" is an imaginary circle with the *mark* or *obstruction* in the center and having a radius of two of the **outside boat's** overall lengths—for instance, 48 feet in a J/24. Rule 42.3(a) simply reads, "A yacht that establishes an inside *overlap* from *clear astern* is entitled to room under Rule 42.1(a) . . . when, at that time, the outside yacht . . . is more than two of **her [emphasis added]** overall lengths from the *mark* or *obstruction.*"

So in order to be entitled to "room," you must have the inside overlap at the moment the outside boat arrives at the "two boat-length circle." Remember, the radius of the circle is two of the **outside** boat's lengths. If you do, then Rule 42.1(b) requires, "An outside yacht *overlapped* when she comes within two of her overall lengths of a *mark* or *obstruction* shall give room as required, even though the *overlap* may thereafter be broken." (See USYRU Appeal

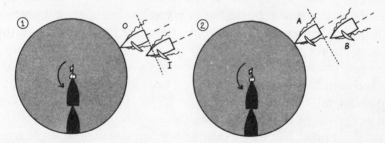

The "two boat-length circle" is a cut-off point for establishing an overlap near a mark or obstruction. The radius of the circle equals two of the outside boat's overall lengths. In situation 1, when O's bow reaches the "two-length circle," I has an inside overlap and is therefore entitled to room, even if O breaks the overlap when inside the "two-length circle." In situation 2, B does not have an overlap on A. Therefore she is not entitled to any room even if she gets an overlap when inside the "two-length circle." The overlap game ends at the "two boat-length circle."

69.) So the game ends at the "two boat-length circle." If you have the inside *overlap,* you are entitled to "room," even if the outside boat pulls ahead of you at one boat-length away.

Remember the definitions of *clear ahead, clear astern,* and *overlap.* (See Chapter 5, Definitions.) Two boats that otherwise are not *overlapped* suddenly become technically *overlapped* when a boat **in between** them *overlaps* both of them. So if you are just *overlapped* on the transom of another boat, and it is just *overlapped* on the transom of a third boat, **you** are technically *overlapped* with the third boat and entitled to "room" if you still have the *overlap* when the third boat arrives at the "two boat-length circle."

Also remember that, by definition, two boats *overlap* when the bow of one is over the line drawn through the aftermost part of the other, **even when the boats are a quarter of a mile apart,** and that for the purposes of Rule 42 they are still considered *overlapped* even when they are on opposite *tacks.*

"Does that mean that I can come zooming up from clear astern and be entitled to 'room' as long as I get the overlap before the boat ahead arrives at the 'two boat-length circle'?"

Exactly, except that the boat ahead has one protective "shield" if they need it. When you get your *overlap* at the zero-moment before the boat ahead enters the "two boat-length circle," the outside boat is **now** required to give you "room." But they are not required to **anticipate** your arrival (Rule 42.2[d]). If you get the *overlap,* but they physically will not be able to **give** you the "room," then you are **not** entitled to it. One obvious example is a tightly packed rounding in light air where a boat astern gets an *overlap* at two and a half boat-lengths, but there's just no way the inside boat can get everyone else to move out in time to create "room" for the new inside boat. Another example is when two boats are going so fast that by the time the outside boat can react and make the "room," the inside boat is already past the *mark* on the wrong side. Twelve knots of boatspeed equals 20 feet per second, so on a windy reach a Hobie 18 will chew up two boat-lengths in less than two seconds!

"What happens when boats on the outside that are keeping clear of overlapped boats on the inside never get to the 'two boat-length circle'

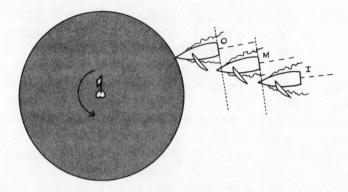

Above: *I is overlapped with O, by defi-nition, when O reaches the "two boat-length circle." Therefore I is entitled to room from O and M.*

Right: *Even though I is about four boat-lengths behind O, she is overlapped on the inside when O reaches the "two-length circle," and therefore is entitled to room from O if she needs it.*

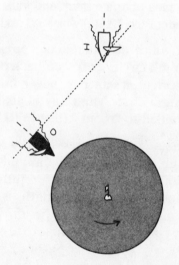

until after they've turned and begun heading for the mark? Now can a boat that was well clear astern suddenly claim room?"
Yes! IYRU Case 127/USYRU Appeal 250 clarifies this very com-mon situation at crowded *marks:*

"FACTS: Five yachts are approaching a leeward mark dead before the wind. Four of them, A1, A2, A3, and A4, are overlapped in line, with A1 inside nearest the mark. The fifth yacht, B, astern of A1, is clear astern of all four of the front line when A1 and A2 come within two lengths of the mark. When the four front yachts reach the mark and turn to round it, the change of bearing of A3 and A4 relative to B results in B becoming overlapped inside them while each of them is more than two lengths from the mark. B rounds the mark behind A1 and A2 but inside of A3 and A4, which are both able to give room to B.

"DECISION: Since B was clear astern of A1 and A2 when each of them came within two lengths of the mark, she was required by Rule 42.2(a) to keep clear of them 'in anticipation of and during the rounding or passing maneuver,' as she did, even though she may have obtained an inside overlap on one or both of them when they altered course to round. However, when A3 and A4 altered course towards the mark, B obtained an inside overlap while each of them was more than two lengths from the mark and thus was entitled by Rule 42.3(a) to room under Rule 42.1(a) which A3 and A4 were able to give."

Notice also that if an outside boat sails into the "two boat-length circle" and then back out again, either intentionally or by accident, it's a whole new game when she reenters the "two boat-length circle," and any boats having the inside *overlap* **then** are entitled to "room." (See IYRU Case 71.)

"How do I know where the 'two boat-length circle' really is?"
Well, at first it's difficult, and then after you've raced more and more it becomes easier to judge. Let's say you race a twenty-five-foot boat. Two boat-lengths is fifty feet. That's about how far the ground is away from the fourth floor of an average building, or just over halfway to first base on a pro baseball diamond. Doing 6 knots (10 feet per second) you'll cover two boat-lengths in 5 seconds. Measure it out and mark it with two orange poles or something at your club so everyone will learn to "guesstimate" it better.

But realizing that there will be disputes, the rule writers designed two very strong "onuses."

Rule 42.1(d) A yacht that claims an inside *overlap* has the onus of satisfying the **protest committee** that she has established the *overlap* in accordance with Rule 42.3.

In other words, if you come up from behind and claim that you got the inside *overlap* **before** the outside boat got to the "two boat-length circle" but the outside boat disagrees, saying that you were

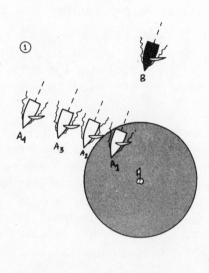

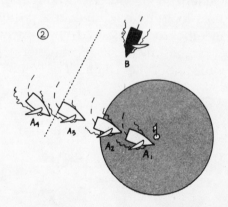

A1, A2, A3, and A4 are in a bunch at a mark. A4 is giving just enough room for the other three boats to gybe and round the mark. As a result, A4 is outside the "two boat-length circle." B is well astern. In position 2, the four boats have gybed and are lined up to round the mark one behind the other. The positions of A1 and A2 make it obvious that A3 and A4 are outside of the "two-length circle." Because B is overlapped on their inside, B is entitled to room from A3 and A4.

still *clear astern* when she arrived at the "two boat-length circle" and that you **subsequently** established the *overlap,* **you** will have to convince the **protest committee** that you are right. (See USYRU Appeal 191.)

Rule 42.1(c) An outside yacht that claims to have broken an *overlap* has the onus of satisfying the **protest committee** that she became *clear ahead* when she was more than two of her overall lengths from the *mark* or *obstruction.*

Here, the shoe is on the other foot. If an inside boat has an *overlap* at, say, five and then four boat-lengths away, the outside boat will be obligated to give her "room" unless she pulls *clear ahead* **before** arriving at the "two boat-length circle." If she claims to have "broken" the *overlap* **just before** she reached "two boat-lengths" but the inside boat disagrees, saying that they were still *overlapped* at "two boat-lengths," then it's the outside boat that must convince the **protest committee** that the *overlap* was broken in time.

These "onuses" are **very tough** to beat, but witnesses help (particularly independent witnesses who were positioned exactly at the "two boat-length circle" and in a position to determine *overlaps*). Remember also Rule 42.1(f): "A yacht that hails when claiming the establishment or termination of an *overlap* ... thereby helps to support her claim." The "onus" is much easier to

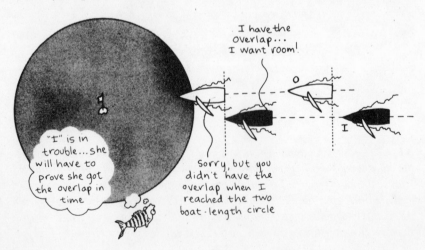

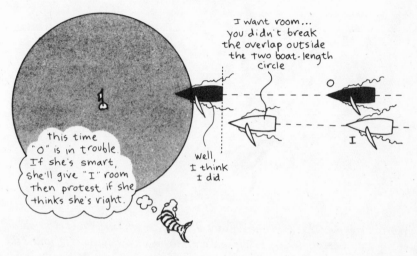

satisfy if appropriate hails have been made as the boats near the "two boat-length circle" to the point where they are almost expected by good **protest committees.**

"C'mon, aren't there any exceptions to all of this?"
Well, yes, there are two exceptions that are simple to remember. One is when a boat *tacks* **within** the "two boat-length circle," and the other is at a "continuing *obstruction.*"

Rule 42.3(a)(ii) However, when a yacht completes a *tack* within two of her overall lengths of a *mark* or *obstruction,* she shall give room as required by rule 42.1(a) to a yacht that, by *luffing,* cannot thereafter avoid establishing a late inside overlap.

If a boat crosses you and completes her *tack* inside the "two boat-length circle" and is **clear ahead of you** upon completion of her *tack,* you are **not** allowed to establish an inside *overlap* on her, unless you **physically cannot luff and get to her outside** (note the new insertion of the phrase "by luffing"). In other words, while she is *tacking* she is required to keep clear of you, and if you have to alter course to avoid her, she has fouled under Rule 41.1. But the moment she completes her *tack,* you must **immediately** try to *overlap* her on the outside (to *windward* if you are on *starboard* approaching a *mark* to be left to port). If you **cannot** get

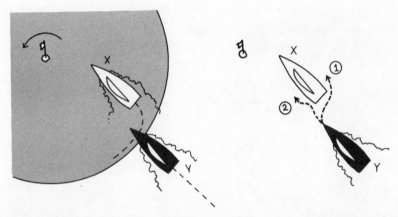

When X completes her tack, she is inside the "two-length circle" and clear ahead of Y. Y must immediately try to luff and overlap her on the outside (1), unless she physically cannot. If she is unable to avoid establishing the overlap on the inside of X (2), she is permitted to do so, and X must give her room at the mark if she can.

to the outside, then you are allowed to establish the late inside *overlap* and be entitled to "room," **provided** the outside boat is able to **give** the "room" (Rule 42.3[a][i]).

A situation that might seem similar, but is not the same thing at all, is when at a windward *mark* a *port-tack* boat *tacks* to *leeward* of a *starboard-tack* boat right at the *mark*. The above exception does **not** apply because the *port-tacker* is **not** establishing an inside *overlap* **from clear astern** (see discussion of Rule 42[a]).

"What about at a 'continuing obstruction'?"
First of all, what is a "continuing *obstruction*"? It is an *obstruction* that a boat "continues" to sail next to, as opposed to one that is passed in a matter of seconds. For instance, a breakwater that a boat is sailing along is a "continuing *obstruction*," whereas a capsized boat that gets sailed by in a few seconds is not a "continuing *obstruction*." When a *windward* boat is sailing parallel to a *leeward* boat for a few boat-lengths, the *leeward* boat as a right-of-way boat is an *obstruction* by definition, and a "continuing" one, as the two boats are sailing side by side for several lengths. (See USYRU Appeal 196 and IYRU Case 67/USYRU Appeal 163.) However,

when a *port-tacker* converges with a *starboard-tacker* upwind, S is **not** a "continuing *obstruction*," as P won't be sailing near her for more than a few seconds. (See IYRU Case 76.)

Because it is impossible to put a "two boat-length circle" around a "continuing *obstruction*," Rule 42.3(a) does not apply and Rule 42.3(b) does.

Rule 42.3(b) Limitation [on establishing an *overlap*] When an Obstruction is a Continuing One:

A yacht *clear astern* may establish an *overlap* between a yacht *clear ahead* and a continuing *obstruction,* such as a shoal or the shore or another vessel, only when, at that time, there is room for her to pass between them in safety.

The question is: When can a boat come up from *clear astern* and establish an inside *overlap* and be entitled to the protection of "room"?

The answer is: A boat *clear astern* (B) can establish the *overlap* **between** the boat *clear ahead* (A) and the "continuing *obstruction*" only when, **at the moment that the overlap is established,** there is enough "room" for her to pass completely between them without touching either. In other words, imagine that the moment the *overlap* on A is made, you could "freeze" the motion of A and the *obstruction*. If there is enough physical space for B to sail through between them without touching either, then the *overlap* is legal and A must give B "room" for as long as they are *overlapped* and B **needs** the "room" to keep from touching the *obstruction*—i.e., running aground, hitting the right-of-way boat, or the like. If B loses the *overlap* on A, then A ceases to be required to give "room" until B reestablishes another legal *overlap* and again **needs** "room." (See USYRU Appeal 257 and IYRU Case 69.)

One sensitive issue here is when A is sailing as close as she dares to shore but it's not obvious how close a boat of her class can really go without running aground. Boat B comes up and wants to establish an inside *overlap*. How do you determine if she could pass inside of A "in safety"?

USYRU Appeal 257 answers: "The determinant of 'safety' is whether under the conditions existing the inside yacht can navigate between the

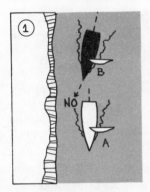
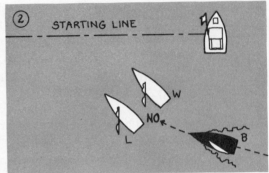

In situation 1, there is not room for B to sail in between A and the shoreline without hitting one or the other. Therefore, she is not allowed to establish an overlap between them and then ask for room from A.

outside yacht and the obstruction without undue risk." IYRU Case 69 continues, "In other words, when [A] is sailing as close to the shore as in the prevailing conditions is prudent, B is not entitled to establish an inside *overlap* [because in A's opinion there is not "room" between her and the "continuing obstruction" for B to pass without running aground] and does so at her own risk."

When she does decide to risk it, USYRU Appeal 257 says, "If the inside yacht, after establishing her inside overlap, promptly runs aground, she has demonstrated that there was not room for her to pass in safety. But after she has sailed inside a couple of lengths, any question of the failure of the outside yacht to give sufficient room is to be answered by the facts found by the protest committee, such as did the inside yacht need the room and if so did she take the appropriate steps so to inform the outside yacht. The outside yacht infringes Rule 42.1(a) if she fails to provide room to the inside yacht entitled to room under 42.3(b)."

"Are there any other times an inside boat is not entitled to room at a mark or obstruction?"
There are two very narrow situations in which Rule 42 does not apply at all, listed as Rules 42(a) and (b).

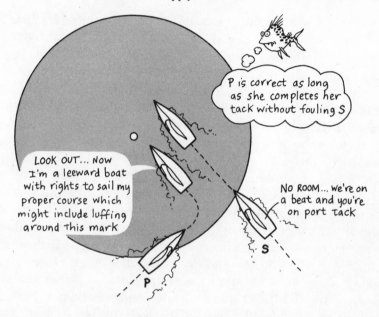

"Rule 42 . . . shall not apply:

(a) between two yachts on opposite *tacks:*
  (i) when they are on a beat, or
  (ii) when one, but not both, of them will have to *tack* either to round or pass the *mark* or to avoid the *obstruction,* or
(b) when rule 42.4 applies."

"Does Rule 42(a) mean that 'buoy room' doesn't apply at the windward mark?"

No. Rule 42(a) means that if two boats are coming in to a windward *mark* on **opposite** *tacks,* Rule 42 doesn't apply. But if the boats are coming into the windward *mark* on the **same** *tack,* then Rule 42 applies just like any other *mark.* A "windward *mark*" implies that at least one of the two boats on **opposite** *tacks* will have to *tack* to round the *mark,* and generally one or both of them will be approaching the *mark* on a *close-hauled* course.

Picture a windward *mark* to be left to port. It would be chaos if suddenly a *port-tack* boat could come in and call for "room" from a *starboard-tack* boat. While the boats are on opposite *tacks,* Rule 36 (*port/starboard*) applies, and if the *port-tack* boat (PI) wants to *tack* to *leeward* of the *starboard-tack* boat (SO), Rule 41, Changing *Tacks,* applies. But once the *port-tack* boat has completed her *tack* without "*tacking* too close" to the *starboard-tack* boat (Rule 41.2), she is on the **same** *tack* and as *leeward* boat she has the right-of-way. Note that the "two-length circle" restriction in Rule 42.3(a) doesn't apply because PI is not establishing an inside *overlap* from *clear astern.*

Once she completes her *tack* onto *starboard-tack* without infringing Rule 41.1 or 41.2, she is "doubly protected" to sail around the *mark,* which might include *luffing* head-to-wind even if she didn't have luffing rights. PI, as a *leeward* boat even without luffing rights, is still free to sail her *proper course,* which might include *luffing* head-to-wind to round the *mark* rather than making two *tacks.* SO would have to stay clear as a *windward* boat (Rules 37.1 and 38). SO, as an outside *overlapped* boat, is likewise required to provide PI room at the *mark* under Rule 42.1(a). Notice this only applies at the windward *mark* (the *mark* that ends the "windward leg"). The reasoning is that at all the other *marks,* even though the boats may be on opposite *tacks,* they are going in the same direction, or at least generally converging at much smaller angles.

The same exception applies when passing an *obstruction.* When two boats on a beat are on **opposite** *tacks,* the inside boat **cannot** ask for "room" to pass an *obstruction.* "On a beat" implies that

both boats are sailing *close-hauled*. Therefore, if in a narrow harbor you are sailing *close-hauled* on *port-tack* as close to the shore or the docks as you can get, you cannot call for "sea-room" from a converging *close-hauled starboard-tack* boat. Rule 36 applies, and you must slow down or *bear off* and take their stern. (See IYRU Case 93.)

USYRU Appeal 80 reads, "When the yachts were some three boat-lengths apart S hailed 'Starboard' to P, who returned a hail for buoy room, to which S correctly replied that P was not entitled to buoy room at a windward mark under the circumstances [opposite *tacks*]. . . . S was the right-of-way yacht approaching the windward mark, and P was attempting to pass between S and a mark although obligated by Rule 36 to keep clear of S." (See also USYRU Appeal 231 and IYRU Case 17.)

IYRU Case 77 is a case where two *starboard-tack* boats were approaching the windward *mark close-hauled*. In an attempt to "make" the *mark* (i.e., round it to port) the *leeward*/inside boat *luffed* hard and went past head to wind, hitting the *starboard-tack*/outside boat. The Appeals Committee ruled, "In attempting to round the mark, P [the leeward/inside boat] luffed and passed beyond head to wind. She was thereafter, by definition, in the act of tacking and, having collided with S while so doing, was properly disqualified under Rule 41.1."

"Does 42(b) mean that I can never get 'buoy room' before the start?"
No. Let me give you the "buoy room" at the start situation in a nutshell. Then I'll go through and explain how the rules permit what they do.

1. IF THE STARTING *MARK* IS **NOT** SURROUNDED BY NAVIGABLE WATER:

If the starting *mark* is not surrounded by navigable water—i.e., enough water so that the inside boat can sail around the *mark* without running aground or hitting a dock or other object—then it ranks as an "obstruction" (see Chapter 5—Definitions). Rule 42 **always applies** at *obstructions* not surrounded by navigable water, and an inside boat is entitled to "room" from any outside boat provided her *overlap* was estab-

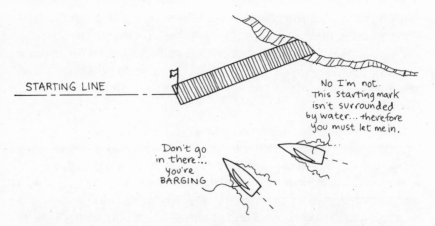

lished in proper time. Though this situation is not common, it will arise when one end of the starting line is the end of a dock or breakwater or a bell buoy that marks some shallow rocks or sandbars.

(The next four situations cover a starting *mark* that is surrounded by navigable water.)

2. IF TWO BOATS WANT TO PASS **TO WINDWARD** OF A STARTING *MARK* THAT IS **NOT** ALSO AN. *OBSTRUCTION:*

In other words, here's the situation at starting *marks* that are small buoys, flagstaffs, etc. **Before** the "starting signal" **Rule 42 does not apply;** however, Rule 40 still does. Therefore, L can slowly *luff* up to *close-hauled* if W has "mast abeam," and all the way to head-to-wind if W does not have "mast abeam." This is generally sufficient for L to pass to windward of the starting *mark*. **After** yachts have *started*—i.e., their bows have crossed the starting line after the starting signal—**Rule 42 applies** and the *leeward*/inside boat is entitled to "room." Note that if she established her *overlap* from *clear astern* she must have done so before the outside boat reached the "two-length circle" and the outside/*windward* boat must be able to give the room. Once entitled, LI can *luff* head-to-wind if necessary, even without luffing rights.

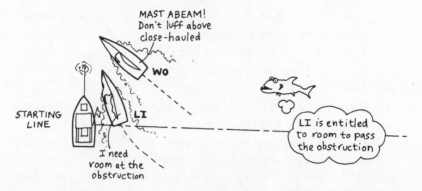

3. IF TWO BOATS WANT TO PASS **TO WINDWARD** OF A STARTING *MARK* THAT **IS** ALSO AN *OBSTRUCTION:*

This covers race committee boats when used as one or both ends of the starting line. **Rule 42 always applies** before, while, and after *starting.* The common situation is when passing the "leeward" end of the line which is a race committee boat. LI is entitled to "room" from WO, and LI can go head-to-wind if necessary regardless of whether she has luffing rights. Again, if LI established her *overlap* from *clear astern,* she must have done so before WO reached the "two-length circle" and WO must be able to give the room.

4. WHEN TWO BOATS WANT TO PASS **TO LEEWARD** OF A STARTING *MARK* THAT IS **NOT** ALSO AN *OBSTRUCTION:*

This would cover when passing to leeward of a starting buoy, flagstaff, etc. **Before** the starting signal a *leeward*/outside boat never has to give "room" to a *windward*/inside boat at such

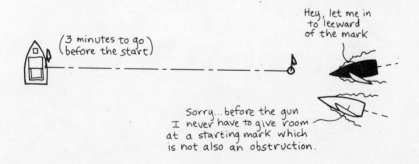

a starting *mark*. **After** the starting signal, the *leeward*/outside boat **cannot** deprive a *windward*/inside boat of "room" by sailing **above** a *close-hauled* course; or if the first leg isn't to windward, by sailing to windward of the compass bearing to the next *mark*.

5. WHEN TWO BOATS WANT TO PASS **TO LEEWARD** OF A STARTING *MARK* THAT **IS ALSO** AN *OBSTRUCTION*:

This covers the common situation of the race committee boat at the windward end of the starting line. If the *leeward*/outside boat is **not** on their final approach to *start*, they must give a *windward*/inside boat "room" to pass to leeward of the *obstruction* (which also happens to be a *mark*). But if the *leeward*/outside boat **is** on their final approach to *start*, they do **not** have to give a *windward*/inside boat "room"; and if WI forces their way in between LO and the race committee boat, we say she has "barged" in there. However, **after** the starting gun the *leeward*/outside boat **cannot** deprive the *windward*/inside boat of "room" by sailing either above *close-hauled* or to windward of the compass bearing to the next *mark*.

Now let's take a closer look at **how** Rule 42 says all this. First, be sure you understand that an object large enough to satisfy the

If Barger tries to squeeze in between the race committee boat and L, and hits L or forces L to bear off to avoid a collision, Barger has infringed Rule 37.1, not Rule 42.4.

definition of *obstruction* is **always** an *obstruction,* even when it is used as a *mark*—e.g., a race committee boat.

Second, notice the removal of the phrase "other than a starting *mark* surrounded by navigable water" from the first line of Rule 42. This clears up the old debate on how to treat an *obstruction* that is also a starting *mark* (e.g., a race committee boat). We now treat it as an *obstruction.* (Notice the inclusion of *"obstruction"* in Rule 42.4.)

Third, note that Rule 42 only applies at *marks* when boats are about to round or pass them on the same **"required"** side. Rule 51.3 says, "A starting line *mark* begins to have a required side for a yacht when she starts." That explains why boats aren't entitled to room

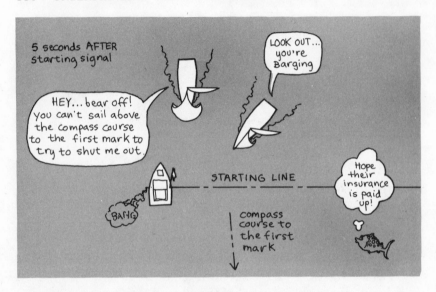

at starting *marks* before they have *started*. Note that when an inside/*leeward* boat wants to pass to windward of a starting *mark*, Rule 40 permits her to slowly *luff* to *close-hauled* if W has "mast abeam," and to head-to-wind if W does not have "mast abeam."

The subtle change caused by the removal of the phrase "other than a starting *mark* surrounded by navigable water" is that now LI, once she has *started*, can *luff* to head-to-wind if necessary to pass to windward of the *mark* even without luffing rights. Note that if LI established her inside *overlap* from *clear astern* she must have done so outside the "two-length circle" and WO must be able to provide the room (Rule 42.3[a]).

Finally, notice that Rule 42 applies "when yachts are about to . . . pass . . . an *obstruction* on the same side." Therefore, whenever two boats are passing an *obstruction* on the **same** side after the preparatory signal, the outside boat must give the inside boat "room" to pass the *obstruction*, which includes a race committee boat. Without a special rule, this would always apply, and at the start, a *leeward*/outside boat would have to give any *windward*/inside boats "room" to pass between her and the race committee boat. Because this would not make for very organized or fair starting, the rule writers devised a special rule, Rule 42.4, for just this situation at the *start*.

Rule 42.4   At a Starting Mark Surrounded by Navigable Water (commonly called the "anti-barging" rule)

When approaching the starting line to *start* until clearing the starting *marks* after *starting,* a *leeward yacht* shall be under no obligation to give any *windward yacht* room to pass to leeward of a starting *mark* surrounded by navigable water including such a mark that is also an *obstruction;* but, after the starting signal, the *leeward yacht* shall not deprive the *windward yacht* of room by *sailing* either:
  (a) to windward of the compass bearing of the course to the next *mark,*
      or
  (b) above *close-hauled.*

Rules 42(b) and 42.4 reinforce the principle that an inside boat **is** entitled to "room" if the starting *mark* is **not** surrounded by navigable water. However, the inside boat must still establish her *overlap* on the outside boat in proper time. "Proper time" is governed by Rule 42.3(a) when the starting *mark* is simply a *mark,* and by Rule 42.3(b) when the *mark* is at the end of "continuing *obstruction*" such as a dock when the inside boat will need room to pass along the *obstruction* prior to reaching the *mark* (i.e., the actual end of the dock or breakwater). (See the discussion of Rules 42.3[a] and [b], USYRU Appeal 8, and IYRU Case 76.)

But when the starting *mark* **is** surrounded by navigable water, Rule 42.4 says that a *leeward*/outside boat does **not** have to give a *windward*/inside boat "room" to pass to leeward of the starting *mark.* This includes the fact that the *mark* may also be an *obstruction*—i.e., a race committee boat. Remember, a *mark* does not cease to be a *mark* just because it is an *obstruction.*

But notice that this exception **only applies** to a *leeward*/outside boat when they are "approaching the starting line to *start* and after *starting.*" **Before** "approaching the line to *start*" an outside boat is not required to give an inside boat "room" to pass a starting *mark* because a starting *mark* doesn't have a "required side" yet, but they **are required** to give an inside boat "room" to pass an *obstruction* (Rule 42.1[a])—for instance, a race committee boat that is being used as a *mark*.

"When is a boat approaching the starting line to start?"
Though this question has never been discussed in an appeal, I would develop my opinion as follows. What is the purpose of the rule? Rule 42.4 is preventing the situation where *windward*/inside boats can reach in and demand "room" at the starting *mark* from *leeward*/outside boats that are trying to *start* there. And "when approaching the starting line to *start*" is establishing the period of time during which these *windward*/inside boats **know** that they are not entitled to any "room." Before LO is "approaching the starting line to *start*," WI is entitled to "room" at the *obstruction* (race committee boat); and the rules are consistently clear in providing predictable and specific times when a boat's rights change. To me, this is no exception. When LO is **clearly** on her final approach toward the line with the intention of *starting*—i.e., crossing the line after the gun—it will be obvious to WI and she will know to keep clear. Furthermore, a boat that is "approaching the starting line to *start*" and is close enough to the starting *mark* to shut out a *windward* boat, will clearly be *starting* in close proximity **distance-wise** to the starting *mark*.

Therefore, to me, a boat that in fifteen knots of breeze goes reaching full-speed by the committee boat with one and a half minutes to go before the starting signal, and ends up *starting* halfway down the starting line, was in no way "approaching the line to *start*" at the moment she went by the starting *mark* (race committee boat). But a boat that is passing the starting *mark* with ten seconds to go certainly is on her final approach to *start* very near to the starting *mark*. In addition, I feel that a boat that in light air sits nearly wayless behind the race committee boat may be approaching the line to *start* at one minute to go, and it will be more obvious and predictable that she plans to *start* near the *mark*, and the *windward*/inside boats can see this and keep clear accordingly.

This is a distinction that in general has caused very few problems, and in general has been very liberally interpreted in the *leeward*/outside boat's favor. But until it is officially interpreted, the safe move on LO's part would be to allow WI "room" up to one minute before the starting signal; and the safe move for WI would be not to try to **force** "room" with much less than two minutes to go. Both boats have the option to protest, and the **protest committee** can then decide whether LO was "approaching the starting line to *start*" in the particular circumstances.

"Now, what about after the starting signal?"

If the first leg is to windward, LO cannot deprive WI of "room" to pass between LO and the starting *mark* by sailing **above** her (LO's) *close-hauled* course after the starting signal. However, if LO is sailing *close-hauled* and there is no "room" for WI to squeeze in there, WI is not allowed to go in there. If, previous to the gun, LO was head to wind holding *windward* boats out, she does not have to **anticipate** her new upcoming obligation. She can wait for the gun and **then** begin to get speed and *bear away* to her *close-hauled* course. While she's responding to her new obligation, *windward* boats must keep clear. (See USYRU Appeal 47.)

If the first leg is **not** to windward, then after the starting signal a *leeward* boat shall not deprive a *windward* boat of "room" at a starting *mark* by sailing "**to windward of the compass bearing of the course to the next *mark*.**" The use of "the compass bearing of the course to the next *mark*" as opposed to the "*proper course*" to the next *mark* is designed to avoid disputes.

However, if L has no intention of passing to leeward of the starting *mark* after the gun, she is certainly under no obligation to do so. In fact, she could exercise her right to *luff* under Rule 40 and pass to windward of the starting *mark*. Because a starting *mark* has no "required" side until a boat *starts,* LO can pass on either side she wants and WI must keep clear. So Rule 42.4 begins to apply the moment it is obvious that LO intends to pass to leeward of the starting *mark* (i.e., *start*).

"If I don't have to give a windward boat room at the committee boat, can I deny her room by luffing head to wind?"

This is a very good question! Rule 42.4 does not give a *leeward*

boat the right to maneuver any differently than she already can under Rules 35, 37, 38, and 40. It is only closing a "loophole" that, in its absence, would force *leeward* boats to have to *bear away* and **give** "room" to *windward* boats right at the *start*.

Rule 37.1 gives L the right-of-way. If W tries to squeeze between L and the *mark* and hits L or forces L to *bear away* to avoid a collision, W has violated Rule 37.1, not Rule 42.4.

Rule 40 tells L how she can *luff*. If W has "mast abeam," then L cannot *luff* above *close-hauled*. If L is sailing *close-hauled* with W in the "mast abeam" position and W can just fit between L and the *mark*, then W is allowed to do so. L cannot *luff* **above** *close-hauled* to deny her "room"—i.e., to try to keep her from "barging."

Rule 35 requires the right-of-way boat not to alter her course if it will prevent the give-way boat from keeping clear. Let's say L and W are "approaching the line to start" and if L holds her course, W will be able to pass between L and the race committee boat without touching either. Just as W sticks her bow in behind the race committee boat, L *luffs* slowly, but W is unable to keep clear due to her proximity to the race committee boat and hits both it and L. W is protected by Rule 38.2(d), and L has infringed Rule 35 by altering her course (*luffing*) such that W was prevented from keeping clear.

So the answer to the question is, yes, you may "close the door" by *luffing* up to head-to-wind, as long as you don't infringe the rules that govern your *luff*.

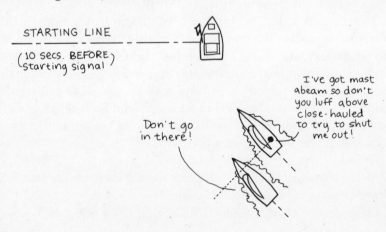

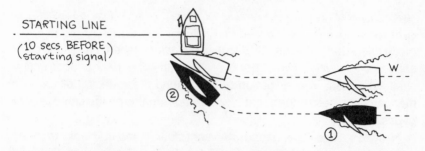

In position 1, W will have room to pass astern of the race committee boat if L holds her course. In position 2, W is passing astern of the race committee boat when L luffs and hits W, who cannot luff out of the way due to her proximity to the race committee boat. W is protected by Rule 38.2(d), and L has infringed Rule 35 by altering course and preventing W from keeping clear. If L wants to luff to "close the door," she must do so before W gets pinned to leeward of the race committee boat.

Finally, remember that Rule 42.4 (the "anti-barging" rule) applies only at a starting *mark*. If, halfway down the line, a *windward* boat bears off on a *leeward* boat in an attempt not to be over the line early, the *windward* boat has **not** "barged" on the *leeward* boat. They have simply infringed Rule 37.1.

Also, especially for big-boat sailors, notice that on downwind starts, **even after the gun** there is no rule that requires a *leeward* boat to *bear away* to her *proper course* or the course to the first *mark* **except** Rule 42.4, which applies only if the *windward* boat is actually being denied "room" to pass between the *leeward* boat and the starting *mark*. Anywhere else on the line, Rule 40 simply applies, and even when W has "mast abeam" L can continue to sail where she pleases provided she doesn't *luff* above a close-hauled course (USYRU Appeal 227). So, on downwind starts, take a good look to leeward before *bearing away* and setting your spinnaker! (See also USYRU Appeal 111 and IYRU Case 54/ USYRU Appeal 143.)

We've discussed thoroughly how Rule 42 applies slightly differently at a windward *mark* and at a starting *mark*. These are its only two exceptions. The rules for "buoy room" are exactly the same at every other *mark* on the course, including the finishing *marks*.

"Now I completely understand when I'm entitled to 'room,' but when I'm clear astern can the boat ahead do anything they want?"

No. Rule 42.2(a) reads, "A yacht *clear astern* when the yacht *clear ahead* comes within two of her overall lengths of a *mark* or *obstruction* shall keep clear in anticipation of and during the rounding or passing manoeuvre, whether the yacht *clear ahead* remains on the same *tack* or *gybes.*"

However, Rule 42.2(c) reads, "A yacht *clear ahead* that *tacks* to round a *mark* is subject to Rule 41, Changing Tacks—Tacking and Gybing."

So if you're *clear astern* when the boat *clear ahead* arrives at the "two boat-length circle," then you must stay clear of that boat until they have rounded or passed **and cleared** the *mark* or *obstruction*. This is true if they stay on the same *tack* or *gybe*. Notice that it is up to them whether they want to *gybe* or not. There is no mention that the *gybe* must be an "integral" part of the rounding or passing maneuver—i.e., "integral" only applies when the boats are *overlapped* when the outside boat arrived at the "two boat-length circle" (Rule 42.1[a]).

An example is when two boats are rounding a windward *mark*

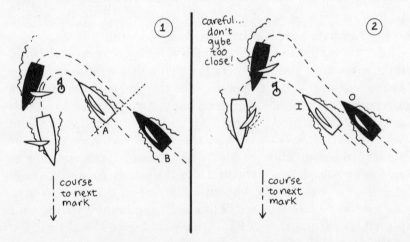

In situation 1, A rounds the mark clear ahead of B and gybes immediately onto port-tack. B must keep clear of A while A gybes (Rule 42.2[a]). In situation 2, I was overlapped with O when O reached the "two-length circle." Therefore, I is not protected while gybing unless gybing is integral to her rounding (Rule 42.1[a]).

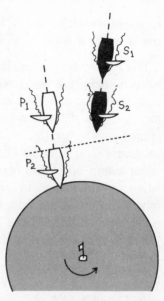

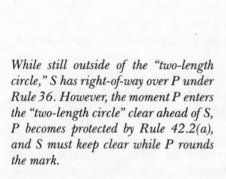

While still outside of the "two-length circle," S has right-of-way over P under Rule 36. However, the moment P enters the "two-length circle" clear ahead of S, P becomes protected by Rule 42.2(a), and S must keep clear while P rounds the mark.

onto a run. If the leading boat was *clear ahead* when she arrived at the "two boat-length circle," she has the right to *gybe* around the *mark* if she chooses, whether or not it's a *proper course*.

But if the leading boat had been *overlapped* on her outside when the **outside boat** arrived at the "two boat-length circle," then the leading/inside boat can only *gybe* if it is an "integral" part of the rounding. IYRU Case 126/USYRU Appeal 245 says, "When a yacht can round a mark onto **a** [emphasis added] proper course to the next mark without . . . a jibe, a . . . jibe is not [integral]." Notice that both *tacks* may be *proper courses* and that the leading boat may **want** to *gybe*. They can only do so if they don't infringe Rule 41 (*gybing* yacht must keep clear) or Rule 36 (*port-tack* yacht must keep clear).

Another example is a boat *clear ahead* on *starboard-tack* that *gybes* to *port-tack* to round the leeward *mark*. Suddenly, the boat astern (SB) calls, "Starboard, get out of my way!" If P is outside of her two overall lengths from the *mark*, she is not yet within the "force-field" of Rule 42 as far as Rule 42.2(a) is concerned. Therefore, outside of the "two boat-length circle," Rule 36 applies, and SB has the right-of-way. But if P is *clear ahead* the moment she **enters** the "two boat-length circle," she is safe and the "force" of Rule 42.2(a) requires that SB keep clear.

IYRU Case 68 discusses an interesting case where a line of boats were running downwind on *starboard-tack* as close to the shore as possible to get out of the current. The leading boat (P) *gybed* to *port-tack* but was still sailing as close to the shore as possible. The boat immediately astern (S), still on *starboard,* then came up and hit the *port-tack* boat. The Appeals Committee decided, "By definition, the terms 'clear astern' and 'clear ahead' apply to yachts on opposite tacks only when they are subject to Rule 42. P and S were passing an obstruction (shore) on the same side, thus bringing Rule 42 into effect and over-riding Rule 36. In this case Rule 42.2(a) applied, under which S, as the yacht clear astern, is disqualified for failing to keep clear of P."

A boat *clear ahead* that wants to *tack* around a *mark* gets no protection from Rule 42 except that Rule 42.2(b) says, "A yacht *clear astern* shall not *luff* above *close-hauled* so as to prevent a yacht *clear ahead* from *tacking* to round a *mark*." Otherwise, Rule 41, Changing Tacks, applies.

Let's say you (A) and another boat (B) are sailing *close-hauled* on *port-tack* into the windward *mark,* **not** *overlapped.* The *mark* must be left to port. You thought you were allowed to just *tack* around the *mark.* As you *tacked,* B had to bear off to miss your transom. Actually, you have fouled by infringing Rule 41.1. But if you two **had** been *overlapped,* then the outside boat would have had to give you "room" to *tack* because *tacking* is an "integral" part of your rounding (Rule 42.1[a]).

Notice, though, that you can *luff* up to head to wind just prior to *tacking* around the *mark,* and a boat close astern is not allowed to do the same thing to prevent you from *tacking.* In this situation, then, tactically speaking for a moment, your best move is to either slow down inside of the "two boat-length circle" and force the trailing boat to *overlap* you on the outside; or *luff* to head to wind, glide up to the *mark,* then *tack* around where you won't "*tack* too close" to the other boat. (See USYRU Appeal 138.)

"I understand when I can and cannot be entitled to 'room,' but what if an outside boat carelessly leaves enough space? Is it a foul to sneak in there?"

Absolutely not, as long as you don't hit the outside boat or force them to alter course to avoid hitting you. USYRU Appeal 38 is clear: "It is an established principle of yacht racing that when a yacht voluntarily or unintentionally makes room available to another yacht that has no right under the rules to such room nor makes or indicates any claim to it . . . the other yacht may take advantage, at her own risk, of the room (freely) given." (See also USYRU Appeal 121.)

"I heard once that it is legal to force someone onto the wrong side of a mark. Is it?"
No, not anymore! There used to be a provision for this under the rules, but that has been removed. In actuality, the occasion to do so rarely presented itself in fleet racing, and only very rarely in team or match racing.

A *leeward* boat with luffing rights can still hold a *windward* boat to windward of the rhumb line, and in fact can "carry" that *windward* boat right on past the *mark* provided L never gets so close to the *mark* that Rule 42 begins to apply. Clearly, when L gets to within two boat-lengths of the *mark*, Rule 42 applies; and it can begin to apply at a farther distance depending on the circumstances (see IYRU Case 55/USYRU Appeal 145). Once Rule 42 begins to apply, L must begin to allow for W to have "room" at the *mark*.

"Does this mean that I now know everything there is to know about the rules at marks and obstructions?"
Almost.

RULE 43   CLOSE-HAULED, HAILING FOR ROOM TO TACK AT OBSTRUCTIONS

Rule 43.1   Hailing

When two *close-hauled* yachts are on the same *tack* and safe pilotage requires the yacht *clear ahead* or the *leeward yacht* to make a substantial alteration of course to clear an *obstruction,* and when she intends to *tack,* but cannot *tack* without colliding with the other yacht, she shall hail the other yacht for room to *tack* and clear the other yacht, but she shall not hail and *tack* simultaneously.

This is the rule that is used when calling for "sea-room" at a shore, breakwater, or dock; however, it is also commonly used when two *port-tack* boats are sailing side by side up a beat and are converging with a *starboard-tacker*. USYRU Appeal 108 reads, "This is primarily a safety rule to permit a close-hauled yacht caught between another close-hauled yacht [on the same tack] and an obstruction to avoid the obstruction without loss of distance when a substantial alteration of course is required to clear it."

Notice that Rule 43 does **not** apply to boats on opposite *tacks*. IYRU Case 93 describes a situation where a *port-tack* boat (P) is sailing *close-hauled* as close to shore as possible. P is on a collision course with a *starboard-tack close-hauled* boat (S). S hails "Starboard" and P hails for "sea-room." The Appeals Committee said, "P is not entitled to hail for room, since this hail is governed by Rule 43, which applies to two yachts, close-hauled on the same tack, approaching an obstruction." Remember also Rule 42(a). So, in this situation P must slow down or *bear away* and pass astern of S.

When all the conditions in Rule 43 are met, a *leeward* boat or one *clear ahead* will be able to call for "room to *tack* at the *obstruction*" when nearby *windward* boats would otherwise be preventing them from *tacking*.

Here is how Rule 43 works:

1. Two boats (or more) must be sailing *close-hauled* on the same *tack* and approaching an *obstruction*.

2. Rule 43.1 is intended for the use of the *leeward* boat (L) or a boat *clear ahead* (A) that is about to hit, or be hit by, an *obstruction*—i.e., a sandbar, a dock, a fishing boat, a *starboard-tack* boat, or the like. When there is any doubt as to whether L or A actually is in imminent danger of colliding with an *obstruction*, IYRU Case 117/USYRU Appeal 147 is clear: "Unless the facts found by the protest committee prove otherwise . . . the judgment of the leeward yacht [or the yacht clear ahead] shall be conclusive."

3. Rule 43.1 can be used only when L or A must make a **"substantial alteration of course"** to go around or keep clear of the *obstruction*. Here, the alteration is simply that needed **not to hit** the *obstruction*. In this case, as my general guideline, a course change of less than 10 degrees is not very "substantial."

That's only 3 feet, 6 inches, in a twenty-foot boat. (See Appendix B2.) Therefore, in a twenty-foot boat, if you can *bear away* and miss an *obstruction* that you would otherwise hit only 3 feet from its edge, you are not entitled to use Rule 43.1; but if you need to **tack** to avoid the last 3 feet, then that's "substantial." USYRU Appeal 81 reads, "If [L] had approached the police launch sufficiently close to its leeward end so that with only a slight alteration of course when near it, she could have safely passed to leeward of it, she should have done so. This situation did not prevail in this case. As is clearly shown by the diagram, L's course brought her close to the windward end of the police launch and she not only had to tack in order to pass it to windward but would have had to bear away substantially below her actual course to pass it to leeward. Inasmuch as she was 'required to make a substantial alteration of course to avoid an obstruction' whichever side she left it, she had a right under Rule 43.1 to hail W for room to tack, as she did." (See also IYRU Case 20.) Notice that even when an *obstruction* is surrounded by open water, L or A can use Rule 43.1. (See USYRU Appeal 81.)

4. When there is a *windward* boat (W) or a boat *clear astern* (B) that is very close by, A or L can hail for "room to *tack*" to keep clear of the *obstruction* **only** when she can't *tack* without **immediately** colliding with B or W. USYRU Appeal 108 says, "If the course of L [or A] is sufficiently to leeward of W's [or B's] course so that, after tacking onto the port-tack she has room to bear

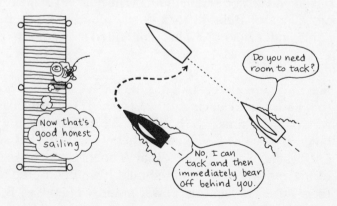

away and pass astern, she is required to do so, since she then is able to 'tack without colliding with the other yacht.'" This means that if A or L can *tack* and **immediately** *bear away* sharply and miss B or W, she must do so and cannot use Rule 43.1. (See IYRU Case 80/USYRU Appeal 189.)

5. So, when L or A is approaching an *obstruction,* and safe pilotage requires her to make a substantial alteration of course to clear the *obstruction,* and when A or L **intends to tack,** but cannot *tack* without colliding with W or B, she can hail W or B for "room to *tack*." Notice four things:

   a. She is **required** to hail—i.e., the hail is mandatory.

   b. Her hail must be **adequate,** which implies that it must be loud enough for B or W to hear it above the wind and noise of the boats, and it must be absolutely clear as to what the hail means. I personally try to quickly turn my head **toward** the other boat, use their skipper's name if I know it, and say to the effect, "I have a dock or a *starboard-tacker* coming, I need 'room' to *tack*." IYRU Case 117/USYRU Appeal 147 reads, "Failure of a windward yacht to hear a properly made hail would not necessarily relieve her of her obligations to a leeward yacht. Where, however, the leeward yacht . . . observed no response after her hail, a second more vigorous hail would be required to constitute proper notice of her intention to tack."

   c. She cannot hail and *tack* simultaneously. USYRU Appeal 246 reads, "The protest committee, having found that L hailed and tacked simultaneously in violation of the express provisions of Rule 43.1, correctly found that she had no rights under Rule 43." This is intended to require L or A to keep a good lookout, so she is not "surprised" by an *obstruction.*

   d. She must adequately hail in time for B or W to respond so that **both boats** can clear the *obstruction.* This will obviously require more time if B or W will have to subsequently hail a boat or boats to *windward* of them. Also, USYRU Appeal 246 reads, "The finding . . . that W should have been aware of the presence of S and should have been prepared to respond as required is unwarranted." Therefore B or W

does not have to anticipate that A or L might be approaching an *obstruction*. If A or L **does not** adequately hail in time and subsequently runs aground or fouls a *starboard-tack* boat, she cannot blame B or W. (See IYRU Case 117/ USYRU Appeal 147.)

"I thought that when two port-tack boats were approaching an obstruction, it was whoever hailed first that got to tell the other what to do."
6. No. The applicable phrase in Rule 43.1 is: ". . . and when she intends to *tack*, . . ." So when A or L will have to make a substantial alteration of course to *bear away* and pass astern of an *obstruction*, it is **her choice** whether to duck or *tack*. When two *port-tack* boats (PW and PL) are approaching a *starboard-tack* boat (S), USYRU Appeal 131 says, "The choice of whether the port-tack yachts will pass astern of S or tack rests with PL. Having made this choice, PW must be bound by such decision." If PL **chooses** to pass astern of S and PW wants to pass astern of S also, then IYRU Case 20 reminds PL that "as an outside yacht passing an obstruction she is bound by Rule 42.1(a) to give room to the windward yacht to pass on the same side." But if PL **chooses** to *tack*, PW must comply even when she'd rather duck.

When A or L adequately hails, Rule 43.2 tells B or W how to respond.

Rule 43.2   Responding

The hailed yacht at the earliest possible moment after the hail shall either:

(a) *tack,* in which case the hailing yacht shall begin to *tack* immediately she is able to *tack* and clear the other yacht; or

(b) reply "You *tack,*" or words to that effect, in which case:

   (i) the hailing yacht shall immediately *tack* and

   (ii) the hailed yacht shall give the hailing yacht room to *tack* and clear her.

   (iii) The onus of satisfying the **protest committee** that she gave sufficient room shall lie on the hailed yacht that replied "You *tack.*"

Notice the phrase "earliest possible moment." Often it will **not** be possible for B or W to respond immediately after hearing a hail. Examples would be: When there are several boats to *windward* or B or W that need to be hailed; when coming in on *port-tack* to a windward *mark* where the boats already going down the first reach are so close that *tacking* is impossible; or when some object in the water such as a log or *mark* momentarily restricts her ability to respond. When it is not possible for B or W to respond immediately, she should so inform A or L.

Another issue is: What if B or W feels A or L's hail is not proper—i.e., she is not really near an *obstruction,* or she will not have to make a substantial alteration of course to go around it. Rule 43.2 says that the hailed yacht **shall** either *tack* or reply, "You *tack.*" B or W has **no other choice** but to do one or the other, and when she feels the hail is improper, she can protest. (See IYRU Case 117/USYRU Appeal 147.)

Notice also that it makes no difference whether the hailed boat can clear the *obstruction* herself (unless it is also a *mark*—see Rule 43.3). If the hailing boat cannot clear it without *tacking* or *bearing away* sharply, she is entitled to hail and to get a response, regardless of whether the hailed boat can clear the **obstruction.**

Now let's say that you are L and have hailed W for room to *tack* because of a converging *starboard-tacker.* Upon hearing your hail,

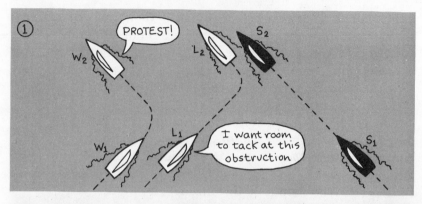

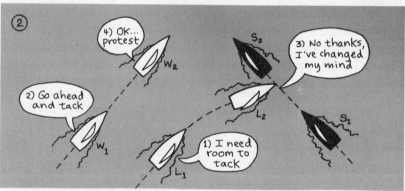

In situation 1, L has infringed Rule 43.2(a) by delaying her tack to starboard. After W begins to tack in response to L's hail, L must begin her tack as soon as she can and still keep clear of W. In situation 2, L infringes Rule 43.2(b)(i) by not immediately tacking after W's verbal response.

W *tacks*. You **must begin** your *tack* (i.e., cross head to wind) **before** W completes her *tack* (i.e., arrives at her *close-hauled* course). In other words, you must put your helm down within a couple of seconds after W puts hers down (Rule 43.2[a]). If in *tacking* so soon you will hit W, you can wait an additional couple of seconds. But you cannot watch W *tack* and then continue another few boatlengths before *tacking*, even though this is commonly done.

If W responds to your hail with the reply "You *tack*," or words to that effect, again you must **immediately** put your helm down and *tack* (43.2[b][i]). Once W hails, "You *tack*," they assume all the obligation to keep clear, so if you hear their reply and immediately put your helm down and hit them, they are wrong (43.2[b][ii]). And if you decide to stop your *tack* or otherwise alter course before completing your *tack* in order to avoid them, **they have the "onus"** to satisfy the **protest committee** that they were in fact keeping clear (43.2[b][iii]).

Finally, let's discuss a common situation. Two *port-tackers* (PW and PL) are sailing *close-hauled* side by side, and on a converging course with a *starboard-tacker* (S). PL hails PW for "room to *tack*," gets no response, and ultimately S must alter course to avoid hitting PL. Who should be penalized?

IYRU Case 6 simply states, "Having hailed three times, PL was entitled to expect that PW would respond and give her room to tack. She was not obliged either to anticipate PW's failure to comply with Rule 43.2 or to bear away astern of S. PL is exonerated as the innocent victim of another yacht's infringement of a rule, under the provisions of Rule 74.4(b)."

However, several USYRU Appeals go into more depth in discussing the primary obligations of PL and her actions in this situation.

USYRU Appeal 11 reads, "When PW failed to respond to PL's hail for room to tack, PL was faced with the necessity of taking alternative action, if she could, to avoid fouling S. This raises the question of whether she should be exonerated as the victim of another yacht's foul as contemplated in Rule 74.4(b). It is reasonable to assume that all yachts in a race know and will obey the rules but discreet to anticipate that in some circumstances they may not. PL claimed that she did not bear away under the stern of S because she thought that with the type of boat and the strength of wind a collision would result. Two expert scow skippers aboard the committee boat, however, gave their opinions that she could have borne off safely or slacked her sheets at four lengths from the mark. The decision of the race committee disqualifying PL for infringement of Rule 36 is therefore sustained."

USYRU Appeal 142 is an excellent summation of the USYRU Appeals on the subject and reads in part, "The situation developed slowly with rights and obligations established at some distance from the point of convergence. In fact PL acknowledged recognizing the problem a minute before S hailed her. Had she taken timely action then, either by hailing PW for room to tack under Rule 43.1 or by bearing away and passing astern of S, she could have avoided S or at least put the major onus on PW. Under the circumstances, the failure of her late reliance on Rule 43.1 does not entitle her to exoneration as an innocent victim, her principal obligation having been to keep clear of S under Rule 36."

USYRU Appeal 116 is a good example of how PL fulfilled her obligation to adequately hail, but then was forced to foul S by PW's failure to respond.

"FACTS: PW and PL were close-hauled on the port-tack. S had been to leeward and ahead of both PW and PL and tacked to starboard . . . in compliance with Rule 41.2. PL thereupon twice hailed PW to come about, so that she could come about and avoid S. PW refused to respond, by which time it was too late for PL to make any alternative maneuver without interfering with oncoming S. PL called to S that it was impossible for her to respond, whereupon S tacked back to avoid a collision.

"DECISION: Inasmuch as PL would have had to make a substantial alteration of course to pass astern of S even if she had borne off instantly as S tacked to starboard, she had the right to hail PW as she did. By the time PW had refused to respond it was too late for PL to clear S by bearing off. Since PL was compelled to foul S in consequence of PW's neglect to observe her obligations under Rule 43, PW was also subject to disqualification under Rule 74.4(b) and PL is correspondingly exonerated thereunder."

The key to all this is that PL must keep a good lookout and begin hailing in time for PW to hear and understand the hail and then respond. If PL waits till the last second to hail PW, and then immediately fouls S, she cannot blame PW. But if after **two clear hails** PW does not respond, PL must make a reasonable effort to keep clear of S. If she cannot keep clear she should be exonerated under Rule 74.4(b), and PW should be penalized for infringing Rules 43.2 and 36. If, however, PL **did** have enough time and room to keep clear of S **after** getting no response from PW but failed to make an effort to use it, she should also be penalized under Rule 36.

This situation commonly occurs at the windward *mark*. When

PW and PL are within the "two boat-length circle," PW is entitled to "buoy room" from PL under Rule 42.1(a). However, the "room" will not be given until the boats reach the *mark*. If PL wants to *tack* to avoid a converging S, she can hail PW for "room to *tack*," and as long as it is possible for PW to respond, **she must do so.** (See USYRU Appeal 11.)

Rule 43.3   When an Obstruction Is also a Mark

(a) When an *obstruction* is a starting *mark* surrounded by navigable water, or the ground tackle of such a *mark*, and when approaching the starting line to *start* and after *starting*, the yacht *clear ahead* or the *leeward yacht* shall not be entitled to room to *tack*.

(b) At other *obstructions* that are *marks*, when the hailed yacht can fetch the *obstruction*, the hailing yacht shall not be entitled to room to *tack* and clear the hailed yacht, and the hailed yacht shall immediately so inform the hailing yacht. When, thereafter, the hailing yacht again hails for room to *tack* and clear the hailed yacht, the hailed yacht shall, at the earliest possible moment after the hail, give the hailing yacht the required room. After receiving room, the hailing yacht shall either retire immediately or exonerate herself by accepting an alternative penalty when so prescribed in the sailing instructions.

(c) When, after having refused to respond to a hail under Rule 43.3(b), the hailed yacht fails to fetch, she shall retire immediately or exonerate herself by accepting an alternative penalty when so prescribed in the sailing instructions.

Notice that a boat can **never** call for "room to *tack*" at an *obstruction* that is also a **starting mark,** and **including** the *mark's* ground tackle. This situation usually develops when there is a race committee boat anchored as the left-hand or "leeward" end of the starting line. A *leeward* boat is truly in "coffin corner" if they sail into a position where they can neither *tack* without fouling the *windward* boat nor *bear away* and pass astern of the race committee boat.

But if the **windward** *mark* is a boat or other object large enough to qualify as an *obstruction*, Rule 43.3(b) applies. Let's say you are

approaching the *mark/obstruction* and cannot get around it on its required side ("fetch" it) without *tacking*, and that you cannot *tack* without colliding with the boat just to *windward* of you. First you must hail W for "room to *tack*" under Rule 43.1. If W **cannot** "fetch" it herself, then she must respond under Rule 43.2. But if she **can** "fetch" it she must immediately tell you so, and she does **not** have to respond under Rule 43.2. In this case you are going to have to *gybe* or *bear away* and *tack* around to try it again. But if after telling you that she is "fetching," she does **not** "fetch it" *on that tack* due to a miscalculation or a windshift, she is wrong and must take her penalty (Rule 43.3[c]). (See also USYRU Appeal 8.)

Now it's possible that, upon learning that the boat just to *windward* of you can "fetch" the *mark/obstruction*, it is too late for you to *bear away* without running into the *mark/obstruction* yourself. In this case you can hail **again** for "room to *tack*," and W **must** give you the "room to *tack*" as soon as she can. Of course, you are in the wrong, so after getting the "room," you must drop out of the race or accept an alternative penalty if one is offered in the sailing instructions.

It's also possible that a competitor might calculate that they will actually lose fewer places by forcing the *windward* boat to give them "room" and then doing a "720" or taking their 20 percent penalty (see Appendix 3), particularly at a crowded windward *mark.* This doesn't work. Appendix 3,1.4, reads, "The protest commit-tee may disqualify a yacht that has accepted an alternative penalty when it finds . . . that she gained a significant advantage." (See also Appendix 3,2.5.)

"Now do I know everything there is to know about room at marks and obstructions?"
Yes!

RULE 44   RETURNING TO START

Rule 44.1 (a) After the starting signal, a premature starter returning to *start,* or a yacht working into position from the course side of the starting line or its extensions, shall keep clear of all yachts that are *starting* or have *started* correctly, until she is wholly on the pre-start side of the starting line or its extensions.

(b) Thereafter, she shall be accorded the rights under the rules of Part IV of a yacht that is *starting* correctly; but when she thereby acquires right of way over another yacht that is *starting* correctly, she shall allow that yacht ample room and opportunity to keep clear.

Rule 44.2 A premature starter, while continuing to *sail* the course and until it is obvious that she is returning to *start,* shall be accorded the rights under the rules of Part IV of a yacht that has *started.*

The rule is clear. If you aren't completely behind the starting line at the starting signal, you are considered a premature starter (PMS). However, even when you and everyone else **knows** you are PMS, you keep all your right-of-way as long as you don't **turn** back. This means that you continue to have rights even while slowing down or *luffing* in order to get clear enough to turn back. When it is obvious that you are **returning** to the starting line, you lose your right-of-way and must keep clear of **all** boats that have *started* properly. Between two or more boats returning to the pre-start side of the line, the rules of Part IV apply in the usual way.

Once you are completely on the pre-start side of the starting line **or its extensions,** you get your normal rights back except that you have a temporary obligation. If you suddenly get the right of way over another boat *starting* correctly, you must give them **ample** "room and opportunity" to keep clear. (See USYRU Appeal 98 and IYRU Case 81.)

"If another boat fouls me and forces me over the starting line just before the gun, I'm PMS, but do I have to go back and restart?"
USYRU Appeal 242 is an interesting case where "Lightning #10807 was sailing in very light air close-hauled on the starboard-tack to cross the starting line. . . . Immediately prior to the start #11738 tacked under #10807 but was too close and collided before completing the tack. Number 10807 attempted to avoid the collision by luffing up and in doing so started prematurely. . . . The district appeals committee concluded that . . . because of the conditions #10807 gained no significant advantage over the others in starting prematurely. Therefore, it exonerated #10807 and directed that she be scored in order of her finish."

The USYRU Appeals Committee said, "The district appeals committee has correctly applied Rule 74.4(b). This rule states that 'the other yachts **shall** be exonerated.' The Introduction to the Rules states that the word 'shall' is mandatory and the provisions of Rule 74.4 apply to 'any' of the rules. A premature starter in this situation who has been properly recalled and does not return to restart takes the chance that the facts may not be found in her favor. In this case the facts are clear and undisputed."

This appeal will be especially useful to a boat wrongfully forced over the line when the race committee is using a stricter "DSQ if you're over early in the last five minutes" type of system to keep boats back.

RULE 45 KEEPING CLEAR AFTER TOUCHING A MARK

Rule 45.1

A yacht that has touched a *mark* and is exonerating herself shall keep clear of all other yachts until she has completed her exoneration and, when she has *started,* is on a *proper course* to the next *mark.*

Rule 45.2

A yacht that has touched a *mark,* while continuing to *sail* the course and until it is obvious that she is exonerating herself, shall be accorded rights under the rules of Part IV.

    The change to Rules 45 and 52 is one of the most major changes in the new rules. To exonerate yourself after touching a *mark,* instead of re-rounding the *mark* you now must do a "720" as soon as possible and well clear of the other boats. (See discussion of Rule 52.2.) When you hit a *mark,* you still have all your rights as long as you continue sailing the course. But the moment it is obvious to other boats that you are clearly beginning to exonerate yourself by sailing well clear of the other boats preparatory to doing your penalty turns, you must stay clear of all other boats in the race. You get your rights back when you have completed your turns and are sailing on a *proper course* to the next *mark.*

    Note that if you touch a starting *mark* before *starting,* you can do your turns immediately (as opposed to waiting for the starting signal before doing them), and you regain your rights the moment you complete your turns.

RULE 46   PERSON OVERBOARD; YACHT ANCHORED, AGROUND, OR CAPSIZED

Rule 46.1

A yacht under way shall keep clear of another yacht *racing* that:

(a) is manoeuvring or hailing for the purpose of rescuing a person overboard, or

(b) is anchored, aground, or capsized.

Rule 46.2

A yacht shall not be penalised when she is unable to avoid fouling a yacht that she is attempting to assist or that goes aground or is capsized.

Rule 46.3

A yacht is capsized from the time her masthead is in the water until her masthead is clear of the water and she has steerageway.

Rule 46.4

A yacht anchored or aground shall indicate the fact to any yacht that may be in danger of fouling her. Under normal conditions, a hail is sufficient indication. Of two yachts anchored, the one that anchored later shall keep clear, except that a yacht dragging shall keep clear of one that is not.

Notice that a boat anchored, aground, capsized, or rescuing a person overboard that is still *racing* has right-of-way over other boats under way, in that boats under way must keep clear of them. The intention is clear: If a boat is anchored, aground, or capsized it cannot very well "move" to get out of another boat's way; and if one boat is in the act of rescuing someone overboard, no other boat should hinder the rescue in any way.

Rule 53.1 reads, "A yacht shall be afloat and off moorings at her preparatory signal, but may be anchored." Rule 53.3 reads in part, "Means of anchoring may include the crew standing on the bottom or any weight lowered to the bottom." Notice the provisions in Rule 46.4 governing boats anchored near each other. Also in Rule 46.4, the word "shall" makes it mandatory that boats anchored or aground indicate this fact to any boat that might hit them.

Finally, Rule 46.2 reemphasizes the principle that a boat with a newly acquired obligation to keep clear is entitled to "room and opportunity" to respond. If a boat goes aground or capsizes and you physically are unable to keep clear, you should not be penalized. It also emphasizes the safety principle in that if you are attempting to assist a boat which otherwise has right-of-way over you, you should not be penalized.

A major addition to the rules is the definition of "capsized" for sailboats. The Sailboard Racing Rules (Appendix 2) have been, and remain, crystal clear on the definition of "capsized," and on the status of a sailboard "recovering" from a capsize. (See Chapter 5, Definitions—Capsized and Recovering; and Appendix 2, 3.3.) New Rule 46.3 now makes it very specific for sailboats.

Notice the fundamental difference in the rules between sailboats and sailboards recovering from a capsize. Appendix 2,3.3, reads, "A sailboard recovering from a capsize shall not obstruct a sailboard or yacht under way." However, a sailboat in the act of recovering is considered as still "capsized," meaning that sailboats under way must keep clear of her (Rule 46.1). She remains protected under Rule 46.1 until her crew is back aboard and she has steerageway.

A boat under way that hits a capsized boat shall be penalized unless the boat capsized such that she was unable to keep clear. However, a boat or sailboard in the **process** of capsizing is not specifically covered by Rule 46. My feeling is that once a boat is to the point where it is obvious that she is going to capsize, then for all intents and purposes under Rule 46 she ranks as capsized. Supporting this opinion is USYRU Appeal 232, where the boat *clear ahead* (A) had difficulty in taking her spinnaker down. Though the boat *clear astern* (B) was twenty feet behind, the head of A's spinnaker hit B's headstay. The Appeals Committee claimed that B was not wrong because "the contact . . . resulted from A's equipment . . . being out of normal position. B was in fact fulfilling her obligations under Rule 37.2 to keep clear." I would apply the same logic to when L capsizes to *windward* and while in the process of capsizing her mast hits W's sail. Similarly, if W loses control and capsizes to *leeward* and her mast rubs against L's shroud, L could protest and then ask the **protest committee** to find the contact minor and unavoidable. (See discussion of Rule 33.)

9

Other Sailing Rules (Part V)

OBLIGATIONS IN HANDLING A YACHT

A yacht is subject to the rules of Part V only while she is *racing*.

Part V contains other rules that govern us while *racing*. Most are straightforward and simple to understand. I'll focus on the two for which an explanation might be helpful, Rules 52, Touching a Mark, and 54, Propulsion.

RULE 52   TOUCHING A MARK

Rule 52.1 A yacht shall neither
    (a) touch:
        (i) a starting *mark* before *starting,* or
        (ii) a *mark* that begins, bounds, or ends the leg of the course on which she is *sailing,* or
        (iii) a finishing *mark* after *finishing* and before clearing the finishing line and *marks,*

    nor

    (b) cause a *mark* or *mark* vessel to shift to avoid being touched.

Rule 52.2 (a) When a yacht infringes rule 52.1, she may exonerate herself by *sailing* well clear of all other yachts as soon as possible after the incident, and remaining clear while she makes two complete 360° turns (720°) in the same direction, including two *tacks* and two *gybes.*

(b) When a yacht touches a finishing *mark,* she shall not rank as having *finished* until she first completes her turns and thereafter *finishes.*

Rule 52.3 When a yacht is wrongfully compelled by another yacht to infringe rule 52.1, she shall be exonerated:
(a) by the retirement of the other yacht (or by the other yacht accepting an alternative penalty when so prescribed in the sailing instructions) in acknowledgement of the infringement, or
(b) in accordance with rule 74.4(b), Penalties and Exoneration, after lodging a valid **protest.**

Prior to the 1969–73 rules, if you touched a *mark* and it was your fault, you had to drop out of the race. In the 1968 Olympics in Mexico, the late Carl Van Duyne, sailing the Finn for the United States, saw the leech of his main touch the windward *mark* in the first race. Despite the claims of the race officer at the *mark* who insisted that Carl did not touch the *mark,* Carl withdrew from the race. From this example and others, the rule writers saw the obvious over-severity of this penalty for the infraction, and changed the rule to permit sailors to take a penalty when they accidentally touch a *mark.*

"I heard that now the penalty for touching a mark is a '720' instead of rerounding the mark. Is this true?"
Yes. From 1969 to 1988 the penalty for touching a *mark* was one penalty rounding of the *mark.* This has now been changed in the new rules. Rule 52.2(a) says that when a yacht has touched a *mark* and wants to exonerate herself, she must sail well clear of all other yachts (not just those rounding the *mark*) **as soon as possible** (not halfway down the next leg) and make two 360-degree turns (720 degrees) in the same direction, including two *tacks* and two *gybes.* See also Rule 45, Keeping Clear after Touching a Mark.

The reason for this significant change is to eliminate the safety hazard caused by yachts' attempting to reround *marks* at the same time other yachts are rounding them, a particularly dangerous situation in heavy air. Furthermore, under the old system it was

often difficult to determine whether a yacht approaching a *mark* for a second time was rerounding (therefore having to keep clear) or making another attempt to round, having failed to "fetch" the first time. Finally, by requiring two turns done as soon as possible, the penalty becomes slightly more severe in most cases.

Notice the requirement of two *tacks* and two *gybes*. This is to prevent a yacht from turning a full 720 degrees without performing the final *gybe,* which is very possible to do. Boardsailors take note that this is a much more severe penalty than a "720" under Appendix 3.1 done for a Part IV infringement. After touching a *mark,* boardsailors must perform two *tacks* and two *gybes,* whereas the "720" in Appendix 3.1 requires only two complete circles of the board itself (Appendix 2,6.1).

So, new Rule 52.1 states that you may not touch a *mark.* If you do, you have two options:

1. Rule 52.2(a): If you think it was **your own fault** that you touched the *mark,* you can get clear of other boats and do a "720" as described in Rule 52.2(a); or

2. Rule 52.3: If you believe **another boat wrongfully forced you** to hit the *mark,* you do **not** have to take a penalty, but you **must protest** the other boat by flying your flag at the first reasonable opportunity and lodging a valid written **protest,** unless the other boat acknowledges fault and retires from the race or exonerates herself by accepting an alternative penalty if one applies.

"Does it count if just my head brushes against the mark?"
Absolutely yes. In fact, if you have a late spinnaker take-down and your spinnaker sheet trails behind the boat and rubs against the *mark* after you're already around and a boat-length away from it, you still have to take your penalty. USYRU Appeal 232 sums it up: "A yacht 'touches' a mark within the meaning of Rule 52 when any part of her hull, equipment, or crew comes into contact with the mark. Rule 52 is not limited in its application to contact that occurs during the actual rounding of the mark; any touching of a mark 'that begins, bounds, or ends the leg of the course on which she is sailing' results in a violation of Rule 52. Thus, it is immaterial here that contact occurred after A 'had rounded and otherwise cleared the mark,' for the mark still 'begins' the next leg of the course which she was then sailing, and contact occurred between the mark and A's equipment. Further, the fact that the contact was inadvertently caused while experiencing maneuvering or sailhandling difficulties does not excuse the foul."

"What if I hit the anchor line and it drags the mark into me?"
USYRU Appeal 59 reads, "If fouling its ground tackle causes the mark to be drawn against the yacht, the mark has been touched and the yacht involved must act in accordance with Rule 52."

"What about when I run aground on an island that I'm required to round or pass on a required side?"
IYRU Case 94 says, "A yacht that goes aground in shoal water near that island is not touching a mark within the meaning of Rule 52. She merely fouls an obstruction. On the other hand, a yacht that touches any above-water part, including a projecting rock or jetty, of an island that ranks as a mark infringes Rule 52 and is subject to the penalty provision of that rule." (See Part 1, Definitions—Mark.)

RULE 54   PROPULSION

Rule 54.1   Basic Rule

Except when permitted by rule 54.3, a yacht shall compete only by *sailing,* and her crew shall not otherwise move their bodies to propel the yacht. Fundamental Rule A, Rendering Assistance, and rule 55, Aground or Foul of an Obstruction, over-ride rule 54.

Rule 54 is the "pumping, rocking, ooching, sculling" rule. The rule specifically tells sailors how they can, and cannot, propel their boats in a sailboat race. The principle behind Rule 54 is simple: The rule writers (and most sailors themselves) want people to race their sailboats and sailboards by "sailing" them, as opposed to by propelling or slowing them in other ways. If you are a bit too early for a start, it is more of a sport if you have to slow down using your sails and rudder than if you could just stick your arms in the water and backpaddle; just as it's more challenging and fun to try to ride the waves on a windy reach as opposed to handing all the sheets to Igor and telling him to "pump" nonstop to the leeward *mark.*

Compliance with this rule continues to be a major problem facing the sport. In response to that, the rule writers have taken many steps toward improving the problem. Their hope is that the rules will become clearer, unambiguous, and as a result more enforceable by both competitors and judges.

They have defined "sailing": "A yacht is *sailing* when using only the wind and water to increase, maintain or decrease her speed, with her crew adjusting the trim of sails and hull and performing other acts of seamanship." This definition has been given great prominence, appearing as the first definition in Part I and in Fundamental Rule C. (See discussion in Chapter 4, Fundamental Rule C, and Chapter 5, Definitions—Sailing.) This definition represents no fundamental change in the way yachts can be raced—i.e., they can be powered only by the natural action of the wind and water. The definition recognizes that the people on boats and boards are going to have to move around in order to adjust the trim of their sails and hull and to otherwise correctly and safely *sail* the boat/board.

Rule 54.1 states the principle of the rule as discussed above. The phrase in Rule 54.1 "her crew shall not otherwise move their bodies to propel the yacht" serves to prohibit any crew action that **in and of itself** propels the yacht (paddling is an obvious example) and serves to prohibit any newly discovered kinetic technique not listed in Rule 54.2. Note that the term "crew" refers to **all sailors on board,** including the helmsman.

For obvious safety reasons, Fundamental Rule A, Rendering

Assistance, and Rule 55, Aground or Foul of an Obstruction, override Rule 54. This reinforces the clear principle that you should get to a boat or person's rescue as fast as you can using any means available, including paddling, rocking, or an engine when you have one. Obviously, this is not intended to be misused as a deceitful way to advance along the race course. IYRU Case 38 and the discussion of Fundamental Rule A (Chapter 4) are clear as to when and how a boat/sailboard that renders assistance should be compensated. Also, you may hop ashore and push your boat off after running aground.

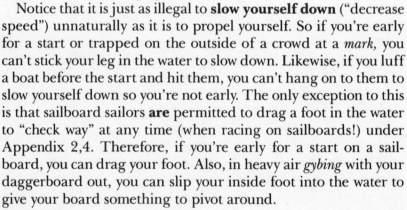

Notice that it is just as illegal to **slow yourself down** ("decrease speed") unnaturally as it is to propel yourself. So if you're early for a start or trapped on the outside of a crowd at a *mark*, you can't stick your leg in the water to slow down. Likewise, if you luff a boat before the start and hit them, you can't hang on to them to slow yourself down so you're not early. The only exception to this is that sailboard sailors **are** permitted to drag a foot in the water to "check way" at any time (when racing on sailboards!) under Appendix 2,4. Therefore, if you're early for a start on a sailboard, you can drag your foot. Also, in heavy air *gybing* with your daggerboard out, you can slip your inside foot into the water to give your board something to pivot around.

"Can I anchor?"

Yes. Generally yachts anchor either as a safety measure or to decrease the speed at which they are moving away from their destination (as in adverse current). Though it is not specifically stated as an exception to Rule 54, I would argue that Rule 53 specifically allows anchoring and therefore it is permissible. Note that a means of anchoring is the crew standing on the bottom (Rule 53.3). Of course if that crew starts walking the boat around, Rule 54 is infringed.

IYRU Case 9 says, "Throwing an anchor forward, except as permitted by rule 55, infringes rule 54.1. Recovering an anchor so as to gather way over the ground and cause the yacht to pass the point at which the anchor is lifted off the ground [also] infringes rule 54.1." Obviously, if you throw your anchor forward, then recover the anchor, you will be "pulling yourself" forward past where you were when you threw out the anchor. Therefore, the anchor must be dropped **straight down** when used while *racing*. Likewise, when you pull the anchor back up, you can't generate momentum that will cause the boat to move **past** the point where the anchor was on the ground—i.e., where it was dropped.

Other permissible means of slowing down include physically holding the boom out so the wind pushes against the sail, and turning the rudder hard over against the flow of the water provided it is not done repeatedly back and forth (see "sculling"—Rule 54.2[d]). USYRU Appeal 132 discusses the question: "On a boat with a trim tab separate from its main rudder, is it permissible to set the two rudders in opposition with each other for the purpose of slowing down? DECISION: Sails are intended to transmit power from the wind to give a vessel forward speed but from the earliest days of square riggers they have also been backed to stop forward motion. Rudders are intended to transmit power from the flow of water to change the direction of the boat and, in the process, drag is increased and the boat slowed. The second rudder is intended to improve performance on some points of sailing and when so used is set at the desired angle while the principal rudder is used to steer with, sometimes being in opposition to the first rudder. Using opposed rudders hard over to slow a boat departs from the regular use only in degree and purpose and is comparable to backing sails. Under these circumstances it is held that such use to slow a boat is not abnormal means of doing so and does not infringe rule 54."

Note also that a yacht can be penalized for infringing Rule 54 only while they are *racing*. USYRU Question 269 says, "Momentum of a yacht after the preparatory signal that is the result of being propelled by her engine before the [preparatory] signal does not cause an infringement of rule 54." Likewise, in light air and adverse current a yacht can just get its bow across the finish line (thereby *finishing*), drift backward, and, when clear of the finishing line and finishing *marks* (i.e., no longer *racing*), turn on her engine and power out of the course area.

"What other modifications have the rule writers made to Rule 54?"
Rule 54.2 is now unambiguous. It lists five specific types of actions which are always prohibited, **regardless of whether they are capable of propelling the yacht or not.** This will make it

easier for sailors to know what they can't do, and for judges to administer the rule on the water and in protest hearings. The five are the major "offenses" and are listed in order of perceived frequency of use (or abuse!).

Rule 54.2   Prohibited Actions

Without limiting the application of rule 54.1, these actions are prohibited:

(a) pumping—repeated fanning of any sail either by trimming and releasing the sail or by vertical or athwartships body movement;

(b) rocking—repeated rolling of the yacht induced either by body movement or adjustment of the sails or centreboard;

(c) ooching—sudden forward body movement, stopped abruptly;

(d) sculling—repeated movement of the helm not necessary for steering;

(e) repeated *tacks* and *gybes* unrelated to changes in the wind or to tactical considerations.

Let me reemphasize: If you do any of these above-listed actions, you have infringed Rule 54.2. It does not matter whether the action propelled the boat! Therefore, it applies to boats and boards of all sizes.

In comprehending these descriptions, notice the use of the word "repeated" throughout, indicating that for the actions to be illegal they must continue nonstop for an extended period of time or for more than just one movement. "Ooching" is the only action that involves a singular movement.

(a) PUMPING—For a sail to be "pumped," it must be trimmed and then released. When a sail is pumped "repeatedly" in short succession, it will look like the sail is being "fanned." This is illegal. This can be done using the sheets, or by using body motions. Bouncing up and down on the rail is an example of "vertical" movement; and crossing the boat quickly from side to side is "athwartships" movement. In a small boat with a flexible mast, bouncing can "pump" the top of the sail. Likewise, movement side to side will commonly cause the angle of heel to change, which in turn can act to "pump" the sail. These means of "pumping" are also illegal. Rule 54.3 allows limited "pumping" in certain conditions.

This rule is not designed to inhibit good sailing techniques. On a puffy windy day, the mainsail can be played constantly to keep the boat flat, provided it doesn't become a "fanning" action. Similarly, downwind, the spinnaker sheet can be played in and out constantly in response to changes in apparent wind.

(b) ROCKING—Your boat is "rocking" when it is rolling back and forth. You may be intentionally doing it with your body, or you may have simply encouraged it by pulling your centerboard up, letting your boom way out, and then starting the action like a pendulum. It doesn't matter whether your body is moving; if your boat is rhythmically rolling back and forth, it's "rocking," and that is illegal at all times. Obviously, waves will cause the boat to toss about. You do not have to run all over the boat counteracting every wave action. If you've ever watched a fleet of boats on a broad reach or run, you know that they all are being tossed in a similar way. If one boat is being intentionally "rocked," she will stand out instantly as being different from the others.

Notice that on a run most boats sail faster when heeled to *windward,* and the crew can position their weight to do this, provided the boat doesn't start "rocking" back and forth as a result. When rounding a leeward *mark* or initiating a *tack,* sailors can heel the boat to *leeward* to "help" the boat head up.

(c) OOCHING—Notice the additions to the description of "ooching" (in bold). It is a "sudden **forward** body movement, **stopped abruptly.**" The key to "ooching" is that it is forward motion, abrupt (sudden), and stopped abruptly. Even just one "ooch" is illegal. Pushing or pulling on the mast or shrouds (forward hand movements), slamming forward on the front of the cockpit, mast shrouds, or forestay, and subtle abrupt forward motions with the rear or feet are all examples of "ooching" and are all now illegal at all times.

(d) SCULLING—"Sculling" is "repeated movement of the helm not necessary for steering." Notice there is no reference to "forceful" or to "crossing the centerline." Simply put, you can not "wiggle" your tiller unless you are attempting to steer the boat.

There are two common situations in which repeated, even force-ful, movement of the helm is often required in normal sailing: (1) When you are trying to bear off on a broad reach when about to broach, pumping the helm helps to prevent the rudder from stalling, thereby increasing steerageway. (2) In very light winds in order to turn a yacht.

(e) REPEATED TACKING AND GYBING UNRELATED TO WIND OR TACTICS—You cannot repeatedly *tack* or *gybe* back and forth in quick succession unless you can justify your maneu-vers based on wind changes (wind shifts, etc.) or tactical consid-erations (covering another boat, etc.). Notice, you can *tack* or *gybe* for any reason you want; but you can't do it "repeatedly" without the specific reasons in the rule.

"Are there any exceptions to this rule?"
Yes, and they are significantly different than in the previous rule. Here is a summary of the changes. (Note, the sailing instructions, and to a more limited extent, the class rules can modify these.)
    You can:

1) Roll-tack and roll-gybe with specific limitations.
2) Have ONE pump per wave or gust on the sheet or wishbone controlling any sail with specific limitations.

    You cannot:

1) Roll your boat to *leeward* immediately prior to a roll-tack or roll-gybe.
2) Ooch at all, not even to initiate surfing or planing.
3) Pump more than ONCE per wave or gust.
4) Pump the spinnaker "guy."
5) Pump using anything but the sheet—i.e., no pumping with the vang or special pumping line.
6) Pump by grabbing all parts of a multi-part mainsheet system. Essentially, you now have to use all parts of the system.
7) Pump to attempt surfing or planing upwind.

Rule 54.3   Exceptions

(a) Immediately before, during and immediately after a *tack* or *gybe*, the yacht's crew may move their bodies to roll the yacht, provided that such movements do not:
   (i) advance the yacht further in the race than she would have advanced in the absence of the *tack* or *gybe*, or
   (ii) move her mast away from the vertical more than once.
(b) On a free leg of the course, when surfing (rapidly accelerating down the leeward side of a wave) or planing is possible, the yacht's crew may, in order to initiate surfing or planing, pump the sheet (or the wishbone on a sailboard), but not the guy, controlling any sail, but only once for each wave or gust of wind. When the mainsail is pumped, only that part of the sheet between the crew member handling the sheet and the first block on the boom shall be used.

"Can I heel my boat to leeward to start my roll-tack?"
Absolutely yes. You may heel your boat slightly to leeward to help the boat head up as you go into your *tack*. Rule 54.3(a) says you can't "roll" the boat in a way that moves the mast away from the vertical more than once. A "roll" is a major change in heel. The definition of *sailing* permits you to move your body to adjust the trim of the hull. The slight heel you need to help turn the boat is permitted by Rule 54.1. This will happen when a hiked or trapezing crew comes in just prior to the *tack* or when the crew leans in to uncleat the jib or simply when the crew intentionally leans in slightly to initiate the turn with a minimum of rudder movement.

Rule 54.3(a)(ii) does permit one major "roll" during the *tack*. This will generally be in the direction of the new *leeward* side. Note that the boat must be brought upright in such a way that the boat doesn't receive enough extra propulsion to carry her further in the race than if she hadn't *tacked* at all. Though tough to judge, this will generally be an issue only in light air and in round-hulled boats. The most important thing is that once the boat is brought up from its roll, the mast cannot immediately make a major dip **again** to *leeward* (i.e., away from vertical). The rule is designed to eliminate these second and third "pumps" to accelerate the boat or sailboard after their *tacks*.

"Why is Rule 54.3(b) now so much more restrictive, and can the rule ever be made more permissive?"

The rule writers have taken this large step to reduce the strength factor required to race sailboats and sailboards successfully, and to ensure that the sport remains a *sailing* contest. Notice that the sailing instructions for a race or event can make this rule more permissive by modifying it with a specific reference to it (Rule 3.1). Furthermore, Rule 54.3(c) reads, "Class rules may alter or add to rule 54.3(b)." (This "permission" is necessary because the IYRR over-ride any conflicting class rules [rule 1.1].) Therefore a class can permit pumping by holding all the parts of the mainsheet, or more than one pump per wave, or ooching, etc. This is an issue all the members of each class should thoroughly discuss.

Notice you are no longer allowed to "ooch" at all. Also, you can "pump" only **once** (not three times, as before) to try to catch a wave or hop up on a plane. Notice that you must be just ready to launch **down** the leeward face of the wave. You can't "pump" up the windward side of the wave claiming it will get you over the top and down the leeward side faster. A "planing" boat will be lifted partly out of the water by its own bow wave, and its stern wave will disappear. Visually it will look like the boat is skimming across the surface of the water. The phrase "on a free leg of the course" prohibits you from "pumping" upwind at all for any reason.

Notice that you can only "pump" using the sheet or wishbone controlling the sail. You cannot therefore "pump" using the vang or a special "pumping" line. Furthermore, you can no longer "pump" the spinnaker "guy," which is the spinnaker sheet that runs through the spinnaker pole.

"Is it true that I can no longer pump the main by grabbing all parts of my mainsheet system?"

Yes. Rule 54.3(b) requires you to use all the "parts" of your mainsheet—i.e., you can't reduce the parts in the system to "pump" 1:1 or whatever. The phrase "only that part of the sheet between the crew member handling the sheet and the first block on the boom" means the following: Let's say you had a 4:1 main-sheet system with two blocks up on the boom. The final part came down through a ratchet block on the cockpit floor or on the traveler and into your hand. Starting with the end that's in your hand (you're the "crew member" referred to in the rule) and working back through the system, the first block you come to is the ratchet block. The next block is the block on the boom which is the "first block on the boom" as you work backward (i.e., reduce purchase) through the system. The rule permits you to grab the part of the sheet between the ratchet and the first block on the boom the sheet passes through. Put another way, the rule permits you to "pump" by bypassing the ratchet block but requires you to use all the other parts of the sheet.

"Does Rule 54.3(b) permit one pump of each sail per wave?"
Rule 54.3(b) permits "pumping" only to initiate surfing or planing. The rule permits one "pump" for each sail (main, spinnaker, and jib if desired, though pumping the jib is generally slow). However, if the "pump" on the main gets the boat surfing, a subsequent "pump" on the spinnaker sheet would not be legal. If the main and spinnaker were "pumped" simultaneously, there would be no problem.

"I also heard that a protest committee can throw me out under Rule 54.2 or 54.3 without a hearing, and that a DSQ under Rule 54 can't be used as a 'throw-out' race. Is this true?"
Rule 70.1(b) of the International Yacht Racing Rules (IYRR) permits a **protest committee** to penalize a yacht for an infringement of Rules 54.2 and 54.3 without a hearing, though Rule 70.1(c) requires that a yacht be notified of such an action, and guarantees them a hearing upon request. **However, the USYRU prescribes that for racing in the United States a protest committee cannot act under Rule 70.1(b) unless the sailing instructions specifically provide that they can.** Furthermore, Rule 74.5(c) prevents a yacht from "dropping" a DSQ under Rule 54, Propulsion. **But the USYRU prescribes that this does not apply in the U.S.**
The thinking is that the rules have been sufficiently improved

so that they are worth using without such other heavy-handed measures to bring about compliance. Furthermore, in the hands of inexperienced or capricious judges, the above-mentioned rules could be more detrimental than useful. However, when racing outside the U.S. and in countries without similar prescriptions, BEWARE!

 "Now I understand what Rule 54 allows and doesn't allow, but what do I do when another competitor starts to rock or pump by me?"
Most active racers believe that the rule itself is clear enough and is not the cause of the problem. The real problem is the enforcement of the rule. Some say the enforcement should be left completely up to judges around the course—i.e., flood the course with referees. Others are strongly arguing that competitors will never police themselves, so therefore the rule should be abolished altogether and the race committees given the authority to proclaim before a race that either "anything" or "nothing" goes.

Fortunately, the majority of us believe that the racing is best when the sailors themselves have the responsibility to sail within the rules. We have seen too many regattas with either too few judges or poorly qualified ones. More to the point, we like the concept of competitor-enforced rules which makes our sport unique from almost all others.

But it takes only a few people in each fleet to ruin it for the rest. If someone decides that doing well in the race by cheating is okay, and they start pumping and sculling off the starting line and rocking downwind, it puts the other sailors in a very awkward position. Either they can join in, or warn and then protest the other boat, or do nothing. To join in, they have to admit that the problem is not worth their effort to fight it. To do nothing is frustrating because the sailor will feel that not only are they being left behind, but that nothing is being done to enforce the rule.

I strongly recommend first warning the other boat, and then protesting if they continue. You are not being the "bad guy" for simply doing what you'd do if a *port-tacker* hit you when you were on *starboard*. It is destructive to the racing when people feel they can get away with cheating; and they will continue to get worse if no one calls them on it.

In the hearing the **protest committee** should (a) find out exactly what the wind and wave conditions were; (b) discuss what the sailing characteristics of the boat are from their shared experiences, competitors' testimony, and expert witnesses when useful; and (c) determine what the exact **actions** of the protestee were. Witnesses are useful to everyone and are desired. Remember, it is permissible for members of the **protest committee** to also be the protestor, but they must be sure to give their entire testimony with evidence while all the **parties to the protest** are present and able to ask questions and otherwise respond. (See Rule 73.4.)

The bottom line to the Rule 54 issue is that everyone who races should make the effort to understand exactly what the rule does and does not allow, and then sail within the rule's limits. The rule is not that complex to understand, and my guess is that most sailors who have studied it have a good sense of what is right and wrong. Where we are weak is where sailors intentionally ignore the rule for their own personal gratification. All fleets of sailors should talk about this issue.

10

Protests, Penalties and Appeals (Part VI)

Part VI contains all the rules governing the procedures on how to protest, how to ask for redress, how and when a protest hearing should be run, what penalties can be applied, and how to appeal. I'll focus on Rules 68, Protests by Yachts, and 75, Gross Infringement of Rules or Misconduct. The other rules of Part VI are either self-explanatory or covered elsewhere in this book. (See Index F.)

RULE 68 PROTESTS BY YACHTS

Rule 68.1 Right to Protest

A yacht can protest any other yacht, except that a **protest** for an alleged infringement of the rules of Part IV can be made only by a yacht directly involved in or witnessing an incident.

If you want to protest another boat for an alleged infringement of any rule(s) in Part IV, you must have been directly involved in or have seen the incident yourself. A **protest** or a hearing **cannot** be initiated by you or the race committee when you or they learn about the incident from a "report" by someone who either was competing in the race or otherwise is an interested party (Rule 70.2[d]).

If you witness an apparent infringement of a Part IV rule and there is no contact, you can still **protest** by flying your flag immediately under Rule 68.3 and otherwise complying with Rule 68.

(See USYRU Appeals 67 and 101.) For example, if you see S duck P and make no contact, you can protest P for an alleged infringement of Rule 36. Presumably you, P, or the **protest committee** will call S in as a witness. If S asserts that she told P to cross her (a common tactic) and that she is satisfied that P did keep clear, then Rule 36 has not been infringed. However, if S does testify that P had in fact not kept clear, then P will probably be penalized.

Notice also that the third boat or the race committee cannot protest S for failing to protest P, even if there was a clear-cut rule infringement but no contact. USYRU Appeal 101 reminds that "the word 'can' is permissive, not obligatory. Therefore S was entirely within her rights not to have protested P."

Rule 68.2   Informing the Protested Yacht

A protesting yacht shall try to inform the yacht she intends to protest that a **protest** will be lodged. When an alternative penalty is prescribed in the sailing instructions, she shall hail the other yacht immediately.

USYRU Appeal 3 says, "In fairness to such competitor he should be notified promptly of his alleged infringement of the rules." It is best when the sailors intending to protest say so right on the spot and clearly identify which boat they intend to protest. (See IYRU Case 100/USYRU Appeal 222.)

But IYRU Case 104 sums it up: "Rule 68.2 is mandatory, only to the extent that an attempt to inform shall be made before the protest is lodged. **It is not mandatory to have succeeded in the attempt** [emphasis added]. The protestor shall try to inform the protested yacht, but an opportunity to do so may not occur until after finishing the race. When the committee is satisfied that the protest flag was displayed at the first reasonable opportunity, failure of the protested yacht to receive notification by hail is not grounds for refusing to hear the protest, but the committee must be satisfied that efforts were made to inform the protested yacht. When a protesting yacht fails to observe Rule 68.2 and does not 'try to inform' the protested yacht, the protest shall be refused. The protesting yacht shall not be disqualified for this reason." (See also Appendix 6,1.4.)

Notice also that the use of the word "will" implies that you try to inform the boat you're protesting **before** you lodge your **protest**.

Rule 68.3 During a Race—Protest Flag

(a) An intention to protest an infringement of the rules occurring during a race shall be signified by the protesting yacht conspicuously displaying a flag. Code flag "B" is always acceptable, irrespective of any other provisions in the sailing instructions. (USYRU prescribes that the flag shall be red, unless otherwise prescribed in the sailing instructions.)

(b) The flag shall be displayed at the first reasonable opportunity after the incident.

(c) (i) Except as provided in Rule 68.3(c)(ii), the flag shall be displayed until the yacht *finishes* or, when the first opportunity occurs after *finishing,* until acknowledged by the race committee.

(ii) In the case of a yacht sailing single-handed, it will be sufficient to display the flag at the first reasonable opportunity after the incident and to have it acknowledged by the race committee when the protesting yacht *finishes.*

(d) When the yacht retires, the flag shall be displayed until she has informed the race committee or has left the vicinity of the course.

The Appeals are loud and clear throughout that if you are required to fly a flag and do not, then only in rare circumstances—for instance, you've been dismasted, capsized, or sunk—will the **protest committee** decide to hear your **protest.** (See USYRU Appeal 153 and Appendix 6,1.3.) Notice that even if your **protest** is for a violation of a class rule, sailing instructions, or the like, you must fly a flag at the point in the race when you first become aware of the alleged violation. (See IYRU Case 88.)

USYRU Appeal 3 (the oldest appeal in the book, dated November 15, 1935) reads in part, "A traditional statement of the principle involved is: that the provisions in the rule requiring the showing of a protest flag are imperative except in exceptional circumstances, and that the race committee is prevented from inquiring, under that rule, into a protest that may be lodged if the protesting yacht has omitted to show a flag; and in all ordinary circumstances when a flag could be flown, if it was not flown, the race committee should refuse to hear the case. The spirit of the rule is that the protesting party must signal his intention at the time prescribed."

In USYRU Appeal 60 a boat had flown a flag following the incident, but it blew overboard during the race so that she wasn't flying it across the finishing line. Her **protest** was not heard.

"Can I just fly anything and call it a protest flag?"
Absolutely not. First of all, notice the major change for sailors in the U.S. The USYRU prescription to Rule 68.3(a) **requires** the flag to be **red,** though Rule 68.3(a) itself does not specify a color for the flag. In responding to a question of interpretation on the word "flag," the USYRU Appeals Committee deleted Appeal 88 (which said that even a red telltale could be considered a protest flag), and wrote a new opinion:

"USYRU QUESTION 277—"QUESTION 1: Is a pair of red shorts acceptable as 'a flag,' as the term is used in rule 68.3(a)? ANSWER: No. A pair of shorts, of any color, is not a flag. One dictionary definition of a flag is 'a (usually rectangular) piece of fabric of distinctive design that is used as a symbol (as of a nation) or as a signalling device.' A pair of shorts will be perceived by most observers to be a pair of shorts rather than a symbol or signalling device. QUESTION 2: What is the test of whether an object can be considered a flag within the meaning of rule 68.3(a)? ANSWER: In the context of rule 68.3(a) a flag is used as a signal to visually communicate the message 'I intend to protest,' or the equivalent. Only if the object used as a flag communicates that message, with little or no possibility of causing confusion on the part of persons on competing yachts, will the object qualify as a flag."

Notice that many sailing instructions will require a more specific flag, so be sure to read them carefully.

Finally, notice that International Code Flag "B" (a red square with a "V" or swallowtail cut from one vertical edge) is always acceptable and often required by the sailing instructions. **To be safe, you should always carry an International Code Flag "B"** or at least a red square flag that can be quickly attached with Velcro straps or the like.

"Does the flag have to be flown on the starboard shroud?"
No. The flag must simply be "conspicuously displayed," and kept displayed until the boat *finishes*. **In USYRU Appeal 162 the flag**

was properly held by a member of the crew. There is no requirement in the rule that the flag need be put anywhere in particular.
For one thing, many boats don't have shrouds. More importantly,
the flag should initially be highly visible to the protested boat. In
many cases the starboard side of the boat may be the worst (least
conspicuous) place to display it.

Also, the flag must be displayed at the first "reasonable opportunity" after the incident. USYRU Appeal 3 says, "While the phrase
'at the first reasonable opportunity' . . . is not synonymous with 'immediately,' it implies that a protest flag must be displayed within a reasonably short time after a contestant has infringed a racing rule while
racing." Obviously, you are not expected to stop sailing to put up
your flag, but you should signal as soon as is reasonable. Delaying
because your flag is in the ditty bag, which is up in the bow under
the anchor, is not reasonable. But waiting forty-five seconds while
your crew finishes putting the pole up and setting the spinnaker
is more reasonable to me, particularly if you've hailed of your
intention to **protest.** You will rarely get in trouble if your crew
keeps the flag in a readily accessible pocket and if the flag is easily
attached to a shroud by Velcro straps so that the flag can be up
within thirty seconds or less of the incident.

Notice that when the "720" or percentage penalty alternatives
are in use, you are **required** to **hail immediately** in addition to
displaying a flag. (See Rule 68.2 and Appendix 3,1.3 and 2.2.)

But USYRU Appeal 162 puts it in perspective: "Recognition of the
need for compliance with the requirements of Rule 68.3, however,
should not lead to strained interpretations that ignore both the purpose
and the spirit of the rule. The purpose of displaying the flag is to signal
the intention of the protesting yacht. Thus, where the protesting yacht's
intention is actually known to those concerned—notably the protested
yacht and the race committee—a less stringent application of Rule 68.3
is appropriate."

Notice that when sailing single-handed you need to show your
flag only to the sailor you're protesting, and again to the race
committee when you **finish.** Sailboard sailors are not required to
display a flag at all, but they must hail the sailor they're protesting

at the time and tell the race committee of their intention to protest when they *finish*. (See Appendix 2.5.) The Inter-Collegiate Yacht Racing Association (ICYRA) has also waived the flag requirement, but it requires hailing the word "protest" at the time of the incident. (See ICYRA Procedural Rules.) You are in smart shoes to always check the sailing instructions before going racing and to always use the word "protest" in your hail.

Rule 68.4   Exception to Protest Flag Requirement

A yacht may **protest** without having displayed a flag when either

(a) she has no knowledge of the facts justifying a **protest** until she has *finished* or retired, or

(b) having been a witness not directly involved in the incident, she learns that a yacht that displayed a protest flag has failed to lodge a valid **protest** in accordance with Rule 33(b), Contact between Yachts Racing, or Rule 52.3(b), Touching a Mark.

It's often heard that a sailor wanted to check his rule book or sailing instructions on shore before being certain if another boat infringed a **rule.** This is not the intent of Rule 68.4(a). IYRU Case 47 reads, "A yacht that has reason to believe another has infringed a rule or sailing instruction and wishes to protest must display a protest flag in accordance with Rule 68.3. When, after finishing, she is satisfied that no infringement occurred, she need take no further action."

An example of when Rule 68.4(a) applies is when a competitor learns after the race that another boat raced without its required anchor.

The subtle change in Rule 68.4(b) is that in order to qualify for the exception, you must have been a witness **and** not directly involved in the incident. Rule 68.4(b) clarifies your obligation to fly a protest flag in the event you see two boats touch each other, or a boat touch a *mark.* If one of the boats involved flies a protest flag, then you need not fly yours. If on shore, you learn that the boat(s) are not going to lodge their protest, you can lodge a protest against them. If, however, neither boat flies a flag at the first reasonable opportunity after the incident, you must fly yours immediately if you want to protest them under any rule. (See the discussion of Rule 33.)

Rule 75   GROSS INFRINGEMENT OF RULES OR MISCONDUCT

Rule 75.1   Penalties by the Race Committee or Protest Committee

(a) The race committee or **protest committee** may call a hearing when it has reasonable grounds for believing that a competitor has committed a gross infringement of the **rules** or a gross breach of good manners or sportsmanship.

(b) When the **protest committee** finds that there has been a gross infringement of the **rules** or a gross breach of good manners or sportsmanship, it may exclude a competitor, and a yacht when appropriate, either from further participation in a series, or from the whole series, or take other disciplinary action. The committee shall report any penalty imposed to its national authority, and to that of the competitor, and to that of the yacht.

(c) No action shall be taken under this rule without a written statement of allegation and a hearing held in accordance with the rules of Section B, Protest Procedure.

(d) Any hearing under this rule shall be conducted by a **protest committee** consisting of at least three members.

Rule 75.2   Penalties by the National Authority

Upon a receipt of a report of gross infringement of the **rules** or a gross breach of good manners or sportsmanship, or a report of a penalty imposed under rule 75.1, a national authority may conduct an investigation and, when appropriate, a hearing and take such action as it deems appropriate against the person or persons or the yacht involved. Such action may include disqualification from participating in any race held in its jurisdiction for any period, or other disciplinary action. The national authority shall report any penalty imposed to the national authority of the competitor, and to that of the yacht, and to the International Yacht Racing

Union. The IYRU shall inform all national authorities, which may also apply a penalty.

Fundamental Rule C, Fair Sailing, states, "A yacht, her owner and crew shall compete . . . in accordance with recognised principles of fair play and sportsmanship." Rule 75.1(a) permits a race or protest committee to call a hearing when it has "reasonable grounds for believing that a competitor has committed a gross breach of good manners or sportsmanship."

Rule 75.1 sets forth the penalty available to the race or **protest committee** that wants to punish a competitor's behavior with something stronger than disqualification from a race. Notice that action must be initiated either by a competitor alleging an infringement of a rule (including Fundamental Rule C, Fair Sailing) or by the race or **protest committee** under Rule 75.1(a). One does not "protest" under Rule 75, though one can suggest in a **protest** that a penalty under Rule 75 be applied.

Note that Rule 75 can be used only when the competitor's infringement or conduct is "gross." "Gross" can be generally interpreted as follows: conspicuously obvious, flagrant, deliberate, referring to offenses or errors so bad they cannot escape notice or be condoned or actions exceeding reasonable or excusable limits.

Notice also that in order for the race or **protest committee** to apply the penalty in Rule 75, there must first be a **written allegation** and a hearing by a **protest committee** of at least three members in full compliance with the rules governing protest hearings (Part VI, Section B, Protest Procedure).

Rule 75.1 requires that the committee report any penalty imposed to its and the competitor's national authority (USYRU in the U.S.), and Rule 75.2 is available to the national authority if they choose to further punish the competitor(s) or yacht(s) with suspension from the sport or other discipline.

Any **deliberate infringement** of the **rules** is a gross infringement. For example: S deliberately rams P causing serious damage (perhaps because the skipper of P had disqualified the skipper of S in a protest hearing the night before). The **protest committee** would decide the **protest** in the normal way, disqualify S under Rule 32, then proceed with a hearing under Rule 75.1. Deciding that the infringement was "gross," they could disqualify her from the entire series if they wanted to. Another example is when a competitor deliberately cuts a *mark* or *starts* ahead of the starting line for the purpose of hindering another competitor's race.

There are obviously many degrees of "gross," and many infringements are not "gross" at all. The use of the word "may" in Rule 75.1 leaves it up to the race and **protest committees** to decide when an infringement is "gross" enough to justify a stronger penalty in their opinion.

To me, examples of a gross breach of good manners or sportsmanship include: **proved lying** in a protest hearing (as opposed to honest differences in recollection of the incident); **intentional cheating**—for instance, *racing* with an unmeasured sail or removing mandatory ballast, as opposed to class or racing rule violations caused by ignorance; **intentional damage to another boat** afloat or on shore—for instance, cutting someone's shrouds in the night; **fighting,** particularly where there is injury or damage; **stealing** from another boat or from private property at a club or elsewhere; and **foul or threatening language,** particularly if it is continued after receiving a clear warning.

Notice also rule Rule 69(d): "a yacht infringing Fundamental Rule C, Fair Sailing, or against which a penalty has been imposed under Rule 75.1." In other words, if a boat materially prejudices you in any way by damaging your boat, by sitting on your wind to slow you, or by any other way, **and** the **protest committee** penalizes them because their action violated the Fair Sailing rule or was a gross infringement or the like, you can apply for redress under Rule 69(d), and as a result you might receive average points, or your place in the race, or other redress under Rule 74.2.

To date, there have been an increasing number of incidents where Rule 75 has been invoked, and slowly precedents for misconduct and appropriate disciplinary measures are being set.

In the 1981 Southern Ocean Racing Circuit (SORC), three of the top finishing boats were remeasured or otherwise found to be out of measurement, and all three were removed from the series. In addition, each of the boat's owners was excluded from racing for two years by USYRU. In at least one boat's case, it was never proved that the owner actually physically did anything **himself** to cause the boat to receive its first "low" rating, but Rule 19.2 strictly provides that "an owner shall be responsible for maintaining his yacht in accordance with her class rules and for ensuring that her certificate is not invalidated by alterations."

In 1982 a one-design sailor was found to have raced with an unmeasured jib in the last race of the series. He was disqualified from the entire series and excluded from racing for six months by the USYRU, which included a major regatta qualifying him for other regattas that following summer, and funding.

In May 1984 a Finn sailor was disqualified under Rule 75 from the Olympic Trials that he had otherwise won. Going into the last race, the only mathematical way he could lose was if the second-place boat won the race. At the start he was PMS, but he continued to sail the course. The **protest committee** found as fact that he deliberately *started* prematurely for the sole purpose of hindering the second-place boat's race. They disqualified him from the entire series, thereby costing him the opportunity to race in the Olympics. IYRU Case 78 is an appeal sent in by the Norwegian Yachting Association, dated 1975, that sets the precedent for judging such deliberate rule infringements.

SUMMARY OF THE CASE

"As the sixth and final race of a championship series began, A's accumulated score was such that the only way she could lose the prize was for B to finish ahead of her and among the first three of the 48 competitors. A started prematurely and was recalled by loud hailer. About 70 to 100 metres beyond the starting line, she turned back, but she had sailed only some 20 to 30 metres toward the line when she met B, which had started correctly. Instead of continuing towards the pre-start side of the line A turned and sailed on top of B. The race committee hailed A again that she was still a premature starter and received a wave of acknowledgement in return, but A continued to sail the course, harassing B throughout the windward leg. When A and B reached the windward mark, they were last but one and last respectively, whereupon A retired. B ultimately finished in 22nd place.

"Since it was obvious to the race committee that A continued to race solely for the purpose of harassing B, it called a hearing on its own initiative under Rule 70.2(a). A was disqualified under Rule 51.1(b),

Sailing the Course, and the Fundamental Rule—Fair Sailing. She then discarded the race and won the championship. She also appealed her disqualification under the Fair Sailing rule, asserting that she believed she had returned and started correctly.

"DECISION: Appeal dismissed. The facts established by the race committee show gross infringements of the rules and of sportsmanship. Such deliberate attempts to win by unfair means should be dealt with severely. To disqualify A in the sixth race only is not enough, since she would then achieve the purpose of her unfair action and become the winner of the championship. Rule 75.1 can be applied to exclude A from the entire series, and such action would be well within the spirit of the racing rules. A, therefore, is excluded from the whole series, and all her results shall be struck from the records as if she had not started in any of the races."

This final point raises the question of what to do with the excluded boat's previous race scores. Rule 74.5(b) reads, "When a yacht is penalised by being removed from a series or a part of a series, no races are to be re-scored and no changes are to be made in the scores of other yachts, except that, when the incident from which the penalty resulted occurred in a particular race, she shall be disqualified from that race and the yachts *finishing* behind her in that race shall each be moved up one place." (See USYRU Appeal 214.)

In the 1987 Admirals Cup series off Great Britain, the crew of a top finishing boat was later found to have stacked plastic Jerry Jugs down below on the windward side and to have filled them with water using their bilge pump system. At some point near the end of one of the races the Jugs were cut up and discarded overboard. When the truth was learned, the penalties included being barred from racing for up to ten years.

Obviously Rule 75 is an important rule, but its effectiveness relies on the integrity of the race or **protest committee** that chooses to invoke it. Each case must be **carefully examined** to determine, as accurately as possible, exactly what happened, what events led up to the incident, and what the probable motives of the individuals involved were. The hearing and deliberations should be conducted as objectively as possible with an effort to keep emotions out. A competitor's previous actions should not be weighed in the case unless germane and accurately represented. Appeals that are cited as precedent must be closely examined to be sure that they are truly nearly identical in all ways. And before invoking Rule 75.1 the **protest committee** must thoroughly consider if the weight of the punishment is justified by the competitor's action.

Disqualification from a series for a gross infringement of the rules or a gross breach of manners or sportsmanship is a strong penalty by itself, due to the effect it generally has on the individual(s) and from the adverse publicity it can create. But in addition, this penalty **must** also be reported to USYRU or the appropriate national authority. In turn they can conduct an investigation and exclude the competitor(s) or yacht(s) from the sport for a period of time. This is extremely strong as it will have an impact on the sailor's life beyond just their sailing, in ways that may extend beyond just the time period of their penalty.

In keeping with the law, a citizen of the United States who feels they have been unjustly penalized under Rule 75 has the right to make an appeal directly to the Executive Committee of USYRU, under Article Fourteen of the USYRU Bylaws. You should contact the USYRU office for exact details if you have the need to use it.

11

The Sailboard Racing Rules and Their Enforcement

Sailboard racing remains one of the fastest-growing areas of our sport. Thousands of sailboards cross starting lines all over the world every weekend, and at the 1984 and 1988 Olympic Games Gold, Silver, and Bronze medals were awarded in the closed-course Olympic sailboard racing event.

Sailboard racing is done under the International Yacht Racing Rules just as for every other class and type of boat, with a few specific modifications. These modifications (Appendix 2 of the IYRR) reflect some of the unique sailing and handling characteristics of a sailboard; and as the sport evolves and more is learned about sailboard racing, the modifications will continue to be refined so that the rules permit the most safe, fair, and challenging racing possible. Appendix 2 also includes rules for multi-mast sailboards and a new section of Funboard Racing Rules for course racing and slalom.

As I discussed in Chapter 3, the rules don't excuse faulty board handling, but they do take into consideration the maneuverability of the boards, the difficulty of the handling required in certain instances, and the speed and sailing characteristics of the board. Just as with sailboats, there is a wide variety in types of sailboards, each having its particular characteristics, and competitors, race officers, and judges should be aware of these differences.

Here are some examples: To *gybe* you must "heel" the board with your feet and "tip" the rig with your arms. Some boards are flat, such as Division 1 boards, and others have more of a "V" bow, such as many of the Division 2 boards. Obviously, the flat board will be less easy to turn, though they are usually more stable, making them easier to stand on—i.e., not fall off.

In light air *gybing* where the board hasn't much momentum, it's very difficult to turn quickly or sharply. In fact, you must rely almost completely on your rig, "tipping" it over nearly parallel with the water to get the board to turn. So at gybe *marks*, especially when sails are blanketing each other, it's common to see boards continue right on by the *mark* even though the sailors are trying their hardest to *gybe*, and for outside boards to get hit as the inside boards "tip" their rigs in order to turn. This problem doesn't exist in boats with rudders and centerboards because in light air the rudder can be wiggled when necessary to turn the boat. (See USYRU Appeal 56.)

Downwind in a breeze, the boards accelerate and slow so fast that the apparent wind jumps around a lot. Because the sailor is usually being supported by the force of the wind in the sail, they have to trim quickly when the wind shifts forward as the board accelerates, or risk falling over. In fact, some Division 2 boards will simply "sink" (i.e., stop planing and just settle into the water) if they slow too much. The similar effect is true upwind, and it's not uncommon to see the sail moving around a lot as the sailors adjust to the apparent wind shifts or simply try to keep their balance.

One feature that is unique to sailboards in general is their ability to stop or slow abruptly when necessary. Therefore, when one board *tacks* just in front of another, it's expected that the other board can "back" her sail momentarily to keep clear, whereas a sailboat might have had to *luff* or *bear away* to keep clear.

The bottom line is that in some instances a sailboard is very maneuverable, in others it isn't; and because they are so narrow and small, often a lot of movement is needed by the boardsailor just to stay on them. The rules and modifications are designed for competitor enforcement, and the racing is clearly the best when everyone sails within the rules. Most average competitors know when they're "pumping" as opposed to sailing, or "pretending to have trouble" when really they're just taking advantage of the rules. This attitude will only result in the need for "referees" on the course, which will inhibit the racing and make it less rewarding for everyone. But when everyone works together to study and share their rules knowledge in informal and formal sessions on shore and on the water, the rules become very easy to learn, understand, and use.

SAILBOARD RACING RULES (APPENDIX 2)

Many of the modifications are explained throughout this book and are marked by the boardsailor in the margin. The other modifications are straightforward and easily understood, though I will focus on a couple of them in more depth here. (See Appendix D of this book for the complete Appendix 2.)

- **1.2, Capsized and Recovering**
  - (a) Capsized—A sailboard is *capsized* when she is not under way due to her sail being in the water or when the competitor is waterstarting.
  - (b) Recovering—A sailboard is *recovering* from a capsize from the time her sail or, when waterstarting, the competitor's body is raised out of the water until she has steerageway.

The fundamental change in the definitions of "capsized" and "recovering" is that the new definitions center on the "way" or motion of the sailboards, whereas the previous definitions were based on the location of the masthead. Notice the inclusion of the concept of "waterstarting" (lying in the water with feet on the rail of the board and the sail held up out of the water such that it will catch some wind and "lift" the sailor right up out of the water). See Appendix 2,3.4, Recovering from a Capsize, and the discussion of Rule 46.

- **2.3, Rule 24 Life-Saving Equipment. A safety device shall prevent the mast separating from the board.**
  This brings up the issue of safety and the "personal flotation device" (PFD) or life jacket. In the United States the states have

different laws, and local sailing areas use different levels of enforcing the laws concerning boardsailing and PFDs. In many, the sailboard itself is considered a PFD **when a "leash" connects the rig to the board.** However, some still require boardsailors to carry or wear a PFD. Regatta officials are often very relaxed about informing sailors of the law or enforcing it, leaving it the sailor's problem if they get caught and fined by the police. **This is not safe or smart.**

The IYRR **require** that you use a "leash" while *racing*—i.e., a race or **protest committee** must penalize you if you are protested by them or a competitor. Of course, that's not the point. The point is safety, and just as all sailboats are required to carry life jackets for everyone on board (Rule 24), boardsailors must use a "leash."

• **3.1, Rule 33 Contact between Yachts Racing. As between each other, Rule 33 shall not apply to sailboards.**

Rule 33 says if two boats "hit" and neither **protests** or acknowledges fault, they both can be penalized no matter which one was right. This doesn't apply to two sailboards that "hit," presumably because there is so much small contact, particularly at the starts and *marks,* that it would be impractical to call every one. However, anyone involved in **or witnessing** an apparent infringement **can protest.** (See Rule 68.1.) So if you drop your rig on a *leeward* boardsailor's head, a third board or race officer can protest you under Rule 37.1—i.e., a rule of Part IV other than Rule 33. (See discussion of Rule 33.)

Clearly, the message is: In boardsailing there is going to be a lot of unintentional, accidental touching. If the boardsailor in the right doesn't care to **protest** or if they choose not to take the time to figure out who hit them, then it is their decision. But this does not mean that rule enforcement is any less important in boardsailing. When a sailor feels that they have been "fouled" they should say so, and the infringer should take their penalty (see Appendix 2,6). Similarly, if a race officer, judge, or another competitor sees or learns about a rule infringement, they can protest if they feel the alleged infringement should be investigated.

• **5.2, Unless otherwise prescribed in the sailing instructions, the 720-degree turns penalty in Appendix 3.1 shall apply.**

This new rule means that the "720 rule" is in effect for all sailboard races unless the sailing instructions specifically say otherwise (and technically, under Rule 3.1, they must refer to Appendix 2,5.2, if modifying this rule).

Notice that a "720" on a sailboard is simply spinning the board around twice; the sail can stay in one place (Appendix 2,6.1). Notice also that when a boardsailor touches a *mark* they must now do two 360-degree turns, including two *tacks* and two *gybes* (Rule 52.2[a]). This is a much more severe penalty than a "720" because of the sail handling involved.

• **3.2, "For 'mainmast' read 'foot of mast.'"**

In other words, for determining when a **windward** board has reached the "mast abeam" position, it is the "universal" or point of attachment between the mast and the board that is used.

• **3.5, Notice that you must have your "sail out of the water and in normal position" when approaching the starting line to *start*, unless you have *capsized* by mistake.**

Though not covered in any appeal, it is my opinion that if you lift your sail from the water and then *start* (i.e., cross the line after the gun) very soon afterward, you were "approaching the starting line to *start*" when your sail was in the water. To be safe, I'd have my sail out of the water in the final minute before the starting signal. (See the discussion of Rule 42.4.)

• **3.6, This makes it clear that if you are a bit early to the line, you cannot "back down" if it will force another sailor to alter course to miss you.**

Again, it begins to apply when you are "approaching the starting line to *start*," which implies your final approach just prior to crossing the line.

12

How to Prepare a Protest and a Defense

by Bill Ficker

Author's Note

In the 1981 Congressional Cup, I was Russell Long's tactician and we were disqualified in a protest for tacking too close. After the series was completed, Bill Ficker, who was on the jury, came over and volunteered some advice on how we could have presented a better defense. Sure enough, two weeks later I was involved in almost exactly the same situation, but this time successfully defended myself, applying the principles Bill had described. To anyone who has ever lost a series by being disqualified in a protest hearing, it's clear that developing excellent protest handling skills is as important to winning regattas as having superior boat speed or brilliant tactics. But it's fair to say that among even the best sailors, the protest handling skills are not as refined as they could be, and this is one area we could all improve in.

Bill Ficker is a welcome authority on the subject, based not only on his successful experiences as both a competitor and a judge, but even more importantly because his success is the result of his very organized and thorough approach to what he does, making his presentation full of useful details and easy to follow. As a competitor, Bill has been racing all his life. Growing up in southern California, he has raced Sabots, Snipes, National One-Designs, Pacific 14-foot dinghies, and finished second in the Intercollegiate national championship. Since then he has won the Star Worlds, Class A of the SORC skippering "Charisma," and the

238 UNDERSTANDING THE YACHT RACING RULES

Congressional Cup. In 1970 he successfully defended the America's Cup as skipper of "Intrepid." As a judge, he has served on the jury for Congressional Cup, California Cup, San Diego Lipton Cup, and numerous other series over the years. He is certified as a Senior Judge by USYRU and has been a member of the USYRU Appeals Committee.

Calmness under pressure is certainly one of the keys to success in a protest hearing, as well as confidence in the rules and an analytical attention to all the details of the incident. Through his experiences, Bill has demonstrated a mastery over these elements, and the insights he shares in this piece, if practiced, should prove extremely helpful.

Before talking about the protest process, let me say a few words about the actions leading up to the need for a protest. It always seems incredible to me that so many world class sailors give so much attention to boat speed, crew training, and development of the state-of-the-art equipment and almost totally ignore an equally significant part of their campaign: learning the rules. The rules are the foil in the art of fencing with sailboats and without the sharpest foil and the understanding of how to use it, you are jeopardizing your entire effort or at least compromising it. Insecurity with the rules leads to hesitation on the race course and not only loss of races, but ultimately the respect of your competitors. As everyone who has sailed in top competition knows, the building of a reputation is important in order to dominate a fleet, and those who want to reach the top have to know the rules cold and act with confidence when engaged in a rules conflict. So study the rules and use the USYRU Book of Appeals Decisions and the IYRU Cases. By carefully studying the appeals, you will not only gain a better understanding of the rules, but you will also be helped tremendously in the preparation of your protest, especially with regard to the diagrams.

As for protesting, I often hear sailors say that protesting is for others and that they have never been in the protest room in their life. That makes good barroom talk, but the hard facts are that each year sailing, like other sports, is becoming more competitive with more good sailors in each fleet. No longer are fleets dominated by one or two good sailors who can easily stay clear of the others. More close situations are occurring on the starting lines, at turning marks, and throughout the race, so you had better be prepared to finish more races and series in the protest room. Finally, if protests are the result of your being involved in or witnessing a foul, or the result of an honest difference of opinion or differences in observation of a particular situation on the water, they should not have the taint of bad sportsmanship. Competitor enforcement of the rules is the tradition in our sport, and when the rules are not followed, we owe it to ourselves and our fellow competitors, for the quality of the racing, to protest. Remember, for your protest to be valid, it must comply with the requirements in Rule 68. (See the discussion of Rule 68.)

PREPARATION FOR THE HEARING

As any lawyer will tell you, the most important step in winning a case is the preparation. If you are thoroughly prepared, everything else will fall into place.

Boat performance table

One tool that will dramatically improve both your protest presentation and your tactical decisions on the race course is a table with all your boat performance precisely worked out in feet and seconds. It should include how many feet-per-second your boat travels in varying wind velocities (see Appendix B), the approximate speed of your boat on all points of sail, how long it takes your boat to go from one tack or gybe to another in varying wind and sea conditions, how far upwind your boat travels in a tack, how long it takes to accelerate to full speed from a standstill, and, especially for match or team racing, how long it takes to make a complete circle in both directions and how large the circle is. Write the table inside the front cover of your rule book. We'll discuss the reasons for this later.

Filing a counter-protest

Obviously, in some incidents there can only be one protest. But in most situations there is an excellent opportunity for a counter-protest, and because the best defense is a good offense, I would suggest that, when possible, a counter-protest always be filed. You might as well go into the hearing with as much indignation at having been fouled as the other person.

Filling out the protest form

The protest form you file will usually be the first encounter the jury has with your incident. Therefore, make sure the first impression you make reflects your thoughtfulness, your knowledge of the rules and the boats you are racing, and your care for detail and doing things the right way. Most regattas use the standard USYRU Protest Form (printed in Appendix 7 of the rule book). Take care in filling out each line on the first page. Print clearly, think first to avoid unnecessary cross-outs, and be sure all the information is correct, particularly the names and sail numbers of the other parties to the protest. Also be sure to use a dark pen, and don't get the protest form wet with soggy cuffs or wet hands. Rule 68.5 lists the minimum amount of information required to make the protest valid. Notice 68.5(c) asks for the rule(s) *alleged* to have been infringed. There is no requirement that you must state the correct rule. Rule 74.4 reads, "Such disqualification or other penalty shall be imposed irrespective of whether the rule which led to the disqualification or penalty was mentioned in the protest."

The diagrams are perhaps a little more difficult if you are not an engineer, architect, or otherwise graphically gifted, but with practice almost anyone can do a good diagram. *Always be sure to work everything out in a rough diagram before putting it on the protest form.* One convenient thing to carry in your rule packet is a small set of boats, as they are useful to trace when preparing your diagrams. Also, a pad of 8½ by 11 quarter-inch graph paper is perfect for this purpose. (It's also useful for studying the rules and doing sample situation analyses.) Usually the three or four boat positions directly preceding the incident are all that is needed to give the jury a clear picture of how the situation developed. In addition, be sure you include all the information, such as the strength and direction of the wind and current, the

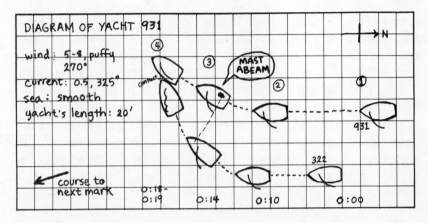

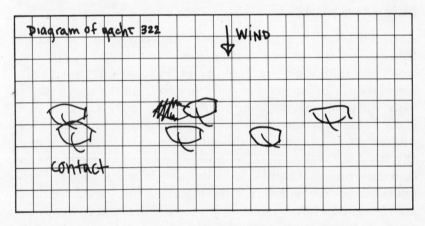

direction to the next or from the previous mark, any topography or other obstructions that had an effect, the compass course and speed your boat was going throughout the incident, and the like. Again, exact awareness of time and distance traveled and their relationship to each other are extremely important. Looking at the example in the diagram, it's important for the defense (Yacht 931) to show that between positions 1 and 2 Yacht 322 went two boat-lengths and the time interval was 10 seconds (indicating Yacht 322 was going about 2½ knots while Yacht 931 was going about 3½). If in the same example the boats were shown to have gone the same two boat-lengths in 4 to 5 seconds, that indicates a speed of 5 to 6 knots, which, because of the light air, would raise a few flags in the minds of the jury. So the more information you have and the more exact your diagram, the more credibility your case will have in the hearing. Use Rule 78.1(b)(ii) as a checklist.

The written part or "description" of the incident should be brief and should stick to the facts. Again, I suggest listing the important facts and points you wish to make in a rough draft before putting them on the protest form. I like to number the sentences as they refer to the diagram, and obviously the diagram and description should match perfectly. (See Description of the Incident.)

Filing the protest

At the outset of the regatta, it's very important to find out where to get the protest forms and where to file them in case of a protest. Don't wait until you're involved in one because things are usually hectic then. Also, as soon as you come in from the race find out when the time ends for filing your protest. This is critical so you know if you have time to shower, eat something, and just relax, without the risk of missing the cut-off time. Unfortunately, usually you don't. When possible, have your crew or friends put the boat away and contact possible witnesses. When you file the protest be sure you note *who* received it and the time, and have them put the time and their name on the form. Finally, keep a copy for yourself. Many clubs can run a copy in their office, but in case they can't, it's a good idea to carry carbon paper in your rule packet.

Witnesses

Good witnesses can be very helpful to your case. The idea behind a witness is to verify the facts you have presented in your testimony. The key attributes of a good witness are: (a) they were in a position to see the incident clearly; (b) they were close by and watching as the incident developed; and (c) (if not a competitor) they understand yacht racing. Obviously the jury should be aware

Description of the Incident

1.) Yacht 322 and Yacht 931 (both 20 ft. long) were sailing down the first reach, both steering slightly above the rhumb line. The wind was west, light and puffy, 5-8 knots; the current was 0.5 knots from NNW (making our apparent wind lighter); the water was smooth. Yacht 931 was one length clear astern and about one length to windward of Yacht 322. Because of better speed and a slight puff, yacht 931 was overtaking Yacht 322.

2.) After about ten seconds of sailing, Yacht 931 overlapped Yacht 322 to windward and pulled up almost bow to bow. Yacht 931 was 1½ lengths to windward, the end of her boom was about five feet beyond her leeward side, and she was keeping clear.

3.) Yacht 322 luffed, and when the helmsman of Yacht 931 was abreast of Yacht 322's mast (sitting in the normal position) he yelled "Mast Abeam." He had responded to the luff, was sailing a parallel course, and his boom was trimmed to within two feet of his leeward side. At the hail, the two boats were ¾ of a boatlength apart.

4.) Yacht 931 continued to keep clear and waited for Yacht 322 to bear away as she's required to do under rule 38.2 (c). However, sailing well above her proper course (her main was luffing) and continuing to luff for another 4-5 secs. after the hail, Yacht 322 made contact with Yacht 931, the bow of Yacht 322 contacting the leeward side of Yacht 931 at the shrouds (located one foot aft of the mast position)

I immediately hailed "protest" and flew our flag. We are protesting under rules 38.2(a) and 38.2(c) and cite Appeal 151.

when a witness is an interested party, such as a crew or teammate, but good juries often learn from these witnesses too.

On the other hand, a poor witness can destroy your case. Don't bring a witness into the hearing who merely told you that they saw the incident and feel you were in the right. Thoroughly screen any witnesses to be sure they understand the protest clearly and that they are definitely on your side. I certainly don't want to imply that you should bring in a witness who has been coached or reflects anything but total integrity, but you must find witnesses who corroborate your observations one hundred percent. There often seems to be a feeling that bringing in a witness you haven't talked to establishes some feeling of credibility. It doesn't. You only look foolish and it usually wastes the time of a lot of people. I can't tell you how many times I've sat in a hearing and the jury has had to ask which boat the witness was for. Also, I would suggest minimizing the number of witnesses. Besides the fact that witnesses are generally poorly prepared, keep in mind that when five people see an incident, they may each see it a little differently; and the more witnesses you call who saw it slightly differently, the more doubt it casts on *your* credibility.

Your right to call and question witnesses, including your crew, is stated in Rules 73.1 and 73.3 and Appendix 6,2.4. If a member of the protest committee intends to bring their observation of the incident into the deliberation, Rule 73.4 and Appendix 6,2.1(c) require them to give their evidence as a witness in front of you and be questioned. A protest committee can, in certain circumstances, limit the number of witnesses it will hear. USYRU Appeal 212 says, "Rule 73.3 permits a protested yacht to present a reasonable number of witnesses. . . . There may be circumstances where the protest committee would be fully justified in limiting the number of witnesses it will hear, particularly when the additional testimony would merely corroborate that of the prior witnesses. However, . . . where additional witnesses are offered from yachts other than those which are parties to the protest, a protest committee should be bound to investigate the nature of their testimony to a greater degree than in the case of additional witnesses from the crews of the yachts involved. Also in this instance the evidence from one of the crew members offered information which the skipper of P could not have supplied from his own knowledge."

Preparing your protest

The final step is to review your facts and how you will substantiate or prove them to be true. One good technique is to role-play the hearing, with friends acting as the judge and protestee. It is key to prepare yourself for any questions the jury or other parties to the protest might ask you. They might include: What was your crew doing as the situation developed? What conversations took place on your boat and between the boats? How fast were you going? How can you be sure there was an overlap? What were the numbers of some of the other boats in the vicinity? How much time was there between the establishment of the overlap and the initial contact? You should be testing yourself and your witnesses with these types of questions before you go into the hearing. Also, review the copies of your protest form to refresh your memory about what you said, and to see if there are any additional points or clarifications you need to make.

Preparing a defense

You should prepare a defense exactly as though you were filing a protest. Write down all the facts that support your claim that you were not in the wrong, as well as the evidence you will use to substantiate or prove your facts. Get all the speeds and distances organized and think through the possible questions. Even if you haven't filed a counter-protest, having everything written out will serve as a good reference. Also, under Rule 72 and section 1.6 of Appendix 6, you are entitled to see a copy of the protest against you *before* the hearing begins. Doing this is very important. The hearing room is not the place to start putting together your defense. The protesting yacht will be extremely well prepared with all the facts written down and thoughtfully organized. You want to go into the hearing just as well prepared.

To get a copy of the protest, *you have to ask for it.* USYRU Appeal 133 says, "Rule 72 only requires that the protest, or a copy, be made available. While as a practical matter, the race committee would be well advised to furnish a copy in any event, there is no obligation to do so unless it is requested by the yacht involved. If a yacht involved after receiving notice of a protest hearing, fails to request a copy, she does so at her own risk." USYRU Appeal 82 says, "Since a copy of the protest was not made available to the protestee, although requested both before the hearing and at it, the disqualification of the protestee is annulled."

One last thought on preparation. Rule 68.2 requires that the protesting yacht *try* to inform the yacht(s) being protested that a protest will be lodged. (See the discussion of Rule 68.2.) Be sure to comply with this and to personally notify the other skipper(s) either on the water or as soon as possible after you come in that you are protesting. If you know it, tell them the time and place of the hearing so it will commence smoothly and on time. It is not to your advantage to have the hearing held up or postponed while people look for the other parties to the protest. Also, be sure you are on time, even a bit early in case the jury is ahead of schedule, and that your witnesses are standing by *right outside the hearing room.* Your case can be weakened if the hearing has to be interrupted while your witnesses are being looked for. If you are the protestee, be *doubly sure* you are there on time, as well as your witnesses. Jury duty is a very demanding, time-consuming activity, which often requires the jury to be in session for hours at a time. So it doesn't endear one to them when they've given up their cocktail hour, dinner, and probably some much more engaging social event to be kept waiting in the hearing room while the competitor is at the bar or elsewhere and unwilling to spend five or ten minutes in readiness to be called.

THE HEARING

Rule 73.1 and Appendix 6,2.2 make it clear that you "have the right to be present throughout the hearing of all the evidence." Rule 73.5 adds that failure to make an effort to attend "may justify the protest committee in deciding the protest as it thinks fit without a full hearing." USYRU Appeal 54 says, "The provisions of Rule 73.1, that the parties to a protest shall have the right to be present at the hearing, represents an important right of which they should not be deprived. Rule 73.5 recognizes that if the interested parties or a representative fail to make an effort to attend the hearing the protest committee may be justified in deciding the protest as it thinks fit without a full hearing." USYRU Appeal 104 explains that this "protects a protest committee against inability to act because of intentional or inadvertent absence from a hearing." USYRU Appeal 144 sums up: "The rule is written as it is, providing the right, but not the necessity, to be present, in order to make it possible to hold a valid hearing without all parties to the protest being present provided each has been properly notified and there are no circumstances justifiably excusing absence."

The rules governing the actions of a protest committee are covered in Part VI and Appendix 6 of the IYRU Rules. If these rules aren't followed, you have the right to object. However, IYRU Case 122/USYRU Appeal 165 makes it clear that you must object at the time the protest committee fails to follow the rules. "An adult yachtsman must take some share of the responsibility for protecting his rights, including the obligation to make a timely objection when a protest committee fails to follow the procedural requirements of the rule; a party to a protest cannot sit by silently in such a case and then, when a decision goes against him, assert the procedural error to overturn that decision."

If the protest committee fails to follow the correct procedures and if you feel your finishing position has been materially prejudiced by their actions or omissions, you may request redress under Rule 69(a) (notice the new insertion of the term "protest committee" in Rule 69[a]). Rule 68.6(a) permits the **protest committee** to extend the time limit for lodging a **protest** (e.g., a request for redress). The USYRU prescription to Rule 69(a) extends the time limit, overriding Rule 68.6.

When the testimony portion of the hearing is over and the parties of the protest have been excused, the first task of the jury is to list the facts they have deduced from the testimonies. Then, based on these facts alone, they apply the rules and make their decision (Rule 74.1 and Appendix 6,3.1 and 3.2). Remembering that in most cases the jury will not have seen your incident or the events leading up to it, the strength of your case lies in your ability to describe the whole scene to them; and the more logical, precise, and complete your description is, the better your chances are that the facts will be found as you have presented them.

Opening testimonies

First the protestor has the opportunity of presenting his case, then the protestee presents his. At this point the questions between them and from the jury are usually restricted to clarifying what each has said (Appendix 6,2.3). There will be differences of opinions, usually due to different points of observation; but after listening to the complete presentations of the competitors and witnesses, the jury can usually tell which observation is most credible (Appendix 6, Duties of the Protest Committee). When making your opening testimony keep it brief and speak slowly and clearly. Obviously, this is an opportunity to transmit information to the jury more directly, so the diagram and description on the protest form can be expanded on. But try not to add any new dimensions orally to what has already been stated in writing unless you have left something off the form that is critical to your case, in which case mention that you are adding it. The important thing is to focus very hard on the facts you are trying to present and prove. Also, be complete. Omitting a part of the overall picture or filling in details later in the response to questions is very unsettling and indicates gaps in your testimony.

Using the Models

When using the models hold your hands so everyone can see what you're showing. If you are explaining that you were two lengths ahead of the other boat, be sure to accurately place your boat two of the model's lengths ahead. If the boats weren't overlapped, don't carelessly place them overlapped; and if the models have booms, be sure the booms are always on the correct side. Here again let me emphasize how important it is to give the exact relationships of the boats, their angles, and their speeds. Remember, if you are going to guess, guess at them before you go into the hearing room, but don't force the jury to interrupt your presentation in order to get these facts. They are absolutely necessary and if you don't know them your case will be severely weakened. (Another reason for precluding interruptions by the jury is that it doesn't give your opponent any tips prior to presenting their testimony.) Also, don't just start moving the boats around the table. Go through the various positions as you did in preparing your diagram, and go back only as far in the evolution of the event as you feel is necessary. If the jury wants you to go back further, they will ask you.

Using notes and the rule book in the hearing

Don't hesitate to bring notes with you into the hearing. In fact, it's a good idea to outline the points you wish to make as well as the possible questions to ask. Also, you should be taking notes while your competitor or the witnesses are giving testimony. You will have the opportunity to make a final statement and if the protest is at all lengthy it is often difficult to recall all the comments that were made. And when making reference to a rule or appeal don't hesitate to open the books. It doesn't diminish your credibility, and you'll always be sure to get it right.

Questions

Before and during the hearing write down the questions you will ask your competitor and witnesses. These should be used for unearthing facts, not making accusations. Also, don't ask your competitor to verify your assumptions, because they are too easily refuted and usually don't have much to do with the facts. During your competitor's testimony listen *carefully* for inconsistencies or statements that can be proven false. If necessary, use questioning to highlight these inconsistencies. And when questioning your own witness never ask a question to which you don't already know the answer. Also, don't feel obligated to ask questions of your competitor or the witnesses. Evaluate their statements, and if you feel that their statements have not been detrimental to your case, don't give them the opportunity to open up new avenues of information.

In responding to questions, there are three basic stages an attorney will advise: First, listen to the question; second, think about it; third, give the answer. It is always important to directly address the question asked. Don't use it as a springboard for adding to your testimony. A good jury will only reprimand you and tell you to stick to the facts in questioning. You'll have the chance to give more testimony later. When answering it's fair to take some time to think about your response. A thoughtful answer is much more useful than a quick one. Also, no matter how bad a question might seem, don't judge the person asking it or give a facetious answer. Sometimes your competitor might merely want to demonstrate that you don't think clearly in a tense situation. That may be all they need to convince the jury that you acted irrationally on the race course. Often a jury member will ask what seems to be an absurd question or might indicate they don't understand the boats or the rules. Some very experienced and clever judges get information by asking questions that might seem way off the track. So always maintain your poise and show you can field tough questions that may even be intended to confuse you.

How to Deal with Suspected Lying

Although protests can sometimes be very disagreeable, my advice is to never take antagonism into the hearing. I think it undermines your case to indicate to the jury that you feel the other person is lying or has acted in an unsportsmanlike manner. Some of the very young competitors will sit and roll their eyes, throw their hands in the air, and make all kinds of gestures and noises while their opponent is giving his testimony. Trying to influence a jury by that kind of action is strictly bush league, and a championship competitor should be more poised than to submit to it. Instead, you should focus on a very precise presentation of your own testimony and, if necessary, focus some direct questioning on certain areas of your opponent's story. If your opponent's story is inaccurate or fabricated, it will usually break down somewhere along the line.

Final Statement

The last step in the hearing of the testimonies is a final statement by each competitor (Appendix 6,2.5). Focus on the key points and be brief. If you have made notes during the testimony, you'll be able to quickly review the facts that support your case and any other key issues. Never introduce new facts or statements. Also, avoid explaining the rules or implying that if you lose your case it will be a miscarriage of justice. If you suspect your competitor was lying or giving distorted facts, avoid facetious remarks but address the fact that in your opinion your opponent presented a very inaccurate description of the incident. Lastly, state the rule(s) you feel should be applied.

One last word about protest hearings. No matter how objective the jury members are, we are all influenced by people's behavior and the way they present themselves in this type of human interaction. It's to your advantage, always, to establish a good rapport with the jury. The best way is to follow the advice above in both your preparation and presentation. Good jurors will immediately pick up your thoroughness and respect you for it. Also, always take yourself seriously, and especially when around the judges. Coming into a hearing after three highballs, horsing around on the water or on shore, or becoming a regular in the hearing room with inane protests will lower the esteem of any judge. Keep in mind that as you get nearer the top of the sport, the names and faces of the competitors start becoming familiar to the top judges, and your reputation will become well known. Be sure it's the kind of reputation you're proud of, and you'll get a lot of mileage from it.

Advanced Rules Quiz

Welcome to the Advanced Rules Quiz. The following questions require an advanced understanding of the 1989–1992 International Yacht Racing Rules to answer completely and correctly. Imagine that you are on the protest committee at the Olympics or a class World Championship and you have to decide each of these cases. To test your understanding I recommend that you read each case carefully, construct your own diagram if it will help, check the applicable rules, and then write up your answer as you would under "Decision and grounds for decision" on a standard protest form. The answers are in Appendix E, and the rules referred to in each answer are thoroughly discussed in this book. I hope you enjoy these. (See Code on page 19 for explanation of abbreviations—L, W, A, B, etc.)

1. W and L are beam reaching on starboard-tack toward the right-hand end of the starting line, which is a large committee boat. They are overlapped bow to bow with forty seconds left before the starting signal. The "720" rule is in effect. L hails W, "Stay clear, you're going to be barging!" W is silent. As L and W begin to pass by the stern of the committee boat there is clearly room for W to keep clear of L and the committee boat if L holds her beam reaching course. L, however, luffs slightly, hitting W, who nearly simultaneously hits the committee boat in an effort to keep clear of L. W hails "protest," immediately sails to windward of the committee boat, and with twenty seconds to go before the starting signal does a "720." L protests W under Rule 42.4 for "barging," and also for doing her "720" before the starting signal. How would you decide this?

2. While rounding the windward mark, Sailboard X accidentally touches the mark. She bears away onto the reach and immediately spins her board in two complete 360-degree turns. Her rig never moves—i.e., she never tacks or gybes the sail. At the gybe mark she calls for room from Sailboard O, who denies her the room

claiming that because she had hit the windward mark and not rerounded it she therefore had no rights and was required to keep clear of him. She hails "protest" to Sailboard O but in the process of gybing she falls off her board. While pulling her sail up out of the water, Sailboard Y alters course to avoid running into her. Sailboard X finally gets up, spins her board again in two full 360-degree circles, finishes the race, and sails straight in without telling the race committee of her intention to protest. Sailboard Y protests Sailboard X for not including two tacks and gybes in her "720." Sailboard O does not show up for the hearing. In the protest hearing Sailboard X tells the committee everything mentioned above. How would you decide all this?

3. While observing a fleet of nineteen-foot boats surfing down the first reach, a judge saw the crew in one boat push abruptly on the front of the cockpit and the helmsman pump twice on the mainsheet just as the bow of the boat was starting to go down the wave. The result was that the boat surfed nicely down that wave. Seeing this same combination of actions repeated several times, the judge "protested" the boat, calling a hearing under Rule 70.2(a). Though a member of the protest committee hearing the case, you were not out on the water. The protested competitor agrees that the testimony of the judge, describing the events as stated above, is accurate. What would your decision be?

4. With three minutes to go before the start, LO and WI are beam reaching on port-tack toward the left-end starting line mark, which is a small buoy. The "720" rule is not in effect. WI calls for room, having read that the new rules have deleted the phrase "other than at a starting mark surrounded by navigable water" from Rule 42. LO holds her course, thereby denying WI of room and WI runs right over the buoy, avoiding any contact with LO. WI immediately does a "720" but never rerounds the mark. WI protests LO for failure to give room, and LO protests WI for failure to reround the mark after the starting signal. How would you resolve this?

5. S is beam reaching behind and parallel with the starting line with about five seconds to go before the starting signal. P is

approaching the starting line close-hauled, and on a course that will take him across S's bow with no problem. With three seconds to go and just as P is crossing her bow, S realizes she is well behind the line and luffs quickly to a close-hauled course, claiming she is assuming her proper course to start. In an attempt to avoid a collision, P puts her helm hard to leeward, but S continues to luff and hits P lightly in the transom. S protests P under Rules 36 and 41, claiming exemption from Rule 35 under the exception in Rule 35(b)(i). What would your decision be?

6. P is approaching the windward mark, to be rounded to port, on a close-hauled course very near to the mark. S rounds the mark (the next leg is a run) and bears away quickly to a dead downwind course, her bow colliding immediately with the port stern quarter of P's hull. P's hull is holed and she is unable to continue in the race. S protests P under Rule 36, claiming Rule 35 permits her to assume a proper course when rounding a mark. What would your decision be?

7. A and B, two twenty-foot boats, are close-reaching on starboard-tack toward the left end of the starting line, which is an anchored committee boat. With ten seconds to go before the starting signal and when A is thirty feet from the committee boat, A lets out her sails to avoid being early for the start. B, moving slightly faster as a result of A's slowing down, sails in to leeward of A from clear astern. With AW in the "mast abeam" position throughout the incident, BL luffs slowly, giving AW time and room to respond. As they approach the committee boat, BL calls for room, luffs head-to-wind, and makes contact with AW, narrowly avoiding contact with the starting mark (committee boat). Both boats protest; what is your decision?

8. W and L are broad reaching on port-tack less than one boat-length apart and both are sailing proper courses. They are bow to bow, but L doesn't have luffing rights because at some point during the overlap W has attained the "mast abeam" position. W, who wants to gybe and assert starboard-tack rights, can't do so while so close to L. W luffs to open the gap and L luffs also,

keeping the distance between them the same. W luffs again and when L follows suit, W protests. In the hearing L is asked whether she luffed above her proper course. She replied "Yes," but that W was not affected by her luff because W was widening the gap of her own volition at the time. What is your decision?

9. Two boats in a match race, LO and WI, are approaching the leeward mark to be rounded to port. They are sailing port-tack broad reaches, and LO's bow is slightly ahead of WI's. They have been overlapped for several boat lengths and LO has luffing rights. When three lengths from the mark, LO tells WI that she intends to pass on the wrong side of the mark. When two lengths from the mark, LO begins a slight luff and WI hails that she needs room at the mark. The two yachts sail into and then out of the two-length circle, winding up on the wrong side of the mark. As they circle back, WI protests LO for failure to give room under Rule 42.1(a). What is your decision?

10. Yacht M is going into the last race of a major U.S. championship; her previous races are such that she will win if Yacht Q finishes eighth or worse. Yacht M can afford to discard her last race. Going down the second reach, Yacht Q is several boats ahead of Yacht M. Yacht M begins pumping nonstop, passes Yacht Q, and proceeds to slow Yacht Q and drive her back in the fleet. With Yacht Q well behind and realizing that she (Yacht M) had pumped illegally, Yacht M retires from the race. Yacht Q protests Yacht M for infringing Rule 54.1, thinking that a DSQ under Rule 54 could not be used as a "drop race." At the outset of the hearing Yacht M tells the protest committee that she had realized at the time she was pumping that she had been pumping illegally, that she had retired from the race, and that the USYRU prescription to Rule 74.5(c) allowed her to "drop" a DSQ under Rule 54. How would you resolve this case?

Appendix A: Significant Changes in the 1989–1992 International Yacht Racing Rules

All changes from the 1985–1988 IYRR, regardless of how minor, are marked in the new rule book by lines in the margin (see Appendix D). The following is a brief summary of the significant changes to both the right-of-way rules (Part IV) and the other rules.

Part I   Rule Changes

- **Fundamental Rule C, Fair Sailing:** The rule now includes the defined term "sailing" and the requirement to comply with recognized principles of fair play and sportsmanship, incorporating those important values into the IYRR.
- **Fundamental Rule D, Accepting Penalties:** The rule, given prominence as a Fundamental Rule, now makes it mandatory to retire or accept an alternative penalty when you know you've infringed a rule.
- **Definition of Sailing:** The rules now define what "sailing" is, building this fundamental concept into the rules and providing a clear counterpoint to Rule 54, Propulsion, which essentially establishes what is not considered "sailing."
- **Definition of Tacking:** This greatly simplified definition eliminates all consideration of whether a yacht is beating to windward or not. Regardless of her point of sail prior to tacking, a yacht's tack is complete when she has borne away to a close-hauled course.

Part IV   Rule Changes

- **Rule 32:** Now it is mandatory to penalize right-of-way yachts that had the opportunity but failed to make a reasonable attempt to avoid a collision resulting in serious damage.
- **Rule 38.2(c):** The hail "obstruction" or words to that effect from a windward boat now carries the same requirement as a hail of "mast abeam"—i.e., that the leeward boat must stop luffing.

- **Rule 42:** The phrase "other than at a starting mark surrounded by navigable water" has been removed from the rule. This clarifies that an inside boat is entitled to room under 42.1(a) at an obstruction that also happens to be a starting mark (i.e., a race committee boat), provided the inside boat attains an overlap on the outside boat in time, etc. This commonly arises when the "leeward" end of the starting line is a committee boat. Inside boats are also entitled to room at starting marks once they have started—i.e., crossed the starting line after the starting signal. Rule 42.4, the anti-barging rule, applies as always.

- **Rule 42.3(a)(ii):** The addition of the phrase "by luffing" clarifies that a boat clear astern need only luff (i.e., alter course to windward) in an attempt to avoid establishing a late inside overlap on a yacht that has tacked clear ahead of her inside the two-length circle. She needn't gybe radically or try other measures.

- **Rule 42.3(c):** This was the rule that permitted outside leeward yachts near marks to take inside yachts to the wrong side of the mark. This rule has been deleted in its entirety. If an outside leeward yacht wishes to try to take an inside windward yacht to the wrong side of the mark, she must exercise her leeward yacht rights and her right to luff before she becomes "about to round the mark."

- **Rule 45:** This rule has been changed to conform to the entirely new form of exoneration for touching a mark (Rule 52). Previously the mark needed to be rerounded. Now the infringing yacht does not need to reround the mark, but she has to make two 360-degree turns, including two tacks and gybes. If she touches a starting mark before the starting signal, she can exonerate herself immediately.

- **Rule 46.3:** This rule is a definition of "capsized" for sailboats, useful for applying Rules 46.1 and 46.2. Essentially you are "capsized" from the time your masthead hits the water until the boat is righted, the crew is on board, and the boat has steerageway.

Part V   Rule Changes

- **Rule 52:** Now when you touch a mark you do not have to reround it. Instead, you must get clear of all other boats as soon as possible after hitting the mark, and do two complete 360-degree turns ("720") in the same direction, including two tacks and two gybes. After hitting a starting mark you can exonerate yourself immediately.

- **Rule 54.1:** The basic rule now says you can compete only by "sailing," which is a new definition in Part I. This, in itself, represents no change to the way yachts are to be sailed.

- **Rule 54.2:** Merely doing any of the actions listed in 54.2 (pumping, rocking, ooching, sculling, and repeated tacks and gybes unrelated to changes in the wind or to tactical considerations) is illegal, whether or not the action is capable of propelling the yacht.

- **Rule 54.3:** The exceptions to Rule 54 have been changed dramatically. You are specifically allowed to roll-tack and roll-gybe with specific limitations, and to have ONE pump per wave on the sheet or wishbone controlling any sail with specific limitations. You cannot roll (dramatically heel, as opposed to a slight heel) your boat to leeward immediately prior to a roll-tack or roll-gybe, **ooch at all** (not even to initiate surfing or planing), pump more than ONCE per wave or gust, pump the spinnaker "guy," pump using anything but the sheet (i.e., no pumping with the vang or special pumping line), pump by grabbing all parts of a multi-part mainsheet system (essentially, you now have to use all parts of the system), and pump to attempt surfing or planing upwind.

- **Rule 64.3:** The tack of the spinnaker no longer needs to be in close proximity to the spinnaker pole when you are hoisting, gybing, or lowering the spinnaker. This clears up the issue of the legality of "gybe sets" and "floater (windward) drops," both done with the pole momentarily off the spinnaker.

Other Rule Changes

- **Rule 4.1, First Substitute—General Recall Signal:** This now means that the preparatory signal will be made one minute after this signal is lowered. Previously, the next signal was the warning signal unless the sailing instructions stated otherwise.

- **Rule 25.2:** This rule, governing the size, shape, and color of sail numbers and national letters has been made stricter and more uniform. Letters and numbers must be a single color and strongly contrasting with the sail, with continuous lines and uniform in thickness, and in roman style (upright) without serifs (the short lines put across the top and bottom of letters and numbers). A table of sizes related to a yacht's overall length is provided.

- **Rule 26, Appendix 14, Rules 2(e), 3.1(iv), 3.2(b)(i):** These all deal with the new concept of classification of events for the purpose of determining how much advertising is permitted. The three classifications from which event organizers can choose are outlined in Appendix 14 (if not otherwise specified by the organizing authority, an event is automatically Category A). In Category A, only event sponsorship is allowed. In Category B, advertising, including event sponsorship, individual boat sponsorship, advertising on sails, hulls and clothing is permitted—but within defined limits. Category C is the no-holds-barred area, intended to encompass pure professional events.

- **Rule 68.3(a):** USYRU prescribes that the protest flag must be red, unless the sailing instructions provide otherwise.

- **Rule 69(a):** "Protest committee" has been added, clarifying that redress can be requested when an action or omission of the protest committee has materially prejudiced a yacht's finishing position through no fault of her own. This will be useful when the protest committee denies a party to a protest their rights or conducts a hearing in contravention to the rules, particularly over the objection of the party to the protest concerned.

- **Rule 69(c):** "Disabled" has been replaced with "damaged," requiring that redress can be sought only when physical damage has occurred to the yacht in question.

- **Rule 70.1(b):** This rule permits the protest committee to penalize a yacht under Rules 54.2 and 54.3, Propulsion, without a hearing. The USYRU prescribes that this rule applies only when the sailing instructions specifically say so.

- **Rule 74.5(c):** This is a significant change. Disqualifications under Fundamental Rules C, Fair Sailing, and D, Accepting Penalties, cannot be "dropped" in series permitting the worst race to be excluded for scoring purposes. Under Rule 74.5(c), Rule 54, Propulsion, is also exempt from exclusion, but the USYRU prescribes that DSQ's under Rule 54 can be "dropped."

- **Rules 77 and 78:** The procedures for filing appeals have been significantly changed. The essence of the changes is that now the parties will send their appeals and materials to the appeals committees, and the appeals committees will gather all the necessary information and circulate it to the parties.

- **Appendix 2—Sailboard Racing Rules:** The definitions of "capsized" and "recovering" are now based on the board's way as opposed to her masthead location. The "720" rule for the exoneration of a Part IV foul is always in effect unless stated otherwise in the sailing instructions. Funboard Racing Rules have been added.

- **Appendix 3—Alternative Penalties:** The appendix has been rewritten. Significant points include: a "720" is not an admission of guilt; a yacht can do an "insurance 720" and protest another yacht in the same incident, claiming it was their fault; a yacht fouling before starting does not have to wait until the starting signal to do her "720"; she can do it immediately; and the second circle no longer is required to follow "immediately" after the first, however, the yacht must remain well clear until her turns are completed, and she can be disqualified if she gains a significant advantage having done her turns.

- **Appendix 4—Team and Match Racing Rules:** Modifications include: some changes to the Team Racing rules; the inclusion of the "Green flag" rule for accepting a penalty; a new section on match racing rules, which include several modifications to Part IV rules; and a section on on-the-water judging particularly applicable to match racing.

Appendix B: Tables

1. DISTANCE, SPEED, AND TIME RELATIONSHIPS (D = R × T)
(1 KNOT = 6,000 FEET PER HOUR)

Boatspeed	Feet per second	Meters per second
1 knot	1.66	0.5
2	3.33	1.0
3	5.00	1.5
4	6.66	2.0
5	8.33	2.5
6	10.00	3.0
7	11.66	3.5
8	13.33	4.0
9	15.00	4.5
10	16.66	5.0

In other words, at 4 knots your boat will travel 6.66 feet per second. One way to determine your boat's speed is to sail by a buoy or other fixed object and count how many seconds it takes for the buoy to go from your bow to stern. If in a J-24 it takes 3 seconds to go by the buoy, you are going 8 feet per second, or just under 5 knots.

It's very useful to know your boat's approximate speed on all points of sail in all wind and wave conditions, particularly in a protest hearing. For instance, in the above example you now know that the "two boat-length circle" is about 6 seconds' worth of sailing before the *mark*. You also know that if you complete your *tack* in front of another boat and they claim they hit you only 3 seconds after your *tack* was completed, you can point out that you completed your *tack* and then they held their course for a full boat-length, by their own testimony.

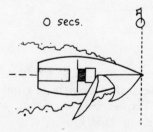
O secs.

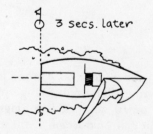
3 secs. later

2. ALTERATION (IN FEET) PER CHANGE IN COURSE (IN DEGREES); X = THE LENGTH OF THE BOAT; Y = THE AMOUNT THE BOW MOVES

10 degrees		15 degrees		20 degrees		
x	y	x	y	x	y	
10'	1' 9"	10'	2' 8"	10'	3' 7"	(add 11" for each 5 degrees more)
15'	2' 7"	15'	3' 11"	15'	5' 3"	(add 16" for each 5 degrees more)
20'	3' 6"	20'	5' 3"	20'	7'	(add 21" for each 5 degrees more)
25'	4' 4"	25'	6' 6"	25'	8' 8"	(add 26" for each 5 degrees more)
30'	5' 3"	30'	7' 10"	30'	10' 5"	(add 31" for each 5 degrees more)
(add 10.5" for each 5' more)		(add 15.5" for each 5' more)		(add 20.5" for each 5' more)		

In other words, when you change your course 10 degrees in a 20-foot boat (x), your bow will move 3'6" (y). See diagram 1. Likewise, when you change your course 20 degrees in a 50-foot boat, your bow moves 17'3".

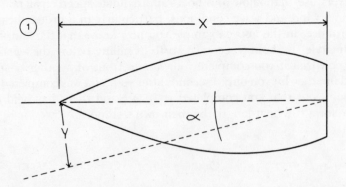

If your 20-foot boat is one length away from a 7-foot log, then the most you will have to change your course at that moment to avoid it is 3'6", or 10 degrees. See diagram 2. This becomes important when defining an *obstruction*, or the applicability of Rule 43.

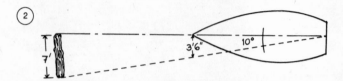

These numbers will also be very useful when you feel a competitor is absolutely exaggerating the facts to their benefit. Let's say that in a protest over *port/starboard,* your competitor (S) said that they had to bear off 45 degrees to pass astern of you (P). You should ask them, (a) where would they have hit you had they held their course; (b) how far from you were they when they altered their course; and (c) how close to your transom did they come. Say they answered "a quarter of a length from your stern," "half a boat-length," and "two feet" to your three questions. If they were sailing a 20-foot boat, you'd now know that they altered course a total of 7 feet and that they were 10 feet away from you at the time, which is the equivalent of a 30-foot boat altering course 7 feet. Therefore, based on your competitor's testimony, they altered their course only by 15 degrees maximum. See diagram 3.

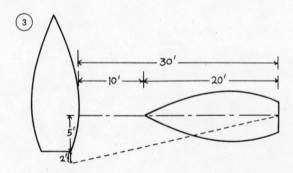

Appendix C: General Information on the Rule Books and Judging

- United States Yacht Racing Union
  Box 209
  Newport, RI 02840
- International Yacht Racing Union
  60 Knightsbridge
  London SW1X 7JX England
- Canadian Yachting Association
  1600 James Naismith Drive
  Gloucester, Ontario K1B 5N4

For rule books (in the U.S.) or for the *USYRU Book of Appeals* and IYRU Cases, write to USYRU.

THE USYRU JUDGES PROGRAM

USYRU administers a voluntary certification program whereby individuals interested in judging submit their qualifications for review by the USYRU Committee on Judges. Those who meet the criteria set by the Committee are certified. Organizing authorities refer to the roster of certified judges for help in obtaining qualified, competent judges.

CRITERIA FOR USYRU CERTIFICATION

None of the following is more important than another, and ordinarily none will be waived by the USYRU Committee on Judges. To be and remain certified a man or woman must:

1. Be a member in good standing of USYRU.
2. Be a member in good standing of a recognized yacht club or class association affiliated with USYRU.
3. Possess judicial temperament and a reputation for mature judgment, and have an outstanding reputation for integrity.
4. Have raced for at least three complete seasons in a position requiring

on-the-water application of the yacht racing rules—such as skipper, tactician, watch captain, or navigator.

5. Have served at least three seasons in a responsible role as a race committee member, including some hearing and deciding of protests.
6. Be highly recommended for USYRU certification by respected members of the yachting community.

Everyone involved in race administration should be familiar with the judges program and own a copy of the *USYRU Judges Manual*. For more information about the program or to order the *Judges Manual*, write to USYRU. Individuals who are interested in learning more about certification should write to the USYRU Committee on Judges, care of USYRU.

Appendix D: The 1989–1992 International Yacht Racing Rules

(Note: The USYRU prescriptions are contained herein and appear in parentheses. All changes from the 1985–1988 IYRR are marked by vertical lines in the margin.)

INTRODUCTION

Translation and Interpretation
In translating and interpreting these rules, it shall be understood that the word "shall" is mandatory, and the words "can" and "may" are permissive.

Note (a) Marginal markings indicate the changes made in the 1985 Racing Rules.
Note (b) No changes are contemplated before 1992.
Note (c) These racing rules supersede all previous editions.

PART I—STATUS OF THE RULES, FUNDAMENTAL RULES AND DEFINITIONS

Status of the Rules

The International Yacht Racing Rules have been established by the International Yacht Racing Union for the organisation, conduct and judging of the sport of yacht racing, and are amended and published every four years by the IYRU in accordance with its Constitution.

A national authority may alter or add to these rules by prescription, with the exception of the rules of Parts I and IV, the definitions of Part VI, rules 1, 3, 26 and 61, and Appendix 14, unless permitted in a rule itself.

The sailing instructions may alter rules only in accordance with rule 3.1, Sailing Instructions.

Fundamental Rules

A. Rendering Assistance

Every yacht shall render all possible assistance to any vessel or person in peril, when in a position to do so.

B. Responsibility of a Yacht

It shall be the sole responsibility of each yacht to decide whether or not to *start* or to continue to *race*.

C. Fair Sailing

A yacht, her owner and crew shall compete only by *sailing,* using their speed and skill, and, except in team racing, by individual effort, in compliance with the **rules** and in accordance with recognised principles of fair play and sportsmanship. A yacht may be penalised under this rule only in the case of a clear-cut violation of the above principles and only when no other **rule** applies, except rule 75, Gross Infringement of Rules or Misconduct.

D. Accepting Penalties

A yacht that realises she has infringed a **rule** shall either retire promptly or accept an alternative penalty when so prescribed in the sailing instructions.

Definitions

When a term defined in Part I is used in its defined sense it is printed in italic type. All preambles and definitions rank as rules. Further definitions will be found at the beginning of Part VI.

Sailing—A yacht is *sailing* when using only the wind and water to increase, maintain or decrease her speed, with her crew adjusting the trim of sails and hull and performing other acts of seamanship.

Racing—A yacht is *racing* from her preparatory signal until she has either *finished* and cleared the finishing line and finishing *marks* or retired, or until the race has been *postponed, abandoned, cancelled,* or a general recall has been signalled.

Starting—A yacht *starts* when, after fulfilling her penalty obligations, if any, under rule 51.1(c), Sailing the Course, and after her starting signal, any part of her hull, crew or equipment first crosses the starting line in the direction of the course to the first *mark.*

Finishing—A yacht *finishes* when any part of her hull, or of her crew or equipment in normal position, crosses the finishing line in the direction of the course from the last *mark,* after fulfilling her penalty obligations, if any, under rule 52.2(b), Touching a Mark.

Luffing—Altering course towards the wind.

Tacking—A yacht is *tacking* from the moment she is beyond head to wind until she has *borne away* to a *close-hauled* course.

Bearing away—Altering course away from the wind until a yacht begins to *gybe.*

Gybing—A yacht begins to *gybe* at the moment when, with the wind aft, the foot of her mainsail crosses her centre line, and completes the *gybe* when the mainsail has filled on the other *tack*.

On a tack—A yacht is *on a tack* except when she is *tacking* or *gybing*. A yacht is on the *tack* (*starboard* or *port*) corresponding to her *windward* side.

Close-hauled—A yacht is *close-hauled* when *sailing* by the wind as close as she can lie with advantage in working to windward.

Clear Astern and *Clear Ahead; Overlap*—A yacht is *clear astern* of another when her hull and equipment in normal position are abaft an imaginary line projected abeam from the aftermost point of the other's hull and equipment in normal position. The other yacht is *clear ahead*.

The yachts *overlap* when neither is *clear astern;* or when, although one is *clear astern,* an intervening yacht *overlaps* both of them.

The terms *clear astern, clear ahead* and *overlap* apply to yachts on opposite *tacks* only when they are subject to rule 42, Rounding or Passing Marks and Obstructions.

Leeward and *Windward*—The *leeward* side of a yacht is that on which she is, or, when head to wind, was, carrying her mainsail. The opposite side is the *windward* side.

When neither of two yachts on the same *tack* is *clear astern,* the one on the *leeward* side of the other is the *leeward yacht*. The other is the *windward yacht*.

Proper Course—A *proper course* is any course that a yacht might *sail* after the starting signal, in the absence of the other yacht or yachts affected, to *finish* as quickly as possible. The course *sailed* before *luffing* or *bearing away* is presumably, but not necessarily, that yacht's *proper course*. There is no *proper course* before the starting signal.

Mark—A *mark* is any object specified in the sailing instructions that a yacht must round or pass on a required side.

Every ordinary part of a *mark* ranks as part of it, including a flag, flagpole, boom or hoisted boat, but excluding ground tackle and any object either accidentally or temporarily attached to the *mark*.

Obstruction—An *obstruction* is any object, including a vessel under way, large enough to require a yacht, when more than one overall length away from it, to make a substantial alteration of course to pass on one side or the other, or any object that can be passed on one side only, including a buoy when the yacht in question cannot safely pass between it and the shoal or object that it marks. The sailing instructions may prescribe that certain defined areas shall rank as *obstructions.*

Postponement—A *postponed* race is one that is not started at its scheduled time and that can be sailed at any time the race committee may decide.

Abandonment—An *abandoned* race is one that the race committee declares void at any time after the starting signal, and that can be re-sailed at its discretion.

Cancellation—A *cancelled* race is one that the race committee decides will not be sailed thereafter.

PART II—ORGANISATION AND MANAGEMENT

1 Organising, Conducting and Judging Races

1.1 GOVERNING RULES

The organising authority, race committee, protest committee and all other bodies and persons concerned with the organisation, conduct and judging of a race, regatta or series shall be governed by these rules, the prescriptions of the national authority when they apply, the class rules (except when they conflict with these rules), the sailing instructions and any other conditions governing the event. Hereinafter the term "race" shall, when appropriate, include a regatta or a series of races.

1.2 ORGANISING AUTHORITY

Races shall be organised by:

(a) the IYRU; or

(b) a member national authority of the IYRU; or

(c) a club or regatta committee affiliated to a national authority; or

(d) a class association either with the approval of a national authority or in conjunction with an affiliated club or regatta committee; or

(e) an unaffiliated body in conjunction with an affiliated club or regatta committee;

which will hereinafter be referred to as the organising authority.
The organising authority shall appoint a race committee and publish a notice of race in accordance with rule 2, Notice of Race.

1.3 RACE COMMITTEE

The race committee shall publish sailing instructions in accordance with rule 3, Sailing Instructions, and conduct the race, subject to such direction as the organising authority may exercise. The term "race committee" whenever it is used shall include any person or committee that is responsible for performing any of the duties or functions of the race committee.

1.4 PROTEST COMMITTEES

The receiving, hearing and deciding of protests and other matters arising under the rules of Part VI, Protests, Penalties and Appeals, shall be carried out by:

(a) the race committee itself; or

(b) a sub-committee thereof appointed by the race committee and consisting of its own members, or others, or a combination of both; or

(c) a jury or a protest committee, separate from and independent of the race committee, appointed by the organising authority or the race committee; or

(d) an international jury appointed by the organising authority in accordance with Appendix 8, International Juries. A national authority may prescribe that its approval is required for the appointment of international juries for events within its jurisdiction other than those of the IYRU.

A jury or protest committee shall not supervise the conduct of the race, or direct the race committee, except when so directed by the organising authority. (The term "jury", as used in yacht racing, means a panel of judges.)

1.5 RIGHT OF APPEAL

Decisions of a protest committee or jury may be appealed in accordance with rule 77.1, Right of Appeal, except that:

(a) there shall be no appeal from the decisions of an international jury constituted in accordance with Appendix 8, International Juries.

(b) when the notice of race and the sailing instructions so state, the right of appeal may be denied when:

(i) it is essential to determine promptly the result of a race that will qualify a yacht to compete in a later stage of the event or a subsequent event (a national authority may prescribe that its approval is required for such a procedure); or

(ii) a national authority so prescribes for a particular event open only to entrants under its own jurisdiction.

1.6 EXCLUSION OF YACHTS AND COMPETITORS

Unless otherwise prescribed by the national authority, the organising authority or the race committee may, before the start of the first race, reject or rescind the entry of any yacht or exclude a competitor, without stating the reason. However, at all world and continental championships, no entry within established quotas shall be rejected or rescinded without first obtaining the approval of the IYRU, the relevant international class association or the Offshore Racing Council.

(USYRU prescribes that neither the organizing authority nor the race committee shall reject or rescind the entry of any yacht, or exclude a competitor, without stating the reason.)

2   Notice of Race

The notice of race shall contain the following information:

(a) The title, place and dates of the event and name of the organising authority.

(b) That the race will be governed by the International Yacht Racing Rules, the prescriptions of the national authority when they apply (for international events, a copy in English of prescriptions that apply shall be available to each yacht), the rules of each class concerned and such other rules as are applicable. When class rules are altered, the alterations shall be stated.

(c) The class(es) to race, conditions of eligibility or entry and, when appropriate, restrictions on numbers of entries.

(d) The times of registration and starts of the practice race or first race, and succeeding races when known.

The notice shall, when appropriate, include the following:

(e) The category of the event in accordance with Appendix 14, Event Classification and Advertising, and, when required, the additional information prescribed in Appendix 14.

(f) The scoring system.

(g) The time and place at which the sailing instructions will be available.

(h) Variations from the racing rules, subject to rule 3.1, Sailing Instructions.

(i) The procedure for advance registration or entry, including closing dates when applicable, fees and the mailing address.

(j) Measurement procedures or requirements for measuring or rating certificates.

(k) The course(s) to be *sailed*.

(l) Alternative penalties for rule infringements.

(m) Prizes.

(n) Denial of the right of appeal, subject to rule 1.5, Right of Appeal.

3 Sailing Instructions

3.1 STATUS

(a) These rules shall be supplemented by written sailing instructions that shall rank as rules and may, subject to the restrictions of rule 3.1(b), alter a rule by specific reference to it.

(b) Except in accordance with rule 3.2(b)(xxix), the sailing instructions shall not alter:

  (i) Parts I and IV,

  (ii) rules 1, 2, 3, 26, 51.1(a) and 61,

  (iii) the definitions and Sections C and D of Part VI,

  (iv) Appendix 14, and

  (v) the provision of rule 68.3(a), Protests by Yachts, that International Code flag "B" is always acceptable as a protest flag.

(c) When so prescribed by the national authority, these restrictions shall not preclude the right of developing and testing proposed rule changes in local races. A national authority may also prescribe that its approval be required for such changes.
(USYRU prescribes that no approval is necessary.)

3.2 CONTENTS

(a) The sailing instructions shall contain the following information:

  (i) That the race will be governed by the International Yacht Racing Rules, the prescriptions of the national authority when they apply (for international events, a copy in English of prescriptions that apply shall be included in the sailing instructions), the rules of each class concerned, the sailing instructions and such other rules as are applicable.

(ii) The schedule of races, the classes to race, and the order and times of warning signals.

(iii) The course to be *sailed* or a list of *marks* from which the course will be selected, describing the *marks,* stating their order and, for each, whether it is to be rounded or passed and on which side.

A diagram or chart is recommended.

(iv) Description of the starting line, the starting system and any special signals to be used.

(v) The procedure for individual and general recalls and any special signals.

(vi) Description of the finishing line and any special instructions for *finishing* a course shortened after the start.

(vii) The time limit, if any, for *finishing*.

(viii) The scoring system, when not previously announced in writing, including the method, if any, for breaking ties.

(b) The sailing instructions shall, when appropriate, include the following:

(i) The category of the event in accordance with Appendix 14, Event Classification and Advertising, and, when required, the additional information prescribed in Appendix 14.

(ii) Variations from the racing rules, subject to rule 3.1, or the class rules for a special race.

(iii) The registration procedure.

(iv) Location(s) of official notice board(s).

(v) Procedure for changes in the sailing instructions.

(vi) Restrictions controlling alterations to yachts when supplied by the organising authority.

(vii) Signals to be made ashore and location of signal station(s).

(viii) Class flags.

(ix) The racing area. A chart is recommended.

(x) The starting area.

(xi) Course signals.

(xii) Approximate course length; approximate length of windward legs.

(xiii) Information on tides and currents.

(xiv) Procedure for shortening the course before or after the start.

(xv) Mark boats; lead boats.

(xvi) Procedure for changes of course after the start and related signals.

(xvii) The time limit, if any, for yachts other than the first yacht to *finish*.

(xviii) Whether races *postponed* or *abandoned* for the day will be sailed later and, if so, when and where.

(xix) The number of races required to complete the regatta.

(xx) Safety, such as requirements and signals for personal buoyancy, check-in at the starting area, and check-out and check-in ashore.

(xxi) Any measurement or inspection procedure.

(xxii) Alternative penalties for rule infringements.

(xxiii) Whether declarations are required.

(xxiv) Protest procedure and times and place of hearings.

(xxv) Restrictions on use of support boats, plastic pools, radios, etc., and limitations on hauling out.

(xxvi) Substitute competitors.

(xxvii) Prizes.

(xxviii) Time allowances.

(xxix) Racing rules applicable between sunset and sunrise and night signals to be used by the race committee.

(xxx) Disposition to be made of a yacht appearing at the start alone in her class.

(xxxi) Denial of the right of appeal, subject to rule 1.5, Right of Appeal.

(xxxii) Other commitments of the race committee and obligations of yachts.

3.3 DISTRIBUTION
The sailing instructions shall be available to each yacht entitled to *race*.

3.4 CHANGES

Changes in sailing instructions shall be made in writing before a race by:

(a) posting in proper time on the official notice board, or

(b) being communicated to each yacht on the water before the warning signal, except that oral instructions may be given only on the water in accordance with procedure prescribed in the sailing instructions.

4   Signals

4.1 VISUAL SIGNALS

Unless otherwise prescribed in the sailing instructions, the following International Code flags (or boards) and other visual signals shall be used as indicated, and when displayed alone shall apply to all classes, and when displayed over a class flag shall apply to the designated class only:

"AP", Answering Pendant—Postponement Signal

Means:

(a) "All races not started are *postponed*. The warning signal will be made one minute after this signal is lowered."
(One sound signal shall be made with the lowering of the "AP".)

(b) Over one ball or shape.
"The scheduled starting times of all races not started are *postponed* fifteen minutes."
(This *postponement* can be extended indefinitely by the addition of one ball or shape for every fifteen minutes.)

(c) Over one of the numeral pendants 1 to 9.
"All races not started are *postponed* one hour, two hours, etc."

(d) Over Code flag "A".
"All races not started are *postponed* to a later day."

"B"—Protest signal.

When displayed by a yacht, means:
"I intend to lodge a protest."

"C"—Change of Course while Racing.

When displayed at or near a rounding *mark,* means:
"After rounding this *mark,* the course to the next *mark* has been changed."

"I"—Round the Ends Starting Rule

When displayed before or with the preparatory signal, means:
"Rule 51.1(c) will be in effect for this start."

When lowered, accompanied by one long sound signal, one minute before the starting signal, means:
"The one-minute period of rule 51.1(c) has begun."

"L"—Means:

(a) When displayed ashore:
"A notice to competitors has been posted on the official notice board."

(b) When displayed afloat:
"Come within hail", or "Follow me".

"M"—Mark Signal.

When displayed on a buoy, vessel, or other object, means:
"Round or pass the object displaying this signal instead of the *mark* that it replaces."

"N"—Abandonment Signal.

Means:
"All races are *abandoned.*"

"N over X"—Abandonment and Re-sail Signal.

Means:
"All races are *abandoned* and will shortly be re-sailed. The warning signal will be made one minute after this signal is lowered."
(One sound signal shall be made with the lowering of "N over X".)

"N over First Substitute"—Cancellation Signal.

Means:
"All races are *cancelled.*"

"P"—Preparatory Signal.

Means:
"The class designated by the warning signal will *start* in five minutes exactly."

"S"—Shorten Course Signal.

Means:
(a) at the starting line:
"*Sail* the shortened course as prescribed in the sailing instructions."

(b) at the finishing line:
   "*Finish* the race either:

   (i) at the prescribed finishing line at the end of the round still to be completed by the leading yacht, or

   (ii) as prescribed in the sailing instructions."

(c) at a rounding *mark:*
   "*Finish* between the rounding *mark* and the committee boat."

"X"—Individual Recall.

When displayed promptly after the starting signal, accompanied by one sound signal, means:
"One or more yachts are recalled in accordance with rule 8.1, Individual Recall."

"Y"—Life Jacket Signal.

Means:
"Life jackets or other adequate personal buoyancy shall be worn while *racing* by all the competitors, unless specifically excepted in the sailing instructions."
When this signal is displayed after the warning signal, failure to comply shall not be cause for disqualification.
Notwithstanding anything in this rule, it shall be the individual responsibility of each competitor to wear a life jacket or other adequate personal buoyancy when conditions warrant. A wet suit is not adequate personal buoyancy.

"First Substitute"—General Recall Signal.

Means:
"The class is recalled for a new start. The preparatory signal will be made one minute after this signal is lowered."
(One sound signal shall be made with the lowering of "First Substitute".)

Red Flag

When displayed by a committee boat, means:
"Leave all *marks* to port."

Green Flag

When displayed by a committee boat, means:
"Leave all *marks* to starboard."

Blue Flag or Shape—Finishing Signal.

> When displayed by a committee boat, means:
> "The committee boat is on station at the finishing line."

4.2 SPECIAL SIGNALS

The sailing instructions shall designate any other special signals and shall explain their meaning.

4.3 CALLING ATTENTION TO VISUAL SIGNALS

Whenever the race committee makes a signal, except "S" before the warning signal or a blue flag or shape when on station at the finishing line, it shall call attention to its action as follows:

(a) Three guns or other sound signals when displaying:

   (i) "N";

   (ii) "N over X";

   (iii) "N over First Substitute".

(b) Two guns or other sound signals when displaying:

   (i) "AP";

   (ii) "S";

   (iii) "First Substitute".

(c) Repetitive sound signals while displaying Code flag "C".

(d) One gun or other sound signal when making any other signal, including the lowering of:

   (i) "AP" when the length of the *postponement* is not signalled;

   (ii) "N over X";

   (iii) "First Substitute".

4.4 SIGNALS FOR STARTING A RACE

(a) Unless otherwise prescribed in the sailing instructions, the signals for starting a race shall be made at five-minute intervals exactly, and shall be either:

System 1 Warning Signal—Class flag broken out or distinctive signal displayed.

Preparatory Signal—Code flag "P" broken out or distinctive signal displayed.

> Starting Signal—Both warning and preparatory signals lowered.

In System 1, when classes are started:

> (i) at ten-minute intervals—
> the warning signal for each succeeding class shall be broken out or displayed at the starting signal of the preceding class.

> (ii) at five-minute intervals—
> the preparatory signal for the first class to start shall be left displayed until the last class starts. The warning signal for each succeeding class shall be broken out or displayed at the preparatory signal of the preceding class.

or

System 2   Warning Signal—White or yellow shape or flag.

> Preparatory Signal—Blue shape or flag.

> Starting Signal—Red shape or flag.

In System 2, each signal shall be lowered one minute before the next is made. Class flags when used shall be broken out not later than the preparatory signal for each class.

When classes are started:

> (i) at ten-minute intervals—
> the starting signal for each class shall be the warning signal for the next.

> (ii) at five-minute intervals—
> the preparatory signal for each class shall be the warning signal for the next.

(b) Although rules 4.1 "P" and 4.4(a) specify five-minute intervals, the sailing instructions may prescribe any intervals.

(c) A warning signal shall not be made before its scheduled time, except with the consent of all yachts entitled to *race.*

(d) When a significant error is made in the timing of the interval between any of the signals for starting a race, the recommended procedure is to signal a general recall, *postponement* or *abandonment* of the race whose start is directly affected by the error and a corresponding *postponement* of succeeding races. Unless otherwise prescribed in the sailing instructions, a new warning signal shall be made. When the race is not recalled, *postponed* or *abandoned* after an error in the timing of the interval, each succeeding signal shall be made at the correct interval from the preceding signal.

4.5 VISUAL STARTING SIGNALS TO GOVERN

Times shall be taken from the visual starting signals, and a failure or mistiming of a gun or other sound signal calling attention to starting signals shall be disregarded.

5 Designating the Course, Altering the Course or Race

5.1 Before or with the warning signal for a class that has not *started,* the race committee:

(a) shall either signal or otherwise designate the course.

(b) may remove and substitute a new course signal.

5.2 Before the preparatory signal, the race committee may shift a starting *mark.*

5.3 Before the starting signal, the race committee may:

(a) shorten the course to one prescribed in the sailing instructions.

(b) *postpone* to designate a new course before or with the new warning signal, or for any other reason.

(c) *postpone* to a later day.

(d) *cancel* the race for any reason.

5.4 After the starting signal, the race committee may:

(a) *abandon* and re-sail the race when there is an error in starting procedure.

(b) when prescribed in the sailing instructions, change the course at any rounding *mark* subject to proper notice being given to each yacht before she begins the changed leg.

(c) shorten the course by finishing a race at any rounding *mark* or as prescribed in the sailing instructions, or *abandon* or *cancel* the race:

(i) because of foul weather, or

(ii) because of insufficient wind making it improbable that the race will finish within the time limit, or

(iii) because a *mark* is missing or has shifted, or

(iv) for any other reasons directly affecting the safety or fairness of the competition.

5.5 After a race has been completed, the race committee shall not *abandon* or *cancel* it without taking the appropriate action under rule 74.2(b), Consideration of Redress.

5.6 The race committee shall notify all yachts concerned by signal or otherwise when and where a race *postponed* to a later day or *abandoned* will be sailed.

6   Starting and Finishing Lines

Unless otherwise prescribed in the sailing instructions, the starting and finishing lines shall be either:

(a) a line between a *mark* and a mast or staff on the committee boat or station clearly identified in the sailing instructions; or

(b) a line between two *marks;* or

(c) the extension of a line through two stationary posts, with or without a *mark* at or near its outer limit, inside which the yachts shall pass.

For types (a) and (c) of starting or finishing lines the sailing instructions may also prescribe that a *mark* will be laid at or near the inner end of the line, in which case yachts shall pass between it and the outer *mark.*

7   Start of a Race

7.1 STARTING AREA
The sailing instructions may define a starting area that may be bounded by buoys; if so, they shall not rank as *marks.*

7.2 TIMING THE START
The *start* of a yacht shall be timed from her starting signal.

8   Recalls

8.1 INDIVIDUAL RECALL
Unless otherwise prescribed in the sailing instructions, when, at her starting signal, any part of a yacht's hull, crew or equipment is on the course side of the starting line or its extensions, or she has not complied with rule 51.1(c), Sailing the Course, the race committee shall promptly display Code flag "X", accompanied by one sound signal, until all such yachts are wholly on the pre-start side of the starting line or its extensions and have complied with rule 51.1(c) when applicable, or for four minutes after the starting signal,

whichever is the earlier. The sailing instructions may prescribe that the race committee will also hail the yacht's sail number.

8.2 GENERAL RECALL

(a) When there is either a number of unidentified premature starters or an error in starting procedure, the race committee may make a general recall signal in accordance with rules 4.1 "First Substitute", Visual Signals, and 4.3, Calling Attention to Visual Signals.

(b) Except as provided in rule 31.2, Rule Infringement, rule infringements before the preparatory signal for the new start shall be disregarded for the purpose of competing in the race to be re-started.

9 Marks

9.1 MARK MISSING

(a) When any *mark* either is missing or has shifted, the race committee shall, when possible, replace it in its stated position, or substitute a new one with similar characteristics or a buoy or vessel displaying Code flag "M"—the *mark* signal.

(b) When it is impossible either to replace the *mark* or to substitute a new one in time for the yachts to round or pass it, the race committee may, at its discretion, act in accordance with rule 5.4(c)(iii), Designating the Course, Altering the Course or Race.

9.2 MARK UNSEEN

When races are *sailed* in fog or at night, dead reckoning alone need not necessarily be accepted as evidence that a *mark* has been rounded or passed.

10 Finishing Within a Time Limit

Unless otherwise prescribed in the sailing instructions, in races where there is a time limit, one yacht *finishing* within the prescribed limit shall make the race valid for all other yachts in that race.

11 Ties

When there is a tie at the finish of a race, either actual or on corrected times, the points for the place for which the yachts have tied and for the place immediately below shall be added together and divided equally. When two or more yachts tie for a trophy or prize in either a single race or a series, the yachts so tied shall, when practicable, *sail* a deciding race; if not, either the tie shall be broken by a method established under rule 3.2(a)(viii), Sailing

Instructions, or the yachts so tied shall either receive equal prizes or share the prize.

12 Races to be Re-sailed

When a race is to be re-sailed:

(a) All yachts entered in the original race shall be eligible to *start* in the race to be re-sailed.

(b) Subject to the entry requirements of the original race, and at the discretion of the race committee, new entries may be accepted.

(c) Rule infringements in the original race shall be disregarded for the purpose of competing in the race to be re-sailed.

(d) The race committee shall notify the yachts concerned when and where the race will be re-sailed.

(Numbers 13, 14, 15, 16 and 17 are spare numbers.)

PART III—GENERAL REQUIREMENTS

Owner's Responsibilities for Qualifying his Yacht

A yacht intending to **race** *shall, to avoid subsequent disqualification, comply with the rules of Part III before her preparatory signal and, when applicable, while* **racing.**

18 Entries

Unless otherwise prescribed either in the notice of race or in the sailing instructions, entries shall be made in the following form:

FORM OF ENTRY

To the Secretary_____Club
Please enter the yacht_____for
the_____race, on the _____
her national letters and sail number are_____
her rig is_____
the colour of her hull is_____
and her rating or class is_____

I agree to be bound by the racing rules of the IYRU, by the prescriptions of the national authority under which this race is sailed, by the sailing instructions and by the class rules.

Name_____

Address_____

Telephone No._____

Club_____

Address during event_____

Telephone No._____

Signed_____Date_____

(Owner or owner's representative)
Entrance fee enclosed

19   Measurement or Rating Certificates

19.1 Every yacht entering a race shall hold such valid measurement or rating certificate as is required by the national authority or other duly authorised body, by her class rules, by the notice of race, or by the sailing instructions.

19.2 An owner shall be responsible for maintaining his yacht in accordance with her class rules and for ensuring that her certificate is not invalidated by alterations. Deviations in excess of tolerances specified in the class rules caused by normal wear or damage and that do not affect the performance of the yacht shall not invalidate the measurement or rating certificate of the yacht for a particular race, but shall be rectified before she *races* again, unless in the opinion of the race committee there has been no practicable opportunity to rectify the wear or damage.

19.3 (a) The owner of a yacht who cannot produce such a certificate when required, may be permitted to sign and lodge with the race committee, before she *starts,* a statement in the following form:

To the Secretary_____Club

UNDERTAKING TO PRODUCE CERTIFICATE

The yacht_____competes in the_____
race on condition that a valid certificate previously issued by the authorised administrative body, or a copy of it, is submitted to the race committee before the end of the series, and that she competes in the race(s) on the measurement or rating of that certificate.

Signed_____

(Owner or his representative)

Date_____

(b) In this event the sailing instructions may require that the owner shall lodge such a deposit as may be required by the organising authority, which may be forfeited when such certificate or copy is not submitted to the race committee within the prescribed period.

20   Ownership of Yachts

20.1 A yacht shall be eligible to compete only when she is either owned by or on charter to and has been entered by a yacht or sailing club recognised by its national authority or a member or members thereof.

20.2 Two or more yachts owned or chartered wholly or in part by the same body or person shall not compete in the same race without the previous consent of the race committee.

20.3 An owner shall not steer any yacht other than his own in a race wherein his own yacht competes without the previous consent of the race committee.

21   Member on Board

Every yacht shall have on board a member of a yacht or sailing club recognised by its national authority to be in charge of the yacht as owner or owner's representative.

22   Shifting Ballast

22.1 GENERAL RESTRICTIONS
Floorboards shall be kept down; bulkheads and doors left standing; ladders, stairways and water tanks left in place; all cabin, galley and forecastle fixtures and fittings kept on board; all movable ballast shall be properly stowed under the floorboards or in lockers and no dead weight shall be shifted.

22.2 SHIPPING, UNSHIPPING OR SHIFTING BALLAST; WATER
From 2100 on the day before the race until she is no longer *racing,* a yacht shall not ship, unship or shift ballast, whether movable or fixed, or take in or discharge water, except for ordinary ship's use and the removal of bilge water. This rule shall not apply to wearing or carrying clothing, equipment or ballast in compliance with Rule 61, Clothing and Equipment.

23   Anchor

Unless otherwise prescribed by her class rules, every yacht shall carry on board an anchor and chain or rope of suitable size.

24 Life-Saving Equipment

Unless otherwise prescribed by her class rules, every yacht shall carry adequate life-saving equipment for all persons on board, one item of which shall be ready for immediate use.

(USYRU prescribes that, irrespective of any provisions in the class rules or sailing instructions, every yacht shall carry life-saving equipment conforming to government regulations.)

25 Class Insignia, National Letters and Sail Numbers

25.1 Every yacht of an international class recognised by the IYRU shall carry on her mainsail and, as provided in rule 25.3(c), on her spinnaker:

(a) The insignia denoting the class to which she belongs.

(b) A letter or letters showing her nationality, thus:

A	Argentina	F	France
AE	Dubai	FL	Liechtenstein
AL	Algeria	G	Federal Republic of
ANU	Antigua		Germany
AR	Egypt	GM	Guam
B	Belgium	GR	Greece
BA	Bahamas	GU	Guatemala
BH	Bahrain	H	Holland
BL	Brazil	HA	Netherlands Antilles
BR	Burma	I	Italy
BU	Bulgaria	IL	Iceland
CB	Colombia	IND	India
CH	China	IR	Ireland
CI	Grand Cayman	IS	Israel
CP	Cyprus	J	Japan
CY	Sri Lanka	K	United Kingdom
CZ	Czechoslovakia	KA	Australia
D	Denmark	KB	Bermuda
DDR	German Democratic	KBA	Barbados
	Republic	KC	Canada
DJ	Djibouti	KF	Fiji
DK	Democratic People's	KH	Hong Kong
	Republic of Korea	KJ	Jamaica
DR	Dominican Republic	KK	Kenya
E	Spain	KP	Papua New Guinea
EC	Ecuador	KS	Singapore

KT	Trinidad and Tobago	RC	Cuba
KV	British Virgin Is.	RI	Indonesia
KZ	New Zealand	RM	Roumania
L	Finland	S	Sweden
LX	Luxembourg	SA	South Africa
M	Hungary	SE	Senegal
MA	Morocco	RSK	Republic of Korea
MO	Monaco	SM	San Marino
MT	Malta	SR	Union of Soviet Socialist
MX	Mexico		Republics
MY	Malaysia	TA	Chinese Taipei
N	Norway	TH	Thailand
OE	Austria	TK	Turkey
OM	Oman	TN	Tunisia
P	Portugal	U	Uruguay
PH	Philippines	US	United States of America
PK	Pakistan	V	Venezuela
PR	Puerto Rico	VI	U.S. Virgin Is.
PU	Peru	X	Chile
PY	Paraguay	Y	Yugoslavia
PZ	Poland	Z	Switzerland
Q	Kuwait	ZB	Zimbabwe
RB	Botswana		

National letters need not be carried in home waters, except in an international championship.

(c) (i) A sail number allotted to her by her national authority or, when so prescribed by the class rules, by the international class association.

(ii) When so prescribed by the class rules, an owner may be allotted a personal sail number by the relevant issuing authority, which may be used on all his yachts in that class instead of the sail numbers allotted to such yachts in accordance with rule 25.1(c)(i).

25.2 The following specifications and minimum sizes of national letters and sail numbers shall apply.

(a) They shall be:

(i) clearly visible, legible and, unless otherwise prescribed by the class rules, of a single colour that strongly contrasts with the sail, and

(ii) in roman style (upright), without serifs, with arabic numerals, and with lines that are continuous and of uniform thickness.

(b) The minimum sizes for national letters and sail numbers shall be related to the yacht's overall length (LOA) and shall be as follows:

LOA	Height	Width excl. number 1 and letter I	Thickness	Space between adjoining letters & nos.
Under 3.5 m	230 mm	150 mm	30 mm	45 mm
3.5 m–8.5 m	300 mm	200 mm	40 mm	60 mm
8.5 m–11 m	375 mm	250 mm	50 mm	75 mm
Over 11 m	450 mm	300 mm	60 mm	90 mm

The size and style requirements of rules 25.2(a) and (b) shall not apply to sails made prior to 1st May, 1989.

(c) National letters shall be placed in front of or above the sail numbers. When the national letters end in "I" (e.g. Italy, U.S. Virgin Islands) and are placed in front of the numbers, they shall be separated from them by a horizontal line approximately 50 mm long.

25.3 The following positioning of class insignia, national letters and sail numbers on the sail shall apply.

(a) Unless otherwise prescribed by the class rules, the class insignia, national letter(s) and sail numbers shall be above an imaginary line projecting at right angles to the luff from a point one-third of the distance, measured from the tack, to the head of the sail; and shall be placed at different heights on the two sides of the sail, those on the starboard side being uppermost.

(b) Where the class insignia is of such a design that, when placed back to back on the two sides of the sail, they coincide, they may be so placed.

(c) The national letters and sail numbers only shall be similarly placed on both sides of the spinnaker, but at approximately half-height.

25.4 Other yachts shall comply with the rules of their national authority or class in regard to the allotment, carrying and size of insignia, letters and numbers, which rules shall, when practicable, conform to the above requirements.

(Consult USYRU rulebook for USYRU prescription.)

25.5 When so prescribed in the notice of race or in the sailing instructions, a yacht chartered or loaned for an event may carry national letters or sail numbers in contravention of her class rules. In all other respects the sails shall comply with the class rules.

25.6 A yacht shall not be disqualified for infringing the provisions of rule 25 without prior warning and adequate opportunity to make correction.

26   Event Classification; Advertising

A yacht and her crew shall *race* in conformity with Appendix 14, Event Classification and Advertising.

27   Forestays and Jib Tacks

Unless otherwise prescribed by the class rules, forestays and jib tacks (not including spinnaker staysails when not *close-hauled*) shall be fixed approximately in the centre-line of the yacht.

(Numbers 28, 29 and 30 are spare numbers.)

PART IV—RIGHT OF WAY RULES

Rights and Obligations when Yachts Meet

The rules of Part IV do not apply in any way to a vessel that is neither intending to **race** *nor* **racing***; such vessel shall be treated in accordance with the International Regulations for Preventing Collisions at Sea or Government Right of Way Rules applicable to the area concerned. The rules of Part IV apply only between yachts that are either intending to* **race** *or are* **racing** *in the same or different races, and, except when rule 3.2(b)(xxix), Race Continues After Sunset, applies, replace the International Regulations for Preventing Collisions at Sea or Government Right of Way Rules applicable to the area concerned, from the time a yacht intending to* **race** *begins to* **sail** *about in the vicinity of the starting line until she has either* **finished** *or retired and has left the vicinity of the course. (See Appendix 9.)*

Section A—Obligations and Penalties

31   Rule Infringement

31.1 A yacht may be penalised for infringing a rule of Part IV only when the infringement occurs while she is *racing*.

31.2 A yacht may be penalised, before or after she is *racing,* for seriously hindering a yacht that is *racing* or for infringing the sailing instructions.

32 Serious Damage

32.1 AVOIDING COLLISIONS
When a collision has resulted in serious damage, the right-of-way yacht shall be penalised as well as the other yacht when she had the opportunity but failed to make a reasonable attempt to avoid the collision.

32.2 HAILING
Except when *luffing* under rule 38.1, Luffing Rights, a right-of-way yacht that does not hail before or when making an alteration of course that may not be foreseen by the other yacht may be penalised as well as the yacht required to keep clear when a collision resulting in serious damage occurs.

33 Contact between Yachts Racing

When there is contact that is not both minor and unavoidable between the hulls, equipment or crew of two yachts, both shall be penalised unless:

either

(a) one of the yachts retires in acknowledgement of the infringement, or exonerates herself by accepting an alternative penalty when so pre-scribed in the sailing instructions,

or

(b) one or both of these yachts lodges a valid **protest.**

34 Maintaining Rights

When a yacht that may have infringed a **rule** does not retire or exonerate herself, other yachts shall continue to accord her such rights as she has under the rules of Part IV.

Section B—Principal Right of Way Rules and their Limitations

These rules apply except when over-ridden by a rule in Section C.

35 Limitations on Altering Course

When one yacht is required to keep clear of another, the right-of-way yacht shall not alter course so as to prevent the other yacht from keeping clear; or so as to obstruct her while she is keeping clear, except:

(a) to the extent permitted by rule 38.1, Luffing Rights, and

(b) when assuming a *proper course:*
either

   (i) to *start,* unless subject to rule 40, Same Tack, Luffing before Clearing the Starting Line, or to the second part of rule 44.1(b), Returning to Start,

   or

   (ii) when rounding a *mark.*

36   Opposite Tacks—Basic Rule

A *port-tack* yacht shall keep clear of a *starboard-tack* yacht.

37   Same Tack—Basic Rules

37.1 WHEN OVERLAPPED
A *windward yacht* shall keep clear of a *leeward yacht.*

37.2 WHEN NOT OVERLAPPED
A yacht *clear astern* shall keep clear of a yacht *clear ahead.*

37.3 TRANSITIONAL
A yacht that establishes an *overlap* to *leeward* from *clear astern* shall initially allow the *windward yacht* ample room and opportunity to keep clear.

38   Same Tack—Luffing after Clearing the Starting Line

38.1 LUFFING RIGHTS
After she has *started* and cleared the starting line, a yacht *clear ahead* or a *leeward yacht* may *luff* as she pleases, subject to the following limitations of this rule.

38.2 LIMITATIONS

(a) Proper Course Limitations:
A *leeward yacht* shall not *sail* above her *proper course* while an *overlap* exists, if when the *overlap* began or at any time during its existence, the helmsman of the *windward yacht* (when sighting abeam

from his normal station and *sailing* no higher than the *leeward yacht*) has been abreast or forward of the mainmast of the *leeward yacht.*

(b) Overlap Limitations:
For the purpose of rule 38 only: An *overlap* does not exist unless the yachts are clearly within two overall lengths of the longer yacht; and an *overlap* that exists between two yachts when the leading yacht *starts,* or when one or both of them completes a *tack* or *gybe,* shall be regarded as a new *overlap* beginning at that time.

(c) Hailing to Stop or Prevent a Luff:
When there is doubt, the *leeward yacht* may assume that she has the right to *luff* or *sail* above her *proper course* unless the helmsman of the *windward yacht* has hailed either:

(i) "Mast Abeam", or words to that effect, or

(ii) "Obstruction", or words to that effect.

The *leeward yacht* shall be governed by such hail and curtail her *luff.* When she deems the hail improper, her only remedy is to protest.

(d) Curtailing a Luff:
The *windward yacht* shall not cause a *luff* to be curtailed because of her proximity to the *leeward yacht* unless an *obstruction,* a third yacht or other object restricts her ability to respond.

(e) Luffing Rights over Two or More Yachts:
A yacht shall not *luff* unless she has the right to *luff* all yachts that would be affected by her *luff,* in which case they shall all respond, even when an intervening yacht or yachts would not otherwise have the right to *luff.*

39 Same Tack—Sailing below a Proper Course after Starting

A yacht that is on a free leg of the course shall not *sail* below her *proper course* when she is clearly within three of her overall lengths of a *leeward yacht* or of a yacht *clear astern* that is steering a course to *leeward* of her own.

40 Same Tack—Luffing before Clearing the Starting Line

Before a yacht *clear ahead* or a *leeward yacht* has *started* and cleared the starting line, any *luff* on her part that causes another yacht to have to alter course to avoid a collision shall be carried out slowly and initially in such a way as to give a *windward yacht* room and opportunity to keep clear. Furthermore, the *leeward yacht* shall not so *luff* above a *close-hauled* course while the helmsman of the *windward yacht* (sighting abeam from his normal station) is abreast or forward of the mainmast of the *leeward yacht*. Rules 38.2(c), Hailing to Stop or Prevent a Luff; 38.2(d), Curtailing a Luff; and 38.2(e), Luffing Rights over Two or More Yachts, also apply.

41 Changing Tacks—Tacking and Gybing

41.1 BASIC RULE
A yacht that is either *tacking* or *gybing* shall keep clear of a yacht on a *tack*.

41.2 TRANSITIONAL
A yacht shall neither *tack* nor *gybe* into a position that will give her right of way, unless she does so far enough from a yacht *on a tack* to enable this yacht to keep clear without having to begin to alter her course until after the *tack* or *gybe* has been completed.

41.3 ONUS
A yacht that *tacks* or *gybes* has the onus of satisfying the **protest committee** that she completed her *tack* or *gybe* in accordance with rule 41.2.

41.4 WHEN SIMULTANEOUS
When two yachts are both *tacking* or both *gybing* at the same time, the one on the other's port side shall keep clear.

Section C—Rules that Apply at Marks and Obstructions and other Exceptions to the Rules of Section B

When a rule of this section applies, to the extent to which it explicitly provides rights and obligations, it over-rides any conflicting rule of Section B, Principal Right of Way Rules and their Limitations, except rule 35, Limitations on Altering Course.

42 Rounding or Passing Marks and Obstructions

Rule 42 applies when yachts are about to round or pass a *mark* on the same required side or an *obstruction* on the same side, except that it shall not apply:

(a) between two yachts on opposite *tacks:*

    (i) when they are on a beat, or

    (ii) when one, but not both, of them will have to *tack* either to round or pass the *mark* or to avoid the *obstruction,* or

(b) when rule 42.4 applies.

42.1 WHEN OVERLAPPED
An Outside Yacht

(a) An outside yacht shall give each inside *overlapping* yacht room to round or pass the *mark* or *obstruction* except as provided in rule 42.3. Room is the space needed by an inside *overlapping* yacht, that is handled in a seamanlike manner in the prevailing conditions, to pass in safety between an outside yacht and a *mark* or *obstruction,* and includes space to *tack* or *gybe* when either is an integral part of the rounding or passing manoeuvre.

(b) An outside yacht *overlapped* when she comes within two of her overall lengths of a *mark* or *obstruction* shall give room as required, even though the *overlap* may thereafter be broken.

(c) An outside yacht that claims to have broken an *overlap* has the onus of satisfying the **protest committee** that she became *clear ahead* when she was more than two of her overall lengths from the *mark* or *obstruction.*

An Inside Yacht

(d) A yacht that claims an inside *overlap* has the onus of satisfying the **protest committee** that she established the *overlap* in accordance with rule 42.3.

(e) When an inside yacht of two or more *overlapped* yachts, either on opposite *tacks* or on the same *tack* without *luffing* rights, will have to *gybe* in order most directly to assume a *proper course* to the next *mark,* she shall *gybe* at the first reasonable opportunity.

Hailing

(f) A yacht that hails when claiming the establishment or termination of an *overlap* or insufficiency of room at a *mark* or *obstruction* thereby helps to support her claim.

42.2 WHEN NOT OVERLAPPED
A Yacht Clear Astern

(a) A yacht *clear astern* when the yacht *clear ahead* comes within two of her overall lengths of a *mark* or *obstruction* shall keep clear in anticipation of and during the rounding or passing manoeuvre, whether the yacht *clear ahead* remains on the same *tack* or *gybes.*

(b) A yacht *clear astern* shall not *luff* above *close-hauled* so as to prevent a yacht *clear ahead* from *tacking* to round a *mark.*

A Yacht Clear Ahead

(c) A yacht *clear ahead* that *tacks* to round a *mark* is subject to rule 41, Changing Tacks—Tacking and Gybing.

(d) A yacht *clear ahead* shall be under no obligation to give room to a yacht *clear astern* before an *overlap* is established.

42.3 LIMITATIONS

(a) Limitation on Establishing an Overlap
A yacht that establishes an inside *overlap* from *clear astern* is entitled to room under rule 42.1(a) only when, at that time, the outside yacht:

  (i) is able to give room, and

  (ii) is more than two of her overall lengths from the *mark* or *obstruction.* However, when a yacht completes a *tack* within two of her overall lengths of a *mark* or *obstruction,* she shall give room as required by rule 42.1(a) to a yacht that, by *luffing,* cannot thereafter avoid establishing a late inside *overlap.*

At a continuing *obstruction,* rule 42.3(b) applies.

(b) Limitation When an Obstruction is a Continuing One
A yacht *clear astern* may establish an *overlap* between a yacht *clear ahead* and a continuing *obstruction,* such as a shoal or the shore or another vessel, only when, at that time, there is room for her to pass between them in safety.

42.4 AT A STARTING MARK SURROUNDED BY NAVIGABLE WATER
When approaching the starting line to *start* until clearing the starting *marks* after *starting,* a *leeward yacht* shall be under no obligation to give any *windward yacht* room to pass to leeward of a starting *mark* surrounded by navigable water, including such a *mark* that is also an *obstruction;* but, after the starting signal, a *leeward yacht* shall not deprive a *windward yacht* of room at such a *mark* by *sailing* either:

(a) to windward of the compass bearing of the course to the next *mark,* or

(b) above *close-hauled.*

43 Close-Hauled, Hailing for Room to Tack at Obstructions

CAN INCLUDE STBD BOAT.

43.1 HAILING

When two *close-hauled* yachts are on the same *tack* and safe pilotage requires the yacht *clear ahead* or the *leeward yacht* to make a substantial alteration of course to clear an *obstruction,* and when she intends to *tack,* but cannot *tack* without colliding with the other yacht, she shall hail the other yacht for room to *tack* and clear the other yacht, but she shall not hail and *tack* simultaneously.

43.2 RESPONDING

The hailed yacht at the earliest possible moment after the hail shall either:

(a) *tack,* in which case the hailing yacht shall begin to *tack* immediately she is able to *tack* and clear the other yacht; or

(b) reply "You *tack*", or words to that effect, in which case:

    (i) the hailing yacht shall immediately *tack* and

    (ii) the hailed yacht shall give the hailing yacht room to *tack* and clear her.

    (iii) The onus of satisfying the **protest committee** that she gave sufficient room shall lie on the hailed yacht that replied "You *tack*".

43.3 WHEN AN OBSTRUCTION IS ALSO A MARK

(a) When an *obstruction* is a starting *mark* surrounded by navigable water, or the ground tackle of such a *mark,* and when approaching the starting line to *start* and after *starting,* the yacht *clear ahead* or the *leeward yacht* shall not be entitled to room to *tack.*

(b) At other *obstructions* that are *marks,* when the hailed yacht can fetch the *obstruction,* the hailing yacht shall not be entitled to room to *tack* and clear the hailed yacht, and the hailed yacht shall immediately so inform the hailing yacht. When, thereafter, the hailing yacht again hails for room to *tack* and clear the hailed yacht, the hailed yacht shall, at the earliest possible moment after the hail, give the hailing yacht the required room. After receiving room, the hailing yacht shall either retire immediately or exonerate herself by accepting an alternative penalty when so prescribed in the sailing instructions.

(c) When, after having refused to respond to a hail under rule 43.3(b), the hailed yacht fails to fetch, she shall retire immediately or exonerate herself by accepting an alternative penalty when so prescribed in the sailing instructions.

44   Returning to Start

44.1 (a) After the starting signal, a premature starter returning to *start*, or a yacht working into position from the course side of the starting line or its extensions, shall keep clear of all yachts that are *starting* or have *started* correctly, until she is wholly on the pre-start side of the starting line or its extensions.

(b) Thereafter, she shall be accorded the rights under the rules of Part IV of a yacht that is *starting* correctly; but when she thereby acquires right of way over another yacht that is *starting* correctly, she shall allow that yacht ample room and opportunity to keep clear.

44.2 A premature starter, while continuing to *sail* the course and until it is obvious that she is returning to *start*, shall be accorded the rights under the rules of Part IV of a yacht that has *started*.

45   Keeping Clear after Touching a Mark

45.1 A yacht that has touched a *mark* and is exonerating herself shall keep clear of all other yachts until she has completed her exoneration and, when she has *started*, is on a *proper course* to the next *mark*.

45.2 A yacht that has touched a *mark*, while continuing to *sail* the course and until it is obvious that she is exonerating herself shall be accorded rights under the rules of Part IV.

46   Person Overboard; Yacht Anchored, Aground or Capsized

46.1 A yacht under way shall keep clear of another yacht *racing* that:

(a) is manoeuvring or hailing for the purpose of rescuing a person overboard, or

(b) is anchored, aground or capsized.

46.2 A yacht shall not be penalised when she is unable to avoid fouling a yacht that she is attempting to assist or that goes aground or is capsized.

46.3 A yacht is capsized from the time her masthead is in the water until her masthead is clear of the water and she has steerageway.

46.4 A yacht anchored or aground shall indicate the fact to any yacht that may be in danger of fouling her. Under normal conditions, a hail is sufficient indication. Of two yachts anchored, the one that anchored later shall keep clear, except that a yacht dragging shall keep clear of one that is not.

(Numbers 47, 48 and 49 are spare numbers.)

PART V—OTHER SAILING RULES

Obligations in Handling a Yacht

*A yacht is subject to the rules of Part V only while she is **racing**.*

50   Ranking as a Starter

A yacht whose entry has been accepted and that *sails* about in the vicinity of the starting line between her preparatory and starting signals shall rank as a starter whether she *starts* or not.

51   Sailing the Course

51.1 (a)   A yacht shall *start* and *finish* only as prescribed in the starting and finishing definitions.

(b)   When any part of a yacht's hull, crew or equipment is on the course side of the starting line or its extensions at the starting signal, she shall thereafter *start* in accordance with the definition.

(c)   When Code flag "I" has been displayed, and when any part of a yacht's hull, crew or equipment is on the course side of the starting line or its extensions during the minute before her starting signal, she shall *sail* to the pre-start side of the line across one of its extensions and *start*.

(d)   Failure of a yacht to see or hear her recall signal shall not relieve her of her obligation to *start* correctly.

51.2   A yacht shall *sail* the course so as to round or pass each *mark* on the required side in correct sequence, and so that a string representing her wake, from the time she *starts* until she *finishes,* would, when drawn taut, lie on the required side of each *mark,* touching each rounding *mark.*

51.3   A *mark* has a required side for a yacht as long as she is on a leg that it begins, bounds or ends. A starting line *mark* begins to have a required side for a yacht when she *starts.* A starting limit *mark* has a required side for a yacht from the time she is approaching the starting line to *start* until she has left the *mark* astern on the first leg. A finishing line *mark* and a finishing limit *mark* cease to have a required side for a yacht when she *finishes.*

51.4   A yacht that rounds or passes a *mark* on the wrong side may exonerate herself by making her course conform to the requirements of rule 51.2.

51.5   It is not necessary for a yacht to cross the finishing line completely; after *finishing,* she may clear it in either direction.

(51.6 USYRU prescribes that, in the absence of the race committee, a yacht shall take her own finishing time and report it to the race committee as soon as possible. If there is no longer an established finishing line, it shall be a line extending from the required side of the finishing mark at right angles to the course from the last mark and of the shortest practical length.)

52   Touching a Mark

52.1 A yacht shall neither:

(a) touch:

   (i) a starting *mark* before *starting,* or

   (ii) a *mark* that begins, bounds or ends the leg of the course on which she is *sailing,* or

   (iii) a finishing *mark* after *finishing* and before clearing the finishing line and *marks,*

nor

(b) cause a *mark* or *mark* vessel to shift to avoid being touched.

52.2 (a) When a yacht infringes rule 52.1, she may exonerate herself by *sailing* well clear of all other yachts as soon as possible after the incident, and remaining clear while she makes two complete 360° turns (720°) in the same direction, including two *tacks* and two *gybes.*

(b) When a yacht touches a finishing *mark,* she shall not rank as having *finished* until she first completes her turns and thereafter *finishes.*

52.3 When a yacht is wrongfully compelled by another yacht to infringe rule 52.1, she shall be exonerated:

(a) by the retirement of the other yacht (or by the other yacht accepting an alternative penalty when so prescribed in the sailing instructions), in acknowledgement of the incident, or

(b) in accordance with rule 74.4(b), Penalties and Exoneration, after lodging a valid **protest.**

53   Casting Off, Anchoring, Making Fast and Hauling Out

53.1 AT THE PREPARATORY SIGNAL
A yacht shall be afloat and off moorings at her preparatory signal, but may be anchored.

53.2 WHEN RACING

A yacht may anchor, but shall not make fast or be made fast by means other than anchoring, nor be hauled out, except for the purpose of rule 55, Aground or Foul of an Obstruction, or to effect repairs, reef sails or bail out.

53.3 MEANS OF ANCHORING

Means of anchoring may include the crew standing on the bottom or any weight lowered to the bottom. A yacht shall recover any anchor or weight used, and any chain or rope attached to it, before continuing in the race, unless, after making every effort, she fails to do so. In this case she shall report the circumstances to the race committee, which may penalise her when it considers the loss due either to inadequate gear or to insufficient effort to recover it.

54 Propulsion

54.1 BASIC RULE

Except when permitted by rule 54.3, a yacht shall compete only by *sailing,* and her crew shall not otherwise move their bodies to propel the yacht. Fundamental Rule A, Rendering Assistance, and rule 55, Aground or Foul of an Obstruction, over-ride rule 54.

54.2 PROHIBITED ACTIONS

Without limiting the application of rule 54.1, these actions are prohibited:

(a) pumping—repeated fanning of any sail either by trimming and releasing the sail or by vertical or athwartships body movement;

(b) rocking—repeated rolling of the yacht induced either by body movement or adjustment of the sails or centreboard;

(c) ooching—sudden forward body movement, stopped abruptly;

(d) sculling—repeated movement of the helm not necessary for steering;

(e) repeated *tacks* and *gybes* unrelated to changes in the wind or to tactical considerations.

54.3 EXCEPTIONS

(a) Immediately before, during and immediately after a *tack* or *gybe,* the yacht's crew may move their bodies to roll the yacht, provided that such movements do not:

(i) advance the yacht further in the race than she would have advanced in the absence of the *tack* or *gybe,* or

(ii) move her mast away from the vertical more than once.

(b) On a free leg of the course, when surfing (rapidly accelerating down the leeward side of a wave) or planing is possible, the yacht's crew may, in order to initiate surfing or planing, pump the sheet, but not the guy, controlling any sail, but only once for each wave or gust of wind. When the mainsail is pumped, only that part of the sheet between the crew member handling the sheet and the first block on the boom shall be used.

(c) Class rules may alter or add to rule 54.3(b).

55   Aground or Foul of an Obstruction

A yacht, after grounding or fouling another vessel or other object, is subject to rule 57, Manual and Stored Power, and may, in getting clear, use her own anchors, boats, ropes, spars and other gear; may send out an anchor in a boat; may be refloated by her crew going overboard either to stand on the bottom or to go ashore to push off; but may receive outside assistance only from the crew of the vessel fouled. A yacht shall recover all her own gear used in getting clear before continuing in the race.

56   Sounding

Any means of sounding may be used, provided that rule 54, Propulsion, is not infringed.

57   Manual and Stored Power

A yacht's standing rigging, running rigging, spars and movable hull appendages shall be adjusted and operated by manual power only, and no device shall be used for these operations that derives assistance from stored energy for doing work. A power winch or windlass may be used in weighing anchor or in getting clear after running aground or fouling any object, and a power pump may be used in an auxiliary yacht.

58   Boarding

Unless otherwise prescribed in the sailing instructions, no person shall board a yacht, except for the purposes of Fundamental Rule A, Rendering Assistance, or to attend an injured or ill member of the crew or temporarily as one of the crew of a vessel fouled.

59   Leaving, Crew Overboard

Unless otherwise prescribed in the sailing instructions, no person on board a yacht when she begins *racing* shall leave, unless injured or ill, or for the purposes of Fundamental Rule A, Rendering Assistance, except that any member of the crew may fall overboard or leave her to swim, stand on the bottom as a means of anchoring, haul her out ashore to effect repairs, reef sails or bail out, or to help her to get clear after grounding or fouling another vessel or object, provided that this person is back on board before the yacht continues in the race.

60 Outside Assistance

Except as permitted by Fundamental Rule A, Rendering Assistance, rule 55, Aground or Foul of an Obstruction, and rule 58, Boarding, a yacht shall neither receive outside assistance nor use any gear other than that on board when her preparatory signal was made.

61 Clothing and Equipment

61.1 (a) Except as permitted by rule 61.2, a competitor shall not wear or carry clothing or equipment for the purpose of increasing his weight.

(b) Furthermore, the total weight of clothing and equipment worn or carried by a competitor shall not be capable of exceeding 15 kilograms, when soaked with water and weighed as provided in Appendix 10, Weighing of Wet Clothing, unless class rules or the sailing instructions prescribe a lesser or greater weight, in which case such weight shall apply, except that it shall not exceed 20 kilograms.

61.2 When so prescribed by the class rules, weight jackets of non-metallic material (excepting normal fasteners), with or without pockets, compartments or containers, shall be permitted, provided that the jacket:

(a) is permanently buoyant,

(b) does not extend more than 30 mm above the competitor's shoulders, and

(c) can be removed by the competitor in less than ten seconds,

and that ballast carried in the pockets, compartments and containers shall only be water. For the purpose of rule 61.1(b), the pockets, compartments and containers shall be filled completely with water and included in the total weight.

61.3 When a competitor is protested or selected for inspection, he shall produce all containers referred to in rule 61.2 that were carried while *racing*.

61.4 Unless otherwise prescribed in the sailing instructions, rule 61.1(b) shall not apply in events for cruiser-racer type yachts required to be equipped with lifelines.

62   Increasing Stability

(a) Unless otherwise prescribed by the class rules, a yacht shall not use any device, such as a trapeze or plank, to project outboard the weight of any of the crew.

(b) When lifelines are required by the class rules or the sailing instructions, no crew member shall station any part of his torso outside them, except when it is necessary to perform a task, and then only temporarily. On yachts equipped with upper and lower lifelines of wire, a crew member sitting on the deck facing outboard with his waist inside the lower lifeline may have the upper part of his body outside the upper lifeline.

63   Skin Friction

A yacht:

(a) shall not eject or release from a container any substance (such as polymer), or

(b) unless otherwise prescribed by her class rules, shall not have specially textured hull or appendage surfaces,

the purpose of which is, or could be, to reduce the frictional resistance of her surface by altering the character of the flow of water inside the boundary layer.

64   Setting and Sheeting Sails

64.1 CHANGING SAILS
While changing headsails and spinnakers, a replacing sail may be fully set and trimmed before the sail it replaces is taken in, but only one mainsail and, except when changing, only one spinnaker shall be carried set.

64.2 SPINNAKER BOOMS
Only one spinnaker boom shall be used at a time and, when in use, shall be attached to and carried only on the side of the foremost mast opposite to the main boom and shall be fixed to the mast.

64.3 SPINNAKERS
A spinnaker, including a headsail set as a spinnaker, shall not be set without a boom. The tack of a spinnaker that is set and drawing shall be in close proximity to the outboard end of the spinnaker boom, except when hoisting, *gybing* or lowering the spinnaker.

64.4 USE OF OUTRIGGERS

(a) No sail shall be sheeted over or through an outrigger, except as permitted in rule 64.4(b). An outrigger is any fitting or other device so placed that it could exert outward pressure on a sheet or sail at a point from which, with the yacht upright, a vertical line would fall outside the hull or deck planking. For the purpose of this rule: bulwarks, rails and rubbing strakes are not part of the hull or deck planking. A boom of a boomed headsail that requires no adjustment when *tacking* is not an outrigger.

(b) (i) Any sail may be sheeted to or led above a boom regularly used for a working sail and permanently attached to the mast from which the head of the working sail is set.

(ii) A headsail may be sheeted or attached at its clew to a spinnaker boom, provided that a spinnaker is not set.

64.5 HEADSAILS
The following distinction shall apply between spinnakers and headsails. A headsail is a sail in which the mid-girth, measured from the mid-points of the luff and leech, does not exceed 50% of the length of the foot, and in which any other intermediate girth does not exceed a value similarly proportional to its distance from the head of the sail. A sail tacked down abaft the foremost mast is not a headsail.

64.6 Class rules may alter or add to this rule.

65   Flags

A national authority may prescribe the flag usage that shall be observed by yachts under its jurisdiction.

(USYRU prescribes that a yacht may display her private signal on the leech of her mainsail or from her mizzen head, and a wind indicator of a solid color or a feather. Other flags shall not be displayed except for signaling. A yacht shall not be penalized for infringing the provisions of this rule without prior warning and adequate opportunity to make correction.)

66   Fog Signals and Lights

Every yacht shall observe the International Regulations for Preventing Collisions at Sea or Government Rules for fog signals and, as a minimum, the exhibition of lights at night.

(USYRU prescribes that the use of additional special purpose lights such as masthead, spreader, or jib luff lights shall not constitute grounds for protest.)

(Number 67 is a spare number.)

PART VI—PROTESTS, PENALTIES AND APPEALS

Definitions

When a term defined below is used in its defined sense, it is printed in **bold type.**
The definitions rank as rules.

Rules—

(a) These racing rules,

(b) the prescriptions of the national authority concerned, when they apply,

(c) the sailing instructions,

(d) the appropriate class rules, and

(e) any other conditions governing the event.

Protest—An allegation by a yacht under rule 68, Protests by Yachts, that another yacht has infringed a **rule** or **rules.**

The term **protest** includes when appropriate:

(a) a request for redress under rule 69, Requests for Redress; or

(b) a request for a hearing under rule 70.1(c), Action by Race or Protest Committee, or Appendix 3, rule 2.6, Alternative Penalties; or

(c) a notification of a hearing under rule 70.2, Action by Race or Protest Committee; or

(d) an investigation of redress under rule 70.3, Yacht Materially Prejudiced; or

(e) a report by a measurer under rule 70.4, Measurer's Responsibility.

Parties to a Protest—The protesting yacht, the protested yacht, and any other yacht involved in the incident that might be penalised as a result of the **protest;** and the race committee when it is involved in a **protest** pertaining to rule 69(a), Requests for Redress, or rule 70, Action by Race or Protest Committee.

Protest Committee—The body appointed to hear and decide **protests** in accordance with rule 1.4, Protest Committees, namely:

(a) the race committee or a sub-committee thereof; or

(b) a separate and independent jury or protest committee; or

(c) an international jury.

Interested Party—Anyone who stands to gain or lose as a result of a decision of a **protest committee** or who has a close personal interest in the result.

Section A—Initiation of Action

68 Protests by Yachts

68.1 RIGHT TO PROTEST

A yacht can protest any other yacht, except that a **protest** for an alleged infringement of the rules of Part IV can be made only by a yacht directly involved in or witnessing an incident.

68.2 INFORMING THE PROTESTED YACHT

A protesting yacht shall try to inform the yacht she intends to protest that a **protest** will be lodged. When an alternative penalty is prescribed in the sailing instructions, she shall hail the other yacht immediately.

68.3 DURING A RACE—PROTEST FLAG

(a) An intention to protest an infringement of the **rules** occurring during a race shall be signified by the protesting yacht conspicuously displaying a flag. Code flag "B" is always acceptable, irrespective of any other provisions in the sailing instructions.

(USYRU prescribes that the flag shall be red, unless otherwise prescribed in the sailing instructions.)

(b) The flag shall be displayed at the first reasonable opportunity after the incident.

(c) (i) Except as provided in rule 68.3(c)(ii), the flag shall be displayed until the yacht *finishes* or, when the first opportunity occurs after *finishing,* until acknowledged by the race committee.

(ii) In the case of a yacht *sailed* single-handed, it will be sufficient to display the flag at the first reasonable opportunity after the incident and to have it acknowledged by the race committee when the protesting yacht *finishes.*

(d) When the yacht retires, the flag shall be displayed until she has informed the race committee or has left the vicinity of the course.

68.4 EXCEPTION TO PROTEST FLAG REQUIREMENT

A yacht may protest without having displayed a protest flag when either:

(a) she has no knowledge of the facts justifying a **protest** until she has *finished* or retired, or

(b) having been a witness not directly involved in the incident, she learns that a yacht that displayed a protest flag has failed to lodge a valid

protest in accordance with rule 33(b), Contact between Yachts Racing, or rule 52.3(b), Touching a Mark.

68.5 PARTICULARS TO BE INCLUDED
A **protest** shall be in writing and be signed by the owner or his representative, and include the following particulars:

(a) the identity of the yacht being protested;

(b) the date, time and whereabouts of the incident;

(c) the particular **rule** or **rules** alleged to have been infringed;

(d) a description of the incident;

(e) unless irrelevant, a diagram of the incident.

68.6 TIME LIMIT
A protesting yacht shall lodge her **protest** with the race committee:

(a) within two hours of the time she *finishes* the race or within such time as may have been prescribed in the sailing instructions, unless the **protest committee** has reason to extend this time limit, or

(b) when she does not *finish* the race, within such time as the **protest committee** considers reasonable in the circumstances.

68.7 FEE
Unless otherwise prescribed in the sailing instructions, a **protest** shall not be accompanied by a fee.

68.8 REMEDYING DEFECTS IN THE PROTEST
The **protest committee** shall allow the protesting yacht to remedy during the hearing:

(a) any defect in the particulars required by rule 68.5, provided that the **protest** identifies the nature of the incident, and

(b) a failure to deposit such fee as may be required under rule 68.7.

68.9 WITHDRAWING A PROTEST
When a written **protest** has been lodged, it shall not be withdrawn, but shall be decided by the **protest committee,** unless prior to the hearing one or more of the yachts acknowledges the infringement, except that, when the **protest committee** finds that contact between two yachts was minor and unavoidable, a protesting yacht may withdraw her **protest.**

(68.10   ADMINISTRATIVE PROTESTS—USYRU prescribes that administrative protests may be lodged in accordance with Appendix 15, paragraph 2, Administrative Protests.)

69   Requests for Redress

A yacht that alleges that her finishing position has been materially prejudiced through no fault of her own by:

(a) an action or omission of the race committee or **protest committee,** or

(USYRU prescribes that a yacht lodging a request for redress alleging prejudice by an action or omission of a protest committee shall do so no later than 72 hours following the action or omission, unless the protest committee has reason to extend this time limit. Rule 68.6 does not apply.)

(b) rendering assistance in accordance with Fundamental Rule A, Rendering Assistance, or

(c) being damaged by another vessel that was required to keep clear, or

(d) a yacht infringing Fundamental Rule C, Fair Sailing, or against which a penalty has been imposed under rule 75.1, Penalties by the Race Committee or Protest Committee,

may request redress from the **protest committee** in accordance with the requirements for a **protest** provided in rules 68.5, 68.6, 68.7 and 68.8, Protests by Yachts. A protest flag need not be displayed. The **protest committee** shall then proceed in accordance with rule 74.2, Consideration of Redress.

70   Action by Race or Protest Committee

70.1 WITHOUT A HEARING

(a) The race committee may act in accordance with rule 74.4, Penalties and Exoneration, without a hearing against a yacht that fails either to *start* or *finish*.

(b) The **protest committee** may act as provided in rule 70.1(a) against a yacht that infringes rule 54.2 or 54.3, Propulsion.

(USYRU prescribes that this rule shall apply only when the sailing instructions so prescribe.)

(c) A yacht so penalised shall be entitled to a hearing upon request, and shall be informed of the action taken, either by letter or notification in the race results, or by such other means as the sailing instructions may prescribe.

70.2 WITH A HEARING

The race committee or the **protest committee** may call a hearing when it:

(a) sees an apparent infringement by a yacht of any of the **rules** (except as provided in rule 70.1), or

(b) learns directly from a written or oral statement by a yacht (including one contained in an invalid **protest**) that she may have infringed a **rule,** or

(c) has reasonable grounds for believing that an infringement resulted in serious damage, or

(d) receives a report not later than the same day from a witness who was neither competing in the race nor otherwise an **interested party,** alleging an infringement, or

(e) has reasonable grounds for supposing, from the evidence at the hearing of a valid **protest,** that any yacht involved in the incident may have committed an infringement.

For such hearings, the race committee or **protest committee** shall notify each yacht involved thereof in writing, delivered or mailed not later than 1800 on the day after:

(i) the finish of the race, or

(ii) the receipt of the relevant information, or

(iii) the hearing of the **protest.**

When rule 70.2(e) applies, or rule 70.2(b) after a **protest** has been declared invalid at a hearing, this notice may be given orally at the hearing. The notice shall identify the incident, the **rule** or **rules** alleged to have been infringed and the time and place of the hearing.

70.3 YACHT MATERIALLY PREJUDICED

The race committee or the **protest committee** may initiate consideration of redress when it is satisfied that any of the circumstances set out in rule 69, Requests for Redress, may have occurred.

70.4 MEASURER'S RESPONSIBILITY

When a measurer concludes that a yacht does not comply with her class rules or measurement or rating certificate:

(a) before a race: he shall request the owner or his representative to correct the defect. When the defect is not corrected, he shall report the matter in writing to the race committee, which shall reject or rescind the yacht's entry or approve the entry in accordance with rule 19, Measurement or Rating Certificates. The yacht shall be entitled to a hearing upon request.

(b) after a race: he shall make a report to the race committee or to the **protest committee,** which shall then notify the yacht concerned and call a hearing.

The measurer shall not have the authority either to rescind an entry or to disqualify a yacht.

Section B—Protest Procedure

71   Procedural Requirements

71.1 REQUIREMENT FOR A HEARING
A yacht shall not be penalised without a hearing, except as provided in rule 70.1, Action by Race or Protest Committee.

71.2 INTERESTED PARTIES

(a) No member of a **protest committee** shall take part in the discussion or decision upon any disputed question in which he is an **interested party,** but this does not preclude him from giving evidence in such a case.

(b) A **party to a protest** who wishes to object to a member of the **protest committee** on the grounds that he is an **interested party** shall do so before evidence is taken at the hearing or as soon thereafter as he becomes aware of the conflict of interest.

71.3 PROTESTS BETWEEN YACHTS IN SEPARATE RACES
A **protest** occurring between yachts competing in separate races organised by different clubs shall be heard by a combined committee of the clubs concerned.

72   Notification of Parties

The **parties to the protest** shall be notified of the time and place of the hearing, and the **protest,** or copies of it, shall be made available to them. A reasonable time shall be allowed for the preparation of a defence.

73   Hearings

73.1 RIGHT TO BE PRESENT
The **parties to the protest,** or a representative of each, shall have the right to be present throughout the hearing of all the evidence and to question

witnesses. When there is an alleged infringement of a rule of Parts IV or V, the representatives of yachts shall have been on board at the time of the incident, unless the **protest committee** has reasonable grounds for ruling otherwise. Each witness, unless he is a member of the **protest committee,** shall be excluded, except when giving his evidence. Others may be admitted as observers at the discretion of the **protest committee.**

73.2 ACCEPTANCE OR REFUSAL OF A PROTEST

When the **protest committee** decides that the requirements of rule 68, Protests by Yachts, and of the sailing instructions have been met, the **protest** is valid, and the **protest committee** shall proceed with the hearing. When these requirements are not met, the **protest** is invalid and shall be refused, but such a decision shall not be reached without giving the protesting party an opportunity of bringing evidence that all requirements have been met.

73.3 TAKING OF EVIDENCE

The **protest committee** shall take the evidence presented by the **parties to the protest** and such other evidence as it deems necessary.

73.4 EVIDENCE OF COMMITTEE MEMBER

Any member of the **protest committee** who speaks of his own observation of the incident shall give his evidence as a witness in the presence of the **parties to the protest,** and may be questioned.

73.5 FAILURE TO ATTEND

Failure on the part of any **party to the protest,** or a representative, to make an effort to attend the hearing may justify the **protest committee** in deciding the **protest** as it thinks fit without a full hearing.

73.6 RE-OPENING A HEARING

(a) A hearing may be re-opened when the **protest committee** decides that it may have made a significant error or when material new evidence becomes available within a reasonable time. A **party to the protest** may request such a re-opening, provided that the request is lodged before 1800 on the day following the decision, unless the **protest committee** has reason to extend this time limit.

(b) When the hearing of a **protest** is re-opened, a majority of the members of the **protest committee** shall, when possible, be members of the original **protest committee.**

74 Decisions and Penalties

74.1 FINDING OF FACTS

The **protest committee** shall determine the facts and base its decision upon them. The finding of facts shall not be subject to appeal.

74.2 CONSIDERATION OF REDRESS

(a) When consideration of redress has been initiated as provided in rule 69, Requests for Redress, or rule 70.3, Yacht Materially Prejudiced, the **protest committee** shall decide whether the finishing position of a yacht or yachts has been materially prejudiced in any of the circumstances set out in rule 69.

(b) If so, the **protest committee** shall satisfy itself by taking appropriate evidence, especially before *abandoning* or *cancelling* the race, that it is aware of the relevant facts and of the probable consequences of any arrangement, to all yachts concerned for that particular race and for the series, if any, as a whole.

(c) The **protest committee** shall then make as equitable arrangement as possible for all yachts concerned. This may be to let the results of the race stand, to adjust the points score or the finishing time of the prejudiced yacht, to *abandon* or *cancel* the race or to adopt some other means.

74.3 MEASUREMENT PROTESTS

(a) A **protest** under rule 19, Measurement or Rating Certificates, or class rules that a measurement, scantling or flotation rule has been infringed while *racing,* or that a classification or rating certificate is invalid, may be decided by the **protest committee** immediately after the hearing, provided that it is satisfied there is no reasonable doubt as to the interpretation or application of the rules. When the **protest committee** is not so satisfied, it shall refer the question, together with the facts found, to an authority qualified to resolve such questions. The **protest committee,** in making its decision, shall be governed by the report of the authority.

(b) In addition to the requirements of rule 74.6, the body that issued the certificate of the yacht concerned shall also be notified.

(c) When an appeal under rule 77, Right of Appeal and Decisions, is lodged, the yacht may compete in further races, but subject to the results of that appeal.

(Consult USYRU rulebook for USYRU prescription.)

74.4 PENALTIES AND EXONERATION

When the **protest committee** after finding the facts, or the race committee or **protest committee** acting under rule 70.1, Action by Race or Protest Committee, decides that:

(a) a yacht has infringed any of the **rules,** or

(b) in consequence of her neglect of any of the **rules,** a yacht has compelled other yachts to infringe any of the **rules,** she shall be disqualified, unless the sailing instructions applicable to that race provide some other penalty, and, in the case of (b), the other yachts shall be exonerated. Such disqualification or other penalty shall be imposed irrespective of whether the **rule** that led to the disqualification or penalty was mentioned in the **protest,** or the yacht that was at fault was mentioned or protested, e.g., the protesting yacht or a third yacht may be disqualified and the protested yacht exonerated.

74.5 POINTS AND PLACES

(a) When a yacht either is disqualified or has retired after *finishing,* the following yachts shall each be moved up one place.

(b) When a yacht is penalised by being removed from a series or a part of a series, no races are to be re-scored and no changes are to be made in the scores of other yachts, except that, when the incident from which the penalty resulted occurred in a particular race, she shall be disqualified from that race and the yachts *finishing* behind her in that race shall each be moved up one place.

(c) When a scoring system provides that one or more scores are to be excluded in calculating a yacht's total score, a disqualification under Fundamental Rule C, Fair Sailing, Fundamental Rule D, Accepting Penalties, or rule 54, Propulsion, shall not be excluded.

(USYRU prescribes that this rule shall not apply to a disqualification under rule 54, Propulsion.)

74.6 THE DECISION

(a) After making its decision, the **protest committee** shall promptly communicate the following to the **parties to the protest:**

(i) the facts found,

(ii) the **rule** or **rules** judged applicable,

(iii) the decision and grounds on which it is based,

(iv) the yacht or yachts penalised, if any, and

(v) the penalty imposed, if any, or the redress granted, if any.

(b) A **party to the protest** shall on request be supplied with:

(i) the above details in writing, and

(ii) unless irrelevant, a diagram of the incident endorsed by the **protest committee.**

Section C—Special Rules

75 Gross Infringement of Rules or Misconduct

75.1 PENALTIES BY THE RACE COMMITTEE OR PROTEST COMMITTEE

(a) The race committee or **protest committee** may call a hearing when it has reasonable grounds for believing that a competitor has committed a gross infringement of the **rules** or a gross breach of good manners or sportsmanship.

(b) When the **protest committee** finds that there has been a gross infringement of the **rules** or a gross breach of good manners or sportsmanship, it may exclude a competitor, and a yacht when appropriate, either from further participation in a series, or from the whole series, or take other disciplinary action. The committee shall report any penalty imposed to its national authority, and to that of the competitor, and to that of the yacht.

(c) No action shall be taken under this rule without a written statement of allegation and a hearing held in accordance with the rules of Section B, Protest Procedure.

(d) Any hearing under this rule shall be conducted by a **protest committee** consisting of at least three members.

75.2 PENALTIES BY THE NATIONAL AUTHORITY

Upon a receipt of a report of gross infringement of the **rules** or a gross breach of good manners or sportsmanship, or a report of a penalty imposed under rule 75.1, a national authority may conduct an investigation and, when appropriate, a hearing and take such action as it deems appropriate against the person or persons or the yacht involved. Such action may include disqualification from participating in any race held in its jurisdiction for any period, or other disciplinary action. The national authority shall report any penalty imposed to the national authority of the competitor, and to that of the yacht, and to the International Yacht Racing Union. The IYRU shall inform all national authorities, which may also apply a penalty.

76   Liability

76.1 DAMAGES

The question of damages arising from an infringement of any of the **rules** shall be governed by the prescriptions, if any, of the national authority.

76.2 MEASUREMENT EXPENSES

Unless otherwise prescribed by the **protest committee,** the fees and expenses entailed by a **protest** on measurement or classification shall be paid by the unsuccessful party.

Section D—Appeals

77   Right of Appeal and Decisions

77.1 RIGHT OF APPEAL

Except when the right of appeal has been denied in accordance with rule 1.5(a) or (b), Right of Appeal, a **party to a protest** may appeal a decision of a **protest committee** to the national authority concerned. A race committee that is a **party to a protest** may appeal only the decision of an independent protest committee or jury.

(USYRU prescribes that a party to a protest wishing to appeal a decision of a protest committee shall submit the appeal to the appeals committee [hereinafter "association appeals committee"] of the USYRU member yacht racing association, class association or affiliated association of which the club or other organizing authority for the race in question is a member. However, a party to a protest in the final series of a USYRU championship, or a party to the protest that has no association appeals committee to which to appeal or that will accept the appeal, may appeal directly to USYRU. Except for the provision of rule 77.6(b) that the decision shall be final, rules 77 and 78 apply to such appeals. A party to a protest may appeal the decision of an association appeals committee to USYRU by complying with the relevant sections of rules 77 and 78.)

77.2 RIGHT OF REFERENCE

A **protest committee** may refer its own decision to (its association appeals committee, and an association appeals committee may refer its decision to) the national authority for confirmation or correction of its interpretation of the **rules.** A reference shall contain the **protest committee**'s decision and the relevant documents listed in rule 78.1(b), Appellant's Responsibilities.

77.3 QUESTIONS OF INTERPRETATION

When no **protest** that may be appealed is involved, a national authority may answer questions from a club or other organisation affiliated to it. A question shall contain sufficient detail for an interpretation to be made.

77.4 INTERPRETATION OF RULES

Appeals, references and questions shall be made only on interpretations of the **rules.** The national authority shall accept the **protest committee**'s finding of facts, except that, when it is not satisfied with the facts presented, it may request further information from the **protest committee** or return the **protest** for a re-hearing.

77.5 INTERESTED PARTIES

No **interested party** or member of the **protest committee** shall take any part in the discussion or decision upon an appeal or reference.

77.6 DECISIONS

(a) A national authority may uphold, reverse or alter a **protest committee**'s decision. When, from the facts found by the **protest committee,** it believes that any yacht that was a **party to the protest** infringed a **rule,** it shall penalise her, irrespective of whether that yacht or that **rule** was mentioned in the decision.

(b) The decision of the national authority shall be final, and shall be transmitted in writing by the national authority to all **parties to the protest** and the **protest committee,** who shall be bound by the decision.

78 Appeal Procedures

78.1 APPELLANT'S RESPONSIBILITIES

(a) Within 15 days of receiving the **protest committee**'s written decision or its decision not to re-open a hearing, the appellant shall transmit to the national authority the dated appeal, which shall include the grounds for the appeal, i.e. why the appellant believes the **protest committee**'s interpretation of the rules to be incorrect, and a copy of the **protest committee**'s decision.

(b) Any of the following documents in the appellant's possession shall be sent with the appeal or as soon as possible thereafter:

(i) the protest form(s);

(ii) a diagram, prepared or endorsed by the **protest committee,** showing the force and direction of the wind; the set and rate of the current or tidal stream, if any; the course to the next *mark,* or the *mark* itself, and the required side; the positions and tracks of all yachts involved; and, if relevant, the depth of the water;

(iii) the notice of race, the sailing instructions, any other conditions governing the event, and any amendments thereto;

(iv) any written statements submitted by the **parties to the protest** to the **protest committee;**

 (v) any additional relevant documents; and

(vi) the names and addresses of all **parties to the protest** and the protest committee chairman.

78.2 NOTIFICATION OF THE PROTEST COMMITTEE

Upon receipt of a valid appeal, the national authority shall transmit a copy of the appeal to the **protest committee,** informing the **protest committee** of the documents supplied by the appellant.

78.3 PROTEST COMMITTEE'S RESPONSIBILITIES

The **protest committee** shall transmit to the national authority the documents listed in rule 78.1(b) not supplied by the appellant. The **protest committee** shall include any comments on the appeal that it may wish to make.

78.4 NATIONAL AUTHORITY'S RESPONSIBILITIES

The national authority shall transmit copies of the appeal and any other relevant documents to the other **parties to the protest.** It shall transmit to the appellant copies of documents that were not supplied by the appellant.

78.5 COMMENTS

All **parties to the protest** may submit comments on the appeal to the national authority within a reasonable time, and at the same time shall transmit copies of such documents to the other **parties to the protest** and the **protest committee.**

78.6 FEE

A national authority may prescribe that a fee be paid for it to consider an appeal, reference or question, and shall allow a reasonable time for payment.

(USYRU prescribes that anyone submitting an appeal, reference or question to USYRU shall include payment of $25 [$65 for non-USYRU members].)

78.7 WITHDRAWAL OF AN APPEAL

An appellant may withdraw an appeal at any time by accepting the decision of the **protest committee.**

APPENDIX 1—DEFINITION OF AN AMATEUR

1   Amateur

1.1 For the purpose of international yacht races in which yachts are required to have one or more amateurs on board and in other races with similar require-ments, an amateur is a yachtsman who engages in yacht racing as a pastime as distinguished from a means of obtaining a livelihood or part-time compensation other than that permitted by the Guidelines to the Eligibility Code. No yachtsman shall lose amateur status by reason of his livelihood being derived from designing or constructing yachts, yacht parts, sails or accessories; or from similar professions associated with the sport; or solely from the maintenance (but not the *racing*) of yachts.

1.2 Competing in a race in which a prize is offered having a value greater than US$300, other than a prize awarded only for temporary possession, is ground for loss of amateur status unless prior to the event:

(i) the competitor assigns to the IYRU, his national authority or his national Olympic committee all his rights to such prize, or

(ii) the organising authority obtains its national authority's consent to a prize having a value greater than US$300.

(USYRU prescribes that any assignment made under paragraph 1.2[i] shall be made to USYRU.)

1.3 Any yachtsman whose amateur status is questioned or is in doubt may apply to his national authority for recognition of his amateur status. Any such applicant may be required to provide such particulars and evidence and to pay such fees as the national authority may prescribe. Recognition may be suspended or cancelled by the national authority granting it, and, upon application by the competitor affected, the authority may reinstate recogni-tion of amateur status following a period of at least two years absence from the sport.

(USYRU prescribes that applications made under paragraph 1.3 shall be referred to the USYRU Committee on Eligibility.)

1.4 The Permanent Committee of the IYRU or any tribunal nominated by the chairman of that committee may review the decision of any national authority affecting the amateur status of a yachtsman for the purpose of competing in international races.

APPENDIX 2—SAILBOARD RACING RULES

Sailboard races shall be sailed under the International Yacht Racing Rules modified as follows:

1   Part I—Definitions

1.1 *Leeward* and *Windward*—The *windward* side of a sailboard is the side that is, or, when head to wind or with the wind astern, was, towards the wind, regardless of the direction in which the sailboard is sailing. However, when *sailing* by the lee (i.e., with the wind coming over her stern from the same side as her boom is on) the *windward* side is the other side.
The opposite side is the *leeward* side.

When neither of two sailboards on the same *tack* is *clear astern,* the one on the *windward* side of the other is the *windward sailboard*. The other is the *leeward sailboard.*

1.2 *Capsized* and *Recovering*

(a) *Capsized*—A sailboard is *capsized* when she is not under way due to her sail being in the water or when the competitor is waterstarting.

(b) *Recovering*—A sailboard is *recovering* from a *capsize* from the time her sail or, when waterstarting, the competitor's body is raised out of the water until she has steerageway.

2   Part III—General Requirements

2.1 Rule 19.1—Measurement or Rating Certificates

When so prescribed by the national authority, a numbered and dated device on the board, daggerboard and sail shall rank as a measurement certificate.

2.2 Rule 23—Anchor

An anchor and chain or rope need not be carried.

2.3 Rule 24—Life-Saving Equipment

A safety device shall prevent the mast separating from the board.

2.4 Rule 25—Class Insignia, National Letters and Sail Numbers

Rule 25.1(a)—The class insignia shall be displayed once on each side of the sail. It shall fit within a rectangle of 0.5 m², the longer dimension of which shall not exceed one metre. It shall not refer to anything other than the manufacturer or class and shall not consist of more than two letters and three numbers. When approved by the IYRU or a national authority within its jurisdiction, this insignia shall not be considered to be advertising.

3   Part IV—Right of Way Rules

3.1 Rule 33—Contact between Yachts Racing

As between each other, rule 33 shall not apply to sailboards.

3.2 Rule 38.2(a)—Proper Course Limitations
Rule 40—Same Tack—Luffing before Clearing the Starting Line

For "mainmast" read "foot of mast".

3.3 Rule 46—Person Overboard; Yacht Anchored; Aground or Capsized

Rule 46.3 does not apply.

3.4 Recovering from a Capsize

A sailboard *recovering* from a *capsize* shall not obstruct a sailboard or yacht under way.

3.5 Sail out of the Water when Starting

When approaching the starting line to *start,* a sailboard shall have her sail out of the water and in a normal position, except when *capsized* unintentionally.

3.6 Sailing Backward when Starting

When approaching the starting line to *start* or when on the course side of the starting line, a sailboard *sailing* or drifting backward shall keep clear of other sailboards and yachts.

4   Part V—Other Sailing Rules

Rule 54—Propulsion

Dragging a foot in the water to check way is permissible.

In rule 54.3(b), for "sheet" read "wishbone" and delete last sentence.

5   Part VI—Protests, Penalties and Appeals

Rule 68—Protests by Yachts

A sailboard need not display a flag in order to signify her intention to protest as required by rule 68.3, but, except when rule 68.4 applies, she shall try to notify the other sailboard or yacht by hail at the first reasonable opportunity and the race committee as soon as possible after *finishing* or retiring.

6   APPENDIX 3—Alternative Penalties for Infringement of a Rule of Part IV

6.1 720° Turns

Unless otherwise prescribed in the sailing instructions, the 720° Turns penalty in Appendix 3.1 shall apply. Two full 360° turns of the board shall satisfy the provision of the 720° turns penalty.

6.2 Percentage

A sailboard need not display Code flag "I" to acknowledge an infringement. She shall notify the other sailboard or yacht by hail immediately and the race committee as soon as possible after *finishing* or retiring.

7   Rules for Multi-Mast Sailboards

7.1 Part IV—Rule 38.2(a) and Rule 40

The normal station of the helmsman is the normal station of the crew member controlling the mainsail. The mainsail is the foremost sail and the mainmast is the foremost mast.

7.2 Appendix 2—Rule 1.2(a) *Capsized*

A multi-mast sailboard is *capsized* when one or more of her sails are in the water or one or more competitors are waterstarting.

7.3 Appendix 2—Rule 1.2(b) *Recovering*

A multi-mast sailboard is *recovering* from a *capsize* from the time her sails or, when waterstarting, the competitors' bodies are raised out of the water until she has steerageway.

7.4 Appendix 2—Rule 3.4—Sail out of the Water when Starting

For "sail" read "sails".

Funboard Racing Rules

These rules apply for alternative sailboard racing only, i.e., course racing and slalom, but not for triangle (Olympic course) racing. Funboard races, both course races and slalom, shall be sailed under the International Yacht Racing Rules, Appendix 2, modified as follows:

A.   The following rules apply for both Course Races and Slalom.

8   Part V—Other Sailing Rules

8.1 Rule 52—Touching a Mark

Rules 52.1(a)(ii) and (iii) do not apply.

8.2 Rule 54—Propulsion

Rule 54 is replaced by: "A sailboard shall be propelled by the action of the wind on the sail, by the action of the water on the hull and by the unassisted actions of the competitor."

9   Part VI—Protests, Penalties and Appeals

9.1 Rule 68—Protests by Yachts

A **protest** does not need to be in writing but can be made orally.

9.2 Rule 77—Right of Appeal and Decisions

Except for a competitor or sailboard penalised under rule 75.1, Gross Infringement of Rules or Misconduct, the right of appeal is denied.

B.   The following rules apply for Slalom only.

10   Part I—Definitions

10.1 *Going Out* and *Coming In*—When *sailing* from the shore against the incoming surf, a sailboard is *going out*. A sailboard *sailing* in the opposite direction is *coming in.*

10.2 *Overtaking*—A sailboard is *overtaking* from the moment she establishes an *overlap* from *clear astern* until she is *clear ahead* of the overtaken sailboard. When an *overlap* exists at the preparatory signal, the *windward* sailboard shall be deemed to be *overtaking*.

11   Part II—Organization and Management

Rule 6—Starting and Finishing Lines

The starting and finishing lines may be positioned on the shore.

12   Part IV—Right of Way Rules

12.1 Except for rule 37.2, rules 36 to 42 do not apply.

12.2 Basic Rules

(a) A sailboard *coming in* shall keep clear of a sailboard *going out.*

(b) When neither *going out* nor *coming in,* a *port-tack* sailboard shall keep clear of a *starboard-tack* sailboard.

12.3 Changing Tacks—Tacking and Gybing

Except when *gybing* around a *mark* in front of another sailboard, a sailboard that is *tacking* or *gybing* shall keep clear of a sailboard *on a tack*.

12.4 Same Tack—Overtaking
An *overtaking* sailboard shall keep clear of the overtaken sailboard.

APPENDIX 3—ALTERNATIVE PENALTIES FOR INFRINGEMENT OF A RULE OF PART IV

Experience indicates that the 720° turns penalty is most satisfactory for small boats in relatively short races, but that it can be dangerous for large yachts and in restricted waters and not sufficiently severe in long races. The 20% penalty is relatively mild and is designed to encourage acknowledgement of infringements and willingness to protest when not acknowledged. Both systems keep yachts racing.

Either of the following alternatives to disqualification may be used by including in the sailing instructions a provision such as the following (or if preferred the selected penalty may be quoted in full):

"The 720° Turns penalty, Appendix 3.1 (or the Percentage penalty, Appendix 3.2) of the racing rules will apply."

1   720° Turns

1.1 A yacht that may have infringed a rule of Part IV may accept an alternative penalty by *sailing* well clear of all other yachts as soon as possible after the incident, and remaining clear while she makes two complete 360° turns (720°) in the same direction, including two *tacks* and two *gybes*.

1.2 When the infringement occurs at the finishing line, she shall make her turns on the course side of the line before she will be recorded as having *finished*.

1.3 A yacht intending to protest shall hail the other yacht immediately and act in accordance with rule 68, Protests by Yachts. A yacht that accepts an alternative penalty may protest with respect to the same incident. She shall not be penalised further for an infringement for which she accepted the penalty, except as provided by paragraph 1.4.

1.4 The **protest committee** may disqualify a yacht that has accepted an alternative penalty when it finds that her infringement resulted in serious damage or that she gained a significant advantage.

1.5 Failure to accept an alternative penalty will make an infringing yacht liable to disqualification or other prescribed penalty. When a yacht complies with some but not all of the requirements of paragraphs 1.1 or 1.2, the yacht infringed against is relieved of further obligations under rule 33, Contact between Yachts Racing.

2 Percentage

2.1 A yacht that may have infringed a rule of Part IV may accept an alternative penalty:

(a) by displaying Code flag "I" at the first reasonable opportunity after the incident, and

(b) except for a yacht *sailed* single-handed, by keeping it displayed until she has *finished,* and

(c) by reporting her acknowledgement and the yacht infringed against to the race committee immediately after *finishing.*

She shall receive a score for the place worse than her actual finishing position by 20% of the number of starters*, but not less than three places, calculated in accordance with paragraph 2.7.

2.2 A yacht intending to protest shall hail the other yacht immediately and act in accordance with rule 68, Protests by Yachts. A yacht that accepts an alternative penalty may protest with respect to the same incident; however, her penalty shall not be affected. She shall not be penalised further for an infringement for which she accepted the penalty, except as provided by paragraph 2.5.

2.3 A yacht may protest without displaying a protest flag against a yacht that has complied with some but not all of the requirements of paragraph 2.1.

2.4 A yacht that does not comply with the requirements of paragraph 2.1, but acknowledges an infringement prior to a hearing, shall be penalised 50%, but not less than six places.

2.5 The **protest committee** may disqualify a yacht that has accepted an alternative penalty when it finds that her infringement resulted in serious damage or that she gained a significant advantage.

2.6 Failure to accept an alternative penalty will make an infringing yacht liable to disqualification or other prescribed penalty. When a yacht complies with some but not all of the requirements of paragraph 2.1, the yacht infringed against is relieved of further obligations under rule 33, Contact between

Yachts Racing. A yacht may request a hearing solely on the point of having complied with the requirements of paragraph 2.1.

2.7 The penalty shall be computed as 20% (or 50%) of the number of starters* in the event to the nearest whole number (round .5 upward), such number to be not less than three (or six), except that a yacht shall not receive a score worse than for one position more than the number of starters*. (Examples: an infringing yacht finishing 8th in a start for 19 yachts would receive a score for 12th place: 8 + (19 × 20% = 3.8 or 4) = 12. Another infringing yacht, finishing 18th, would receive the score for 20th place.) The imposition of a percentage penalty shall not affect the scores of other yachts. Thus, two yachts may receive the same score.

2.8 A yacht infringing a rule in more than one incident shall receive a penalty for each incident.

* When scoring a regatta, these calculations shall be based on the number of yachts entered in the series, not the number of starters in the race in question.

APPENDIX 5—SCORING SYSTEMS

The two scoring systems most often used are the Olympic and the Low-Point. The Olympic system has been adopted for many class championships; the Low-Point system is suitable both for championships and for club and other small fleet racing, and is somewhat easier to use for race committees and competitors.

In both systems, lower points designate better finishing places. The Low-Point system uses a "straight line" points schedule that rewards performance in direct proportion to finishing place; the Olympic system uses a "curved" points schedule that provides an additional reward in the top six finishing places. Although designed primarily for scoring regattas, either system may be used for other series; see paragraph 3, Suggested Alterations for a Non-Regatta Series.

The sailing instructions may include a complete system verbatim or may incorporate either system by reference, with or without alterations, as explained in the Note following each system. See also Appendix 12, Sailing Instructions Guide, Instruction 18.

1 The Olympic Scoring System

1.1 NUMBER OF RACES, MINIMUM REQUIRED, AND RACES TO COUNT There will be seven races, of which five shall be completed to constitute a series. Each yacht's total score will be the sum of her scores for all races, excluding her worst score in accordance with rule 74.5(c), Points and Places. The lowest total score wins.

1.2 POINTS

Each yacht *finishing* in a race and not thereafter retiring or being disqualified will be scored points as follows:

Finishing Place	Points
First	0
Second	3
Third	5.7
Fourth	8
Fifth	10
Sixth	11.7
Seventh and thereafter	Place plus six

All other yachts, including a yacht that *finishes* and thereafter retires or is disqualified, will be scored points for the finishing place one more than the number of yachts entered in the series.

1.3 TIES

When there is a tie on total points between two or more yachts, the tie will be broken in favour of the yacht or yachts with the most first places, and, when the tie remains, the most second places, and so on, if necessary, for such races as count for total points. When the tie still remains, it shall stand as part of the final results.

Note: (a) The sailing instructions can incorporate the Olympic system by stating "The Olympic Scoring System, Appendix 5.1 of the racing rules, will apply."

(b) When the number of races is not seven, add "except that ____ races are scheduled, of which ____ shall be completed to constitute a series." (Insert the numbers of races.)

(c) When all races are to be counted, add "except that each yacht's total score will be the sum of her scores for all races."

2 The Low-Point Scoring System

2.1 NUMBER OF RACES, MINIMUM REQUIRED, AND RACES TO COUNT

The number of races scheduled and the number required to constitute a series shall be prescribed in the sailing instructions. Each yacht's total score will be the sum of her scores for all races, excluding her worst score in accordance with rule 74.5(c), Points and Places. The lowest total score wins.

2.2 POINTS

Each yacht *finishing* in a race and not thereafter retiring or being disqualified will be scored points equal to her *finishing* place, minus one-quarter point for first place, as follows:

Finishing Place	Points
First	$^3/_4$
Second	2
Third	3
Fourth	4
and so on.	

All other yachts, including a yacht that *finishes* and thereafter retires or is disqualified, will be scored points for the finishing place one more than the number of yachts entered in the series.

2.3 TIES

When there is a tie on total points between two or more yachts, the tie will be broken in favour of the yacht or yachts with the most first places, and, when the tie remains, the most second places, and so on, if necessary, for such races as count for total points. When the tie still remains, it shall stand as part of the final results.

Note: (d) The sailing instructions can incorporate the Low-Point system by stating "The Low-Point Scoring System, Appendix 5.2 of the racing rules, will apply, with _____ races scheduled of which _____ shall be completed to constitute a series." (Insert the numbers of races.)

(e) When all races are to be counted, add "except that each yacht's total score will be the sum of her scores for all races."

3 Suggested Alterations for Non-Regatta Series

3.1 In a regatta all yachts are expected to compete in all races, and the difference between the number of entrants and the number of starters is usually insignificant. However, in a longer series there may be a number of yachts that compete in fewer races than others, in which case it is suggested that the following be substituted for the last paragraph in either 1.2 or 2.2:

A yacht that does not *start* or rank as a starter in accordance with rule 50, Ranking as a Starter, will be scored points for the finishing place one more than the number of yachts entered in the series. All other yachts, including a yacht that *finishes* but thereafter retires or is disqualified, will be scored points for the finishing place one more than the number of yachts that *started* or ranked as starters in accordance with rule 50 in that race.

3.2 When it is desired to increase the number of races to be excluded from each yacht's series score, change the second sentence in 1.1 or 2.1 to read: "excluding her _____ worst scores". (Insert the number.)

4 Guidance for Race and Protest Committees

4.1 ABBREVIATIONS FOR SCORING RECORDS
The following abbreviations are recommended to record the various occurrences that may determine a particular score:

DNC Did not compete; i.e., did not *start* or rank as a starter under rule 50, Ranking as a Starter.

DNS Did not *start;* i.e. ranked as a starter under rule 50 but failed to *start*.

PMS Started prematurely or otherwise failed to comply with the starting procedure.

DNF Did not *finish*.

RET Retired after *finishing*.

DSQ Disqualified.

DND Disqualification not discardable under rule 74.5(c); Points and Places.

YMP Yacht materially prejudiced.

4.2 REDRESS
In applying rule 74.2, Consideration of Redress, when it is deemed equitable to adjust the score of the prejudiced yacht by awarding points different from those she received for the race in question, the following possibilities are to be considered:

(i) Points equal to the average, to the nearest tenth of a point (round .05 upward), of her points in all the races in the series except [her worst race and]* the race in question.

(ii) Points equal to the average, to the nearest tenth of a point (round .05 upward), of her points in all the races before the race in question.

(iii) An arbitrary number of points based on the position of the yacht in the race in question at the time she was prejudiced.

(Author's note: consult USYRU rulebook for USYRU prescription 5A, Club Series Scoring System.)

* Delete these words when all scores count for series results, or alter when more than one race is to be excluded.

APPENDIX 6—RECOMMENDED PROTEST COMMITTEE PROCEDURE

In a protest hearing, the **protest committee** should give equal weight to all testimony; should recognize that honest testimony can vary and even be in conflict as a result of different observations and recollections; should resolve such differences as best it can; should recognize that no yacht is guilty until her infringement has been established to the satisfaction of the **protest committee;** should keep an open mind until all the evidence has been submitted as to whether the protestor or the protestee or a third yacht, when one is involved in the incident, has infringed a **rule.**

1 Preliminaries

1.1 Note on the **protest** the time at which it is received.

1.2 Determine whether the **protest** contains the information called for by rule 68.5, Particulars to be Included, in sufficient detail to identify the incident and the protested yacht, and to tell the recipient what the **protest** is about. If not, ask the protestor to supply the information (rule 68.8, Remedying Defects in the Protest). When a **protest** by a yacht does not identify the nature of the incident, it shall be refused (rule 68.8(a) and 73.2, Acceptance or Refusal of a Protest).

1.3 Unless the **protest** already provides the information;

Inquire whether the protestor displayed a protest flag in accordance with rule 68.3, unless rule 68.4 applies or the protestor is seeking redress under rule 69, and note his answer on the **protest.** When a protest flag has not been properly displayed, the **protest** shall be refused; rule 73.2, Acceptance or Refusal of a Protest, refers, except when the **protest committee** decides either:

(a) rule 68.4 applies; or

(b) it was impossible for the yacht to have displayed a protest flag, because she was, for example, dismasted, capsized or sunk.

1.4 Unless the **protest** already provides the information;

Inquire whether the protestor tried to inform the protested yacht(s) (the protestee(s)) that a **protest** would be lodged (rule 68.2, Informing the Protested Yacht) and note his answer on the **protest.** Rule 68.2 is mandatory with regard to the attempt to inform, but not with regard to its success.

See that the protest fee, if any, required by the sailing instructions is included and note its receipt on the **protest** (rule 68.7, Fee).

1.5 When the **protest** conforms to the requirements of rule 68, arrange to hold a hearing as soon as possible. Notify the representative of each yacht involved of the time and place of the hearing (rule 72, Notification of Parties).

1.6 The **protest** and any written statement regarding the incident (preferably photocopies) shall be available to all **parties to the protest** and to the **protest committee** for study before the taking of evidence. A reasonable time shall be allowed for the preparation of defence (rule 72, Notification of Parties).

2 The Hearing

2.1 The **protest committee** shall ensure that:

(a) a quorum is present as required by the organising authority. The quorum is not affected when it is considered desirable that some members of the **protest committee** leave the hearing during the discussion and decision.

(b) no **interested party** is a member of the **protest committee** or takes part in the discussion or decision. Ask the **parties to the protest** whether they object to any member on the ground of "interest". Such an objection shall be made before the **protest** is heard (rule 71.2, Interested Parties).

(c) when any member of the **protest committee** saw the incident, he shall give his evidence as a witness only in the presence of the **parties to the protest** and may be questioned (rule 73.4, Evidence of Committee Member).

(d) when a hearing concerns a request for redress under rule 69, Requests for Redress, or rule 70.3, Yacht Materially Prejudiced, involving a member of the race committee, it is desirable that he is not a member of the **protest committee** and would therefore appear only as a witness.

2.2 The **parties to the protest** or a representative of each (with a language interpreter, when needed) shall have the right to be present throughout the hearing. Each witness, unless he is a member of the **protest committee,** shall be excluded, except when giving his evidence. Others may be admitted as observers at the discretion of the **protest committee** (rule 73.1, Right to be Present).

2.3 Invite first the protestor and then the protestee(s) to give their accounts of the incident. Each may question the other(s). Questions by the **protest committee,** except for clarifying details, are preferably deferred until all accounts have been presented. Models are useful. Positions before and after the incident itself are often helpful.

2.4 Invite the protestor and then the protestee to call witnesses. They may be questioned by the protestor and protestee as well as by the **protest committee.** The **protest committee** may also call witnesses. It may be appropriate and prudent to ask a witness to disclose any business or other relationship through which he might have an interest or might stand to benefit from the outcome of the **protest.**

2.5 Invite first the protestor and then the protestee to make a final statement of his case, including any application or interpretation of the **rules** to the incident as he sees it.

2.6 The **protest committee** may adjourn a hearing in order to obtain additional evidence.

3 Decision

3.1 The **protest committee,** after dismissing those involved in the incident, shall decide what the relevant facts are (rule 74.1, Finding of Facts).

3.2 The **protest committee** shall then apply the **rules** and reach a decision as to who, if anyone, infringed a **rule** and what **rule** was infringed (rule 74, Decisions and Penalties).

3.3 Having reached a decision in writing, recall the protestor and the protestee and read to them the facts found, the decision and the grounds for it (rule 74.6).

3.4 Any **party to the protest** is entitled to a copy of the decision (rule 74.6), signed by the chairman of the **protest committee.** A copy should also be filed with the committee records.

APPENDIX 14—EVENT CLASSIFICATION AND ADVERTISING

(No changes are contemplated before 1993. However, the Permanent Committee may approve changes in the interim.)

1 General

1.1 This appendix shall apply when *racing* and, in addition, unless otherwise prescribed in the notice of race, from 0700 on the first race day of a regatta or series until the expiry of the time limit for lodging protests following the last race of the regatta or series.

1.2 Events shall be classified as Category A, B or C in accordance with paragraphs 2, 3 and 4 of this appendix.

Unless otherwise prescribed in the notice of race and the sailing instructions, an event shall be classified as Category A.

1.3 The notice of race and the sailing instructions for any category of event may prescribe more restrictive criteria than are otherwise required for that category.

1.4 The IYRU, a national authority, the Offshore Racing Council (ORC) or a class association may develop rules for sanctioning events within its jurisdiction in any or all categories, as well as for giving consent for individual advertisements. Fees may be required.

1.5 Advertised products shall comply with moral and ethical standards.

1.6 In world and continental events, unless so prescribed by the class rules, a competitor shall not be required or induced to display advertising on a yacht, clothing or equipment.

1.7 Governmental requirements affecting yachts shall override this appendix only to the extent that they are inconsistent with it.

2 Category A

Except as permitted in accordance with paragraphs 1.8 and 1.9, a yacht competing in a Category A event shall not display advertising on her hull, spars, sails and equipment and, while aboard the yacht, on the clothing and equipment worn by the crew.

1.8 The following advertising is permitted at all times:

(a) one sailmaker's mark (which may include the name or mark of the manufacturer of the sail cloth and pattern or model description of the sail) may be displayed on each side of any sail. The whole of such a mark shall be placed not more than 15% of the length of the foot of the sail or 300 mm from its tack, whichever is the greater. This latter limitation shall not apply to the position of marks on spinnakers.

(b) one builder's mark (which may include the name or mark of the designer) may be placed on the hull, and one maker's mark may be displayed on spars and equipment.

(c) such marks (or plates) shall fit within a square not exceeding 150 mm × 150 mm.

(d) one maker's mark may be displayed on each item of clothing and equipment worn by the crew, provided that the mark fits within a square not exceeding 100 mm × 100 mm.

(e) the yacht's type may be displayed once on each side of the hull, provided that the lettering shall not exceed 1% in height and 5% in length of the overall length of the yacht, but not exceeding a maximum height of 100 mm and a maximum length of 700 mm.

(f) a sailboard's type may be displayed on the hull in two places. The lettering shall not exceed 200 mm in height.

1.9 After obtaining the approval, when relevant, of the national authority, ORC and/or class association, the organising authority of a sponsored event may permit or require advertising by the sponsor on yachts and sailboards only within the following limits:

(a) On yachts: the display of a flag and/or the application to the hulls of a decal or sticker, neither of which shall be larger than 45 cm × 60 cm.

(b) On sailboards: the display of not more than two stickers, one on each side of the sail, each of which shall fit within a rectangle of 2,500 cm², no side of which shall exceed 80 cm in length. The notice of race shall state whether one or both sides of the sail are to be used. When both sides are used, the stickers shall be placed back to back. The stickers shall be placed above the wishbone and at least partly in the lower half of the sail.

(c) such permission or requirement shall be prescribed in the notice of race.

1.10 When a protest committee after finding the facts decides that a yacht or her crew has infringed this appendix, rule 74.4, Penalties and Exoneration, shall not apply, and the **protest committee** shall:

(a) warn the infringing yacht that a further infringement will result in action under rule 70.2, Action by Race or Protest Committee, or

(b) disqualify the yacht, or

(c) when the infringement occurs when the yacht is not *racing,* disqualify the yacht from the race most recently *sailed* or from the next race *sailed* after the infringement, or

(d) when it decides that there was a gross breach of the appendix, disqualify the yacht from more than one race or from the whole series.

3 Category B

In addition to the advertising permitted by paragraphs 1.8 and 1.9, a yacht competing in a Category B event may display advertising only in accordance with paragraphs 3.1 to 3.4, and a sailboard in accordance with paragraph 3.5.

3.1 ADVERTISING ON YACHTS—GENERAL

(a) A yacht shall not display the advertisements of more than two organisations at one time.

(b) Each advertisement shall consist of one or two of the following:

(i) the name of the organisation;

(ii) one brand or product name;

(iii) one logo.

3.2 ADVERTISING ON HULLS

(a) The forward 25% of the length overall of the hull, including the deck, shall be clear of any individual advertising. This area is reserved for the requirements of the IYRU, national authorities, the ORC or class associations.

(b) 50% of the remaining 75% of the length overall of the hull may be used for individual advertising.

3.3 ADVERTISING ON SAILS

(a) Advertising on spinnakers is without restriction, except as provided in paragraph 3.3(c).

(b) On other sails, only one advertisement may be carried at any one time, and it may be on both sides of one sail. It shall be placed below an imaginary line between the mid-points of the luff and leech of the sail, and have a width of not more than two-thirds of the length of the foot of the sail, and a height of not more than one-third of that width.

(c) Advertisements on all sails shall be clearly separated from, and below, the sail numbers.

3.4 ADVERTISING ON SPARS

(a) One-third of the main mast may be used.

(b) Two-thirds of the main boom may be used.

(c) Advertising on the mast or boom shall be limited to the name, brand or product name, or logo of one of the organisations.

3.5 ADVERTISING ON SAILBOARDS

(a) The upper half of the sail above the wishbone may carry only the logo of a sailboard manufacturer or a sailmaker.

(b) The tack corner on each side of the sail may carry one label or logo either of a sailboard manufacturer or a sailmaker.

(c) The lower half of the sail above the wishbone may carry only the logo of a sailmaker.

(d) The space below the wishbone is at the disposal of the competitor for advertising. Any advertising shall fit within a rectangle of 4000 cm^2.

3.6 ADVERTISING ON CLOTHING AND PERSONAL EQUIPMENT
In addition to the advertisements carried on the yacht or sailboard, advertisements limited to the organisation(s) advertising on the yacht or sailboard and one or two additional organisations may be displayed on clothing and personal equipment worn by the crew.

4 Category C

In addition to the advertising permitted by paragraphs 1.8 and 1.9, a yacht competing in a Category C event may display advertising in accordance with special advertising rules. Such rules shall be:

(a) prescribed or approved by the national authority for an event within its jurisdiction;

(b) subject to approval by the IYRU; and

(c) stated in the notice of race and the sailing instructions.

Appendix E: Answers to the Advanced Rules Quiz

1. With just forty seconds to go, L and W were certainly "approaching the starting line to start." W was required to keep clear of L under Rule 37.1. Rule 42.4 tells L she is not obligated to give W room at the obstruction (committee boat); if W forces room, she infringes 37.1, not 42.4. However, of her own volition, L was giving W room to pass to leeward of the obstruction. Once W was committed to passing along the obstruction, L, the right-of-way boat, then altered her course in such a way that W was prevented from keeping clear, in clear infringement of Rule 35. W was further protected by Rule 38.2(d). Nothing in Rule 42.4 gives L any rights different from those given by the rules in Section B. L is penalized.

Immediately after the incident and before the starting signal W did a "720" and also protested L for the same incident. Appendix 3,1.1 permits a "720" to be done as soon as possible after the incident. You do not have to wait until the starting signal. Appendix 3,1.3 permits a yacht to do an "insurance 720"—i.e., having done her "720," W could not be penalized further in this incident; however, W can still protest L, and L can be penalized. (See discussion of Rules 35 and 42.4.)

2. For boardsailors, there is a significant difference between the penalty for touching a mark and the "720" alternative penalty after infringing a rule of Part IV. When any boat or sailboard touches a mark, Rule 52.2(a) states that the penalty is two complete 360-degree turns in the same direction, including two tacks and two gybes. When a sailboard wants to do a "720" for a Part IV rule infringement, Appendix 2,6.1 states that two full 360-degree turns of the board shall satisfy the provisions of the 720-degree turns penalty (in Appendix 3.1).

By obstructing Sailboard Y while recovering from her capsize, Sailboard X infringed Appendix 3,3.4, which is a Part IV rule. She properly did a "720" and is exonerated. As for her protest against Sailboard O, she did not try to report it to the race committee after finishing, as is required by Appendix 3,5. Rule 73.2 requires that the protest be deemed invalid and refused, even though Sailboard X was entitled to all her rights for as long as she continued to race (Rule 34).

Having heard the oral self-incriminating statement by Sailboard X that she touched a mark and failed to exonerate herself properly, the protest committee has the option (notice the word "may" in 70.2) to call a hearing, under Rule 70.2(b), and to prosecute Sailboard X for this infringement. Notice that in this case they can give oral notice that a hearing will be called. I always recommend that the protest committee make a policy decision prior to the start of a race or series on when they will act under Rule 70.2 to ensure consistency and an unbiased policy.

3. The hearing is valid, under Rule 70.2(a), because a member of the protest committee has seen an apparent infringement of the rules. Though Rule 70.1(b) permits the protest committee to penalize the yacht under Rule 54.2 without a hearing, the USYRU prescription does not permit it in the U.S. unless the sailing instructions so provide. The action of pushing abruptly on the cockpit was "ooching." "Ooching" is never allowed under Rule 54. In surfing conditions, Rule 54.3(b) permits sailors only one pump per wave in order to initiate surfing. The protested sailor has infringed Rule 54.1 by performing actions specifically prohibited by Rules 54.2(a) and 54.2(c) and is therefore penalized. Note that Rule 74.5(c) prohibits a disqualification under Rule 54 from being used as a "drop race"; however, the USYRU prescribes that this portion of Rule 74.5(c) shall not apply in the U.S. (See discussion of Rule 54.)

4. The removal of the phrase "other than a starting mark . . ." leaves Rule 42 saying, "Rule 42 applies when yachts are about to round or pass a mark on the same **required** side . . ." (emphasis added). Rule 51.3 says that a starting mark begins to have a required side for a yacht when she starts—i.e., first crosses the starting line after the starting signal. Therefore, Rule 42 did not apply to WI and LO as they were passing the starting mark before the starting signal, and WI was required to keep clear of LO under Rule 37.1, which she did. Rule 52.1(i) requires that boats not hit starting marks before starting. Rule 52.2(a) allows boats to exonerate themselves by doing two complete 360-degree turns (720) as soon as possible after touching the mark. Boats do not need to reround the mark, nor wait until after the starting signal to do their turns. Neither boat is penalized. (See discussion of Rule 52.)

5. While P was keeping clear of S, S, as the right-of-way boat, was required by Rule 35 not to alter her course in such a way that P was prevented from keeping clear. There is no proper course before the starting signal (see definition of proper course); therefore, the excep-

tion in Rule 35(b)(i) does not begin to apply until after the starting signal. Clearly in this case, S infringed Rule 35 by altering course so close to P that P was prevented from keeping clear.

6. Rule 35(b)(ii) permits S, the right-of-way boat, to assume a proper course when rounding the mark; and P must anticipate this potential alteration of course and keep clear under Rule 36. Because the next leg was a run, a dead downwind course was certainly a proper course for S. P is penalized. Rule 74.1 requires the protest committee to find the facts and base their decision on them. The facts indicate that there was a collision. Upon investigation the protest committee concludes that P sustained serious damage in the collision, that S had the opportunity to attempt to avoid the collision (she could have not borne away as far), and that S failed to make a reasonable attempt to avoid the collision. Given these findings, Rule 32.1 requires the protest committee to also penalize S, and Rule 74.4 permits them to do so. (See discussion of Rules 32 and 35.)

7. The removal of the phrase "other than a starting mark surrounded by navigable water" clarifies that when two boats are about to pass an obstruction on the same side, including an obstruction that also happens to be a mark, the outside boat must give the inside boat room under Rule 42.1(a). However, in order to be entitled to such room, an inside boat that establishes an overlap from clear astern must do so while the outside boat is outside the "two boat-length circle" (Rule 42.3[a][ii]). When BL established her overlap to leeward of AW from clear astern, Rule 37.3 required her to initially provide AW ample room and opportunity to keep clear—which she did. When she luffed, Rule 40 required her to luff slowly, and to initially provide AW room and opportunity to keep clear—which she did. With AW in the "mast abeam" position, Rule 40 permitted BL to luff up to BL's close-hauled course, but not beyond. Therefore, up to the point of close-hauled BL was doing everything legally.

When BL established her overlap on AW, AW was 30 feet from the obstruction (less than two boat-lengths); therefore BL was not entitled to room under Rule 42.1(a) and is penalized under Rule 40 for luffing above close-hauled while AW was in the "mast abeam" position. Furthermore, even if BL had luffed after the starting signal, claiming she was assuming a proper course to start, she was still subject to Rule 40, making her "ineligible" for the exception in Rule 35(b)(i).

8. Rule 38.2(a) specifically prohibits L from sailing above her proper course at all while overlapped with W because at some point in their overlap, W had attained the "mast abeam" position. When L luffed above her proper course she infringed Rule 38.2(a). Notice that had W sailed more than two lengths away from L, the boats would not have been overlapped for the purposes of Rule 38.2(a). This, however, was not the case. (See discussion of Rule 38.) L is penalized.

9. The rule that governed taking another yacht to the wrong side of the mark (Rule 42.3[c]) has been deleted in its entirety. Once the boats reached the two-length circle, Rule 42 clearly applied, and LO, as outside boat, was required to give WI, as inside boat, room to round the mark under Rule 42.1(a). The fact that WI hailed for more room than she was getting supports her claim (Rule 42.1[f]). Therefore LO is penalized.

Had LO started to luff, under Rule 38.1, at, say, four lengths from the mark, she could have effectively taken WI to the wrong side of the mark because WI would be required to keep clear under Rule 37.1. But once the yachts become "about to round the mark," Rule 42 begins to override Rules 37 and 38, and LO has to begin to prepare to give WI room.

10. Based on her own testimony, Yacht M realized she had infringed Rule 54 and she did not retire promptly. She therefore infringes Fundamental Rule D, Accepting Penalties, and must be disqualified under Rule 74.4. Rule 74.5(c) prevents her from "dropping" her DSQ under Fundamental Rule D; therefore she must add the DSQ points and drop her next worse score in calculating her final points. This is a severe penalty in itself; however, the protest committee has the option to call a hearing under Rule 75, Gross Infringement of Rules or Misconduct, to consider further action against Yacht M for her deliberate infringement of the rules.

Appendix F: Index of Rule Numbers and Titles, with Cross-Reference Chart for New Rule Numbers

1985–88 Rule	1989–92 Rule
1.1	1.2
1.2	1.3
1.3	1.6
1.4	1.1
1.5	1.4
1.6	1.4(d)
1.7	1.5
3.5	3.4(b)
4.2	4.4
4.3	4.2
4.4	4.3
13	deleted
25.1(c)	25.2(c)
25.1(d)(i)	25.3(a)
25.1(d)(ii)	25.3(b)
25.1(d)(iii)	25.3(c)
25.1(e)	25.1(b)
25.1(f)	25.2
25.2	25.4
25.3	25.5
25.4	25.6
33.1	Fund. D & 34
33.2	33
34.1	32.2
34.2	42.1(f)
38.2	38.2(a)
38.3	38.2(b)
38.4	38.2(c)
38.5	38.2(d)
38.6	38.2(e)
42.3(c)	deleted

APPENDIX 2

1985–88 Rule	1989–92 Rule
3.3	3.4
3.4	3.5
3.5	3.6

APPENDIX 3

1985–88 Rule	1989–92 Rule
1.1	1.3
1.2	1.1
1.3	1.1
1.4	deleted
1.5	1.2
1.6	1.3
1.7	deleted
1.8	1.5
1.9	1.4
1.10	1.4

1985–88 Rule	1989–92 Rule
52.1	52.1 & 52.3
68.2	68.3
68.3	68.4
68.4	68.2
70.1(a)	70.1(a) & (c)
70.1(b)	deleted
72.1	73.2
72.2	73.2
72.3	72
73.2	73.3
73.3	73.4
73.4	73.5
73.5	73.6
74.5	deleted
74.6(a)	deleted
74.6(b)	74.5(a)
74.6(c)	74.5(b)
74.7	74.6
77.1(a)	77.1
77.1(b)	77.1
77.1(c)	77.2
77.1(d)	77.1
77.1(e)	preamble Part VI, Sec. D
77.1(f)	deleted
77.1(g)	preamble Part VI, Sec. D
77.1(h)	deleted
77.1(i)	77.2
77.2	78.1(a) & 78.6
77.3	77.4
77.7	77.6(b)
78.4	78.5
79	77.3

APPENDIX 3

1985–88 Rule	1989–92 Rule
2.2	2.5
2.3	2.2
2.4	2.1
2.5	2.4 & 2.6
2.7	deleted
2.8	2.7

Part I—STATUS OF THE
RULES, FUNDAMENTAL
RULES AND DEFINITIONS

                                    page
Status of the Rules 269
Fundamental Rules
A   Rendering Assistance 51
B   Responsibility of a
    Yacht 55
C   Fair Sailing 56
D   Accepting Penalties 60
Definitions
Sailing 62
Racing 63
Starting 64
Finishing 66
Luffing 68
Tacking 68
Bearing Away 69
Gybing 69
On a Tack 70
Close-hauled 70
Clear Astern and Clear
    Ahead; Overlap 71
Leeward and Windward 72
Proper Course 75
Mark 78
Obstruction 79
Postponement 82
Abandonment 82
Cancellation 84

Part II—ORGANISATION
AND MANAGEMENT

Rule   page
 1 Organising, Conducting
    and Judging Races 272
 2 Notice of Race 274

 3 Sailing Instructions
    3.1 Status 275
    3.2 Contents 275
    3.3 Distribution 277
    3.4 Changes 278
 4 Signals
    4.1 Visual signals 278
    4.2 Special signals 281
    4.3 Calling attention to
        visual signals 281
    4.4 Signals for starting a
        race 281
    4.5 Visual starting signals
        to govern 283
 5 Designating the Course,
    Altering the Course or
    Race 283
 6 Starting and Finishing
    Lines 284
 7 Start of a Race
    7.1 Starting area 284
    7.2 Timing the start 284
 8 Recalls
    8.1 Individual recall 284
    8.2 General recall 285
 9 Marks
    9.1 Mark missing 285
    9.2 Mark unseen 285
10 Finishing within a Time
    Limit 285
11 Ties 285
12 Races to be Re-sailed 286

Part III—GENERAL
REQUIREMENTS

**Owner's Responsibilities for
Qualifying his Yacht**

18 Entries 286
19 Measurement or Rating
    Certificates 287

20 Ownership of Yachts 288
21 Member on Board 288
22 Shifting Ballast 288
    22.1 General restrictions 288
    22.2 Shipping, unshipping
         or shifting ballast;
         water 288
23 Anchor 288
24 Life-Saving Equipment ... 289
25 Class Insignia, National Letters
    and Sail Numbers 289
26 Event Classification; Advertis-
    ing 292
27 Forestays and Jib Tacks 292

Part IV—RIGHT OF WAY RULES

Rights and Obligations when Yachts Meet

Section A
Obligations and Penalties

31 Rule Infringement 93
32 Serious Damage 94
33 Contact between Yachts
    Racing 102
34 Maintaining Rights 108

Section B
Principal Right of Way Rules and their Limitations

35 Limitations on Altering
    Course 110
36 Opposite Tacks—Basic
    Rule 120
37 Same Tack—Basic Rules
    37.1 When overlapped 122
    37.2 When not overlapped
         124
    37.3 Transitional 125

38 Same   Tack—Luffing   after
    Clearing the Starting Line
    38.1 Luffing rights 127
    38.2 (a) Proper course
         limitations 128
    38.2 (b) Overlap limitations
         131
    38.2 (c) Hailing to stop or pre-
         vent a luff 132
    38.2 (d) Curtailing a luff 135
    38.2 (e) Luffing rights over two
         or more yachts 136
39 Same Tack—Sailing below
    a Proper Course after
    Starting 136
40 Same   Tack—Luffing before
    Clearing the Starting Line 138
41 Changing Tacks—Tacking
    and Gybing
    41.1 Basic rule 142
    41.2 Transitional 142
    41.3 Onus 145
    41.4 When simultaneous 147

Section C
Rules that Apply at Marks and Obstructions and other Exceptions to the Rules of Section B

42 Rounding or Passing Marks and
    Obstructions 151
    42.1 When overlapped   154
    42.2 When   not   overlapped
         186
    42.3 Limitations 163
    42.4 At a starting mark sur-
         rounded by navigable
         water 181
43 Close-Hauled, Hailing for Room
    to Tack at Obstructions
    43.1 Hailing 189

43.2 Responding 194
43.3 When an obstruction is
      also a mark 198

44 Returning to Start 200
45 Keeping Clear after Touching a
    Mark 201
46 Person Overboard; Yacht
    Anchored, Aground, or Cap-
    sized 202

**Part V—OTHER SAILING
RULES**

Obligations in Handling a Yacht

50 Ranking as a Starter 301
51 Sailing the Course 301
52 Touching a Mark 205
53 Casting Off, Anchoring, Making
    Fast and Hauling Out 302
    53.1 At the preparatory signal
         302
    53.2 When racing 303
    53.3 Means of anchoring 303
54 Means of Propulsion
    54.1 Basic Rule 208
    54.2 Prohibited actions 212
    54.3 Exceptions 215
55 Aground or Foul of an Obstruc-
    tion 304
56 Sounding 304
57 Manual and Stored Power 304
58 Boarding 304
59 Leaving, Crew Overboard 304
60 Outside Assistance 305
61 Clothing and Equipment 305
62 Increasing Stability 306
63 Skin Friction 306
64 Setting and Sheeting Sails
    64.1 Changing sails 306

64.2 Spinnaker booms ... 306
64.3 Spinnakers 306
64.4 Use of outriggers 306
64.5 Headsails 307
65 Flags 307
66 Fog Signals and Lights 307

**Part VI—PROTESTS,
PENALTIES AND APPEALS**

Definitions
Rules 85
Protest 85
Party to a Protest 85
Protest Committee 87
Interested Party 87

Section A
Initiation of Action

68 Protests by Yachts
    68.1 Right to protest 220
    68.2 Informing the protested
         yacht 221
    68.3 During a race—Protest
         flag 222
    68.4 Exception to protest flag
         requirement 225
    68.5 Particulars to be included
         310
    68.6 Time limit 310
    68.7 Fee 310
    68.8 Remedying defects in the
         protest 310
    68.9 Withdrawing a protest
         310

69 Requests for Redress 311

70 Action by Race or Protest Committee
  70.1 Without a hearing 311
  70.2 With a hearing 312
  70.3 Yacht materially prejudiced 312
  70.4 Measurer's responsibility 312

Section B
Protest Procedure

71 Procedural Requirements
  71.1 Requirement for a hearing 313
  71.2 Interested parties ... 313
  71.3 Protests between yachts in separate races 313

72 Notification of Parties 313

73 Hearings
  73.1 Right to be present 313
  73.2 Acceptance or refusal of a protest 314
  73.3 Taking of evidence 314
  73.4 Evidence of committee member 314
  73.5 Failure to attend 314
  73.6 Re-opening a hearing 314

74 Decisions and Penalties
  74.1 Finding of facts 315
  74.2 Consideration of redress 315
  74.3 Measurement protests 315
  74.4 Penalties and exoneration 316
  74.5 Points and places 316
  74.6 The decision 316

Section C
Special Rules

75 Gross Infringement of Rules or Misconduct
  75.1 Penalties by the race committee or protest committee 226
  75.2 Penalties by the national authority 226

76 Liability
  76.1 Damages 318
  76.2 Measurement expenses 318

Section D
Appeals

77 Right of Appeal and Decisions
  77.1 Right of appeal 318
  77.2 Right of reference 318
  77.3 Questions of interpretation 319
  77.4 Interpretation of rules 319
  77.5 Interested parties ... 319
  77.6 Decisions 319

78 Appeal Procedures 319

APPENDICES

1 Definition of an Amateur 321
2 Sailboard Racing Rules 322
3 Alternative Penalties for Infringement of a Rule of Part IV 326
5 Scoring Systems 328
6 Recommended Protest Committee Procedure 332
14 Event Classification and Advertising 334

About the Author

Dave Perry grew up sailing on Long Island Sound. Learning to sail in Sunfish, Blue Jays, and Lightnings from his parents and in the junior program at the Pequot Yacht Club in Southport, Connecticut, he won the Clinton M. Bell Trophy for the best junior record on L.I.S. in 1971. While at Yale (1973–77) he was captain of their National Championship Team in 1975, and was voted All-American in 1975 and 1977. Other racing accomplishments include: 1st, 1978 Tasar North Americans; 5th, 1979 Laser Worlds; 1st, 1979 Soling Olympic Pre-Trials (crew); 10th overall 1981 SORC (crew); 3rd, 1982 Soling Worlds; 1st, 1982 Prince of Wales Match Racing Championship; 1st, 1983 Star South American Championship (crew); 1st, 1983 and 1984 Congressional Cup; 2nd, 1984 Soling Olympic Trials; 6th, 1985 Transpac Race (crew); and 1st, 1988 Knickerbocker Match Race Cup.

Dave has been actively working for the sport since 1977. He has led over one hundred USYRU instructional seminars in over fifty one-design classes; directed U.S. Olympic Yachting Committee Talent Development Clinics; coached the 1981 World Champion U.S. Youth Team; and given seminars in Japan, Australia, Sweden, Argentina, Brazil, and Canada. He has been the Youth Representative on the USYRU Board of Directors and the Chairman of the U.S. Youth Championship Committee, and has served on the following other USYRU committees: Olympic, Training, Class Racing, and O'Day Championship. He is currently a member of the USYRU Appeals Committee and a USYRU senior certified judge.

About the Illustrator

Brad Dellenbaugh grew up in Fairfield, Connecticut, where he learned to sail at the Pequot Yacht Club. He studied art at Brown University, and after graduation taught art for four years at the Hotchkiss School. During the summers he continued to direct junior sailing programs on Long Island Sound. Brad returned to

Brown, where he coaches the sailing team and has been pursuing his freelance career in art and writing at the same time, contributing frequently to *Sailing World* and *Yachting* magazines, and collaborating with Dave Perry on *Winning in One-Designs*. He is a USYRU Certified Judge and helped coach the U.S. Women's 470 Team as it prepared for the 1988 Olympic Games, in which it won the Gold Medal. He has raced Solings and competed in the Congressional Cup with Dave, and he also races other one-design and offshore boats, winning the 1987 and 1988 USYRU Team Racing Championships.